THE CITY

Patterns and Processes in the Urban Ecosystem

Also of INTEREST

Making Cities Work: The Dynamics of Urban Innovation, David Morley, Stuart Proudfoot, and Thomas Burns

Preservation in American Towns and Cities, Nathan Weinberg

Planning the Total Landscape: A Guide to Intelligent Land Use, Julius Gy. Fabos

The Federal Government and Urban Problems: HUD: Successes, Failures, and the Fate of Our Cities, M. Carter McFarland

† *Prisoners of Space? Exploring the Geographical Experience of Older People*, Graham D. Rowles

† Available in hardcover and paperback.

About the Book and Authors

*The City: Patterns and
Processes in the Urban Ecosystem*
Christopher H. Exline, Gary L. Peters,
and Robert P. Larkin

This text introduces urban geography from an ecosystem perspective, encouraging a synthesis of the diverse elements that form the modern city. The authors discuss the physical geography of cities, patterns of human residence, the economic basis of cities, and transportation and mobility both within and between cities. They also look at systems of cities, suburbanization, urban planning, and the controversial issue of growth restriction and speculate on the future of U.S. cities.

Throughout, the authors are concerned with the application of models and concepts, linking them in ways that can be used in urban planning and in solving – or at least better understanding – urban problems.

This is an ideal textbook for upper-division and graduate-level courses in urban geography, urban studies, and urban design and planning.

Dr. Christopher H. Exline is associate professor and chairman of the Department of Geography at the University of Nevada in Reno. **Dr. Gary L. Peters** is a professor in the Department of Geography at California State University in Long Beach. **Dr. Robert P. Larkin** is a professor in the Department of Geography and Environmental Studies at the University of Colorado in Colorado Springs.

THE CITY

Patterns and Processes in the Urban Ecosystem

Christopher H. Exline
Gary L. Peters
Robert P. Larkin

Westview Press / Boulder, Colorado

The essay "Reflections on South Chicago" in Chapter 3 was written especially for this book by Professor Thomas J. Napierkowski of the University of Colorado, Colorado Springs.

Published in 1982 in the United States of America by
  Westview Press, Inc.
  5500 Central Avenue
  Boulder, Colorado 80301
  Frederick A. Praeger, Publisher

Library of Congress Cataloging in Publication Data
Exline, Christopher H.
  The city: patterns and processes in the urban ecosystem.
  Includes bibliographical references and index.
  1. Cities and towns. 2. Urban ecology. I. Peters, Gary L. II. Larkin, Robert P.
III. Title.
HT151.E9   307.7'6   81-7528
ISBN 0-89158-904-X   AACR2
ISBN 0-89158-905-8 (pbk.)

Printed and bound in the United States of America

CONTENTS

PART 2
SYSTEMS OF CITIES

Tables

FiGURES

PREFACE

Diversity is the keystone of the study of urban places. Accordingly, questions often asked by students in courses dealing with urban phenomena are, Does order coexist with such diversity? Can one truly understand something as complex as a city?

One method of answering the question of how to study the city is to demonstrate that the city is fundamentally a system that is the product of a series of interrelationships and interactions among a myriad of social, economic, political, historical, and physical variables. The functioning of the city as a system, the concepts of growth and decay for example, can be related to processes found in a natural ecosystem. An investigation of cities that is based on analogy to the physical ecosystem is a procedure that relates all parts to the whole. A holistic conceptual framework is woven throughout this volume.

The use of the urban ecosystem concept allows great flexibility in the subject matter covered in an urban-oriented course. Topics of interest can be explored and expanded upon in this organizational scheme while maintaining the perspective of an overview. In this volume, for instance, the importance of the suburb in the North American urban landscape, new dimensions in urban planning, the physical city, and the recent trend toward growth restriction policies are added, in context, to the more traditional topics found in other works that deal with the city.

In addition to its analytical potential, the systems, or

ecosystem, approach can help make an observer aware that the beauty and harmony found in nature may also be found in the city. For the observer trained in ecosystem analysis, then, the urban area can take on new forms and meaning. The flexibility of the approach means that it may be used to observe cities of any size and cultural composition.

This book has been designed to serve a dual purpose. First, the volume may be used as an introduction and a basic approach to the study of cities. Second, through the use of the integrating ecosystem concept, this text could be used in conjunction with a book of readings or a more highly specialized volume to focus on a specific field of interest. The material from the more specialized text could be phased into its appropriate place in the systematic coverage of the city offered in this work without any loss of continuity or disruption of the focus on the city as an ecosystem.

The authors wish to thank the many students and colleagues who aided in the development of this project. The effort and talent of the staff of Westview Press are also greatly appreciated. Finally, we wish to express a special note of gratitude to Dean Thomas J. Napierkowski for his contribution of an excellent essay and for his support and encouragement of this work. The authors, of course, remain responsible for any shortcomings or errors found in the book.

From the inception of this project we have had one overriding goal. It is our hope that this volume will be of assistance and interest to those people who explore the matchless diversity that is to be found in the urban landscape.

Christopher H. Exline
Gary L. Peters
Robert P. Larkin

PART 1

THE CITY AS AN ECOSYSTEM

AN INTRODUCTION
TO THE URBAN ECOSYSTEM

Cities are enigmatic. For several thousand years people increasingly have been living in them; yet even today city dwellers are often ambivalent about their attitudes toward city life. Since the Industrial Revolution got under way in eighteenth-century England, cities have grown, some into such urban behemoths as New York, London, and Tokyo. However, cities continue to be both praised and damned. Sir Kenneth Clark caught the essence of recent urban growth in the following comment:

> Imagine an immensely speeded up movie of Manhattan Island during the last hundred years. It would look less like a work of man than like some tremendous natural upheaval. It's godless, it's brutal, it's violent—but one can't laugh it off, because in the energy, strength of will and mental grasp that have gone to make New York, materialism has transcended itself. [Clark, 1969, p. 321]

If you examine any city from a high vantage point or look at an aerial photograph of an urban area (Figure 1.1), you will most probably note the residential and commercial structures, the roads, the industrial areas, the parks, and the landforms that together compose the physical form of the city. Such an overview makes us aware of the obvious spatial patterns found in cities, or what is usually termed urban morphology. Not so apparent is the myriad of political, social, behavioral, and political processes and decisions that are con-

FIGURE 1.1. Aerial View of New York City Looking Toward Central Park. Source: HUD.

stantly interacting to create and shape the urban landscape. A knowledge of the interrelations and interworkings among the various components of the city is the key to understanding urban dynamics and the diversity of urban places.

If we are to make sense of an entity as complex as a city, a special method of study is needed. The use of systems analysis and the ecosystem concept provides a vehicle through which the interrelated processes that give life to a city can be examined.

The systems approach is essentially a formalized method of determining the part that even the most minute component plays in the operation of an entire system. A system is a collection of interrelated parts that forms an integrated whole. The terms *systems method* and *systems approach* describe the orderliness or methodical planning used in the investigation of the ways in which systems function.

The systems approach can hardly be considered new; in essence it simply treats something as a complex integrated whole that exists as more than just the sum of its parts. General systems theory has evolved mainly as a response to the increasing specialization and compartmentalization that have occurred in both the natural and the social sciences in the twentieth century. The systems approach, thus, is an attempt to unify the social and natural sciences.

Without getting bogged down in the scientific jargon of systems theory, a few basic concepts should be considered. Any system, for example, exists in an environment. An open system interacts with its environment; a closed system is isolated from it. Cities, obviously, are open systems, because they exchange energy and materials with their environment. Air pollution is one obvious manifestation of such an exchange.

Cities must also be viewed as holons, as parts of holarchies, as developed by Koestler (1978). According to Koestler "holons are, by definition, sub-wholes, so all branches of a hierarchy are sub-hierarchies, and whether you treat them as 'wholes' or 'parts' depends on the task at hand" (Koestler, 1978, p. 56). For our purpose it is essential to recognize that in the study of cities we are looking at a complex array of systems and subsystems.

On the one hand, a city is composed of numerous subsystems, such as neighborhoods, commercial districts, and manufacturing districts. On the other hand, a city is one subsystem in a regional, national, or global system of cities. Thus, although our focus is the city, we must be able to move from one scale to another, from neighborhood to systems of cities. Furthermore, we must remain aware of the interrelationships that exist among the various scales, a point that merits repeated emphasis.

Consider an example from the world of medicine. A physician is trained in the analysis of the human body as a system. The body is simply a collection of subunits, which we will call subsystems—the cardiovascular (heart), respiratory (lungs), central nervous, and digestive subsystems, for instance. Suppose a person is having difficulty digesting food and seeks help from a doctor. Once the symptoms have been explained, the physician begins a systematic analysis of the patient's complaint. The skilled medical practitioner understands the manner in which each part of the body affects the other subunits; thus he or she can dismiss the factors that are not involved in the problem and isolate the appropriate subsystem. In some cases the cause-and-effect nature of the interrelationships among the subsystems of the body is obvious; in other instances the manner in which one element of the system affects the other components is difficult to detect.

Many other examples of the systems approach to analysis and problem solving can be found. The mechanic repairing an automobile uses a knowledge of the way in which the parts of an automobile function in concert with each other to diagnose problems and take corrective action. An ecologist could never understand a forest without a highly systematic method of describing the manner in which diverse variables interact to form the whole forest. Those people who study urban areas often draw analogies or comparisons between the processes that occur in cities and those that are found in natural ecosystems. The term *urban ecosystem* stems from the practice of comparing cities to biological ecosystems.

Let's go back to the example of a forest for a moment. In order to understand that biosystem, ecological processes as well as physical features need to be considered. The arrangement of the elements of the forest ecosystem is not the result of chance occurrence but is instead the product of a highly structured sequence of events. We must discover the parts that local landforms, soils, and plant and animal communities have played in forest development. Likewise, local patterns of weather and climate must be considered and human influences reviewed in order to form a complete picture of the ecosystem. Our knowledge of the workings of the forest ecosystem provides us with a schematic framework for analyzing changes in the system, such as growth, transition, and decay. The systems approach offers a clearly defined hierarchical method for illuminating the relationship of each

FIGURE 1.2. Decay in the Urban Ecosystem (New York City). Source: HUD.

part to the totality of the system.

The process of analyzing and dissecting an urban ecosystem is similar to the method used in studying the forest. The components of the urban ecosystem interact, as do the elements of the biological system. In both systems energy flows are important. Those people who study the city are concerned with the manner in which economic, social, political, and decision-making processes work together to produce a city. The city is viewed as a living organism – as a dynamic place with a vitality that causes growth and allows decay – just as the forest is (Figure 1.2).

We have simplified the notion of the urban ecosystem to a great extent in order to introduce the concept. Four general warnings about the use of ecosystem analogies in such basic form should be issued at this juncture. First, everything in life is not harmoniously adjusted to everything else; thus the elements of an urban ecosystem may have a much higher degree of autonomy than the elements of a natural ecosystem have. Predicting the inevitability of events that result from a change in one element of the ecosystem is often a more difficult task in the urban setting than in the natural ecosystem.

Second, the scale at which studies are undertaken is of great importance. One should not assume that the processes that occur on the neighborhood or local community level are the same as those that occur on the city, metropolitan, or state level. In 1970 a strong positive relationship was found in the city of Cincinnati, Ohio, between the percentage of voters selecting Republican political candidates and the percentage of voters with a high income. It is tempting to project such local-level associations into predictions about patterns occurring on a statewide basis. However, if the relationship between high income and the Republican vote in 1970 for the entire state of Ohio is considered, a significant negative relationship is found (Palm and Exline, 1976). This is a basic example of the manner in which relationships that hold true at one scale can change as the scale increases or decreases. Because an ecological approach to urban study is dependent upon an examination of the interrelationships between variables, an awareness that these associations can fluctuate as the scale changes is of great importance.

Third, in using ecological analysis in urban studies we must remember that as cultural boundaries are crossed, urban models and assumptions that hold true in one cultural setting may not be appropriate in other parts of the globe. Our focus in this book is primarily on the North American city, so some of the concepts discussed will be of only marginal use in an examination of a Third World city, for example.

The final consideration in using ecological analysis is that it is often extremely difficult to correctly describe the process that led to the formation of some spatial pattern by simply observing that pattern. For example, a certain social group or industrial activity may be clustered in a particular area, thus forming a pattern of spatial location. Upon observing such a distribution, we may want to cite some form of economic or social discrimination as the agent responsible for the grouping. Yet it may well be that group preference, or any one of a vast number of other factors, was the real cause of such clustering.

Although caution must be exercised, when the systems approach is used with care in combination with an ecological analogy, it can be a powerful tool for describing and analyzing urban places. This method of study is often employed by those charged with the responsibility for city planning.

THE SYSTEMS APPROACH TO URBAN PLANNING

The most fundamental aspect of land use planning is the consideration of the interrelationships among all possible variables (physical, social, political, and economic) that are involved in the question of how best to use the land. Inherent in the planner's decision-making process are many of the basic concepts of urban ecology.

Balance, in the ecological sense of the term, must be a factor in urban planning. A planner must decide how his or her decision will affect the balance found in the urban ecosystem. Is there a balance in the transportation subsystem, for example? If that subsystem is out of balance, is the greatest emphasis placed on the automobile and would the planner's decision exaggerate the disharmony?

Competition is another concept of ecology that applies to the urban setting. In some types of economic systems the user willing to pay the greatest price will acquire the right to use a particular piece of land. The planner may intervene in this purely competitive market and determine that cultural, social, or historical factors should take precedence over pure market economics.

Those people who are charged with urban redevelopment or community-scale land use policy formation must consider the ecological processes of invasion, succession, and dominance. We will explore these concepts in far more detail later in this book, but at this point we can briefly define invasion, succession, and dominance as the sequence of events that may occur if a social group or industrial activity moves into an area. If a manufacturing plant invades (locates in) a residential area, that action may trigger a movement of people from the area, which in turn would provide space for more nonresidential land users to invade. This ongoing process can lead to changes in the activity patterns or social composition of large areas of a city.

Along with identifying all relevant variables, developing a statement of objectives and priorities of a plan is essential to the planning process. Determining the manner in which a plan affects the urban ecosystem can be accomplished through developing measures and standards that act as feedback or indicator devices. If the intent of a plan is to provide more low-cost housing in a city, then one measure of effectiveness would be the amount of low-cost housing actually provided in the urban area as a result of the plan. If the low-cost housing segment of the city's housing stock did not increase, then the plan would have to be modified.

Again using the example of low-cost housing, a planner must make assumptions and projections about the need for low-cost housing in the urban ecosystem. If he or she assumes that more low-cost housing will be needed than the natural workings of the system will provide, then a plan will be needed that focuses on alleviating the expected deficit of that particular category of housing.

In addition to an analysis of interrelationships and the establishment of goals, the extent of the region for which planning is needed must be determined. It may be that a plan designed to have impact on a single neighborhood will have to consider the surrounding city and suburbs as well as that particular community. It makes little sense to plan for urban traffic patterns without taking into account the commuter flows into the city from the surrounding suburbs, for example. The extent of the area that will have an effect on a plan is an essential consideration.

A plan, once formulated, can serve the urban ecosystem in many ways, and it should be a source of information regarding the way in which the system functions. Those creating a plan are designing a program for change, an estimate for the future, and a technique for coordinating the elements of the urban system. Obviously the use of the ecosystem concept has broad applications not only in the study of urban areas but also in the development of plans for cities.

AN APPROACH TO THE STUDY OF CITIES

We will use the framework provided by the ecosystem method of the study of urban places in the remainder of this book. The dynamics of urban growth, and conversely of growth restriction, are also major topics to be investigated. Our discussion of urban growth will be based on a model developed by James E. Vance, Jr.

In discussing the process of urban growth Vance identified several stages of urban development (Vance, 1966). The following processes were suggested as making up the general urban growth sequence: inception, exclusion, segregation, extension, relocation and readjustment, and redevelopment. Vance was examining the "downtown" or central business district (CBD); however, these processes also relate to the city in its entirety.

Inception refers to the key element that gives rise to a city in a particular place. It may be that some type of resource or transportation factor, climate, or health served as the impetus for urban location. River cities, such as Pittsburgh, are excellent examples of the former, and Phoenix is an example of the latter.

We often use such terms as mining town, mill town, agricultural service center, or fishing village to describe particular towns and cities. The terms indicate the types of activities that help support such cities and were perhaps responsible for their initial location. Town names also sometimes provide clues to the reasons for a town's location. For example, there is Martins Ferry, Ohio, and Leadville, Colorado.

Exclusion describes the forcing of activities out of an area. The rent costs in the central business district are often so great that many types of activities cannot locate there. For example, a lumberyard might find it uneconomical to pay the costs of locating in the central business district and would, therefore, be excluded from a location in the CBD.

Similar types of industries tend to locate in a particular region or section of a city. This process, much like association, is referred to as segregation. Vance observed that "In New York we find the stock exchange on Wall Street, the shop company area on Park Row, advertising several miles away on Madison Avenue, and corporate headquarters, other than those noted, on Park Avenue" (Vance, 1966, p. 116). Segregation refers to the manner in which separate functional districts within a city evolve.

Extension is the outward, often radial, movement of activities from the center. Innovations in transportation generally explain the extension of a city (see Figure 1.3). In a city that was founded as a seaport, most activity at the time of inception would have taken place near the actual harbor. In time, as fixed-rail transportation came into existence, the city

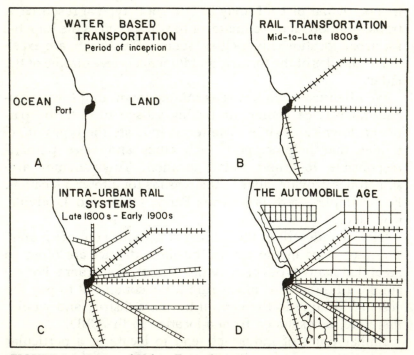

FIGURE 1.3. Stages of Urban Extension.

would have expanded, creating a skeletal transportation network. Trolley lines and other intraurban transportation systems, which became a widespread part of the American urban scene in the late nineteenth century, served to fill in the framework created by the previous transportation systems. The widespread use of the automobile as the primary means of transportation in the United States allowed such flexibility that a vast web of roadways has developed and is a part of virtually all American urban landscapes.

Readjustment and relocation are exemplified by the large shopping centers and malls found in American suburbs. Historically, the downtown area of most cities was generally the major area of retail sales activity. The urban to suburban shift of population, which took place during the past forty years, in part caused many activities to move from the central city to suburban locations. The San Francisco Bay area provides an example of the relocation and evolution of retail sales establishments in the suburbs (see Figure 1.4).

As a consequence of relocation, the downtown areas of many cities have had to readjust their functions in an attempt to maintain economic and social viability. In many cases that has meant urban redevelopment and the construction of high-rise buildings, both residential and commercial, in downtown areas.

Quite obviously, urban growth and development result from the workings of the urban ecosystem, even though the elements of a city ecosystem may function so discreetly that little activity seems to be occurring. It may therefore be useful to consider Vance's processes of inception through readjustment as major, highly visible results of the interactions of the urban system. Using Vance's framework much like an outline of major headings, we can use the ecosystem concept to fill in the spaces between the most distinct subheadings of the outline and to understand the factors that create such phenomena as segregation and exclusion. The major concepts of geography and spatial analysis are also of considerable utility in the study of the urban ecosystem and the stages of urban development.

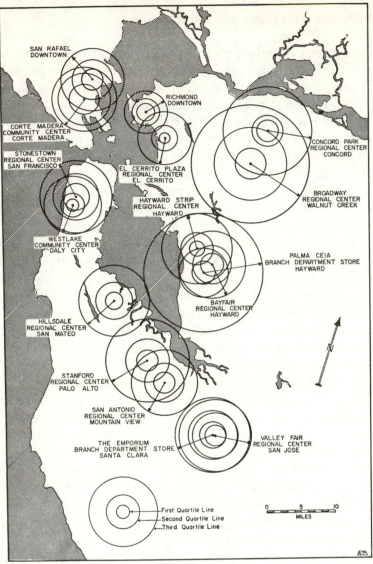

This map shows the location and nature of the tributary area for the twelve discrete regional shopping centers in the Bay Area, as well as several community centers and downtown areas of older satellite towns. The three concentric circles centered on each shopping area enclose the residence of (1) the nearest quarter of the customers of that center, (2) the nearer half, and (3) the closest three-quarters of the customers, respectively, Thus, the space between successive quartile circles helps indicate the density of customer-residence. The radial spacing of the circles shows the peripheral extent of the tributary area. From this graphic summation of tributary areas we find that the Palma Ceia Center in Hayward has the greatest radial extent, whereas the El Cerrito Plaza has the most restricted tributary area.

FIGURE 1.4. Outlying Shopping Centers of the Bay Area, 1959. Source: James E. Vance, *Geography and Urban Evolution in the San Francisco Bay Area* (Berkeley: Institute of Governmental Studies, University of California, 1964), p. 73.

ELEMENTS OF SPATIAL ANALYSIS

Models in Geography

A model is, by definition, a hypothetical or stylized representation of reality, and throughout this book the use of urban models will be demonstrated. Chorley and Haggett have observed that "a model is thus a simplified structuring of reality which presents supposedly significant features and relationships in a generalized form. Models are highly subjective approximations in that they do not include all associated observations and measurements, but . . . they are valuable in obscuring incidental detail and in allowing fundamental aspects of reality to appear" (Chorley and Haggett, 1967, p. 22).

Some models have applications in a wide range of circumstances and a high probability of successfully describing, explaining, or predicting phenomena. The majority of models, however, are used in a rather limited context and have only a marginal probability of success. The terms *approximations, selective, structured, pattern seeking, suggestive, analogies,* and *reapplication* are frequently used to describe models (Chorley and Haggett, 1967).

A vast number of categories exist into which models can be organized. We have selected four groups of models as being representative of general land use models. The first classification is the static model. A map is a prime example of a static model in that it essentially represents a simplification of spatial reality as it exists at a given moment. If you ask virtually anyone what tool is most associated with the geographer, the answer would most likely be the map. It is used to reduce large areas of the earth's surface into readily observable form. The making of maps, cartography, is a fascinating process that involves the "real world" as it is perceived by the map author and put on paper by the cartographer. The map is printed and becomes a source of information used for a variety of purposes (see Figure 1.5).

As a map reader sifts through the information on a map, his or her biases, attitudes, and knowledge become factors that influence the way in which the map is used. Maps, as well as

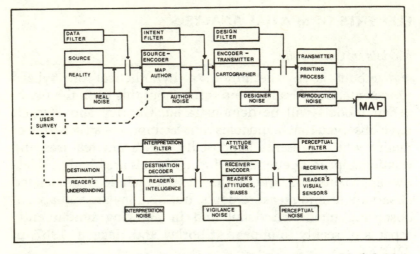

FIGURE 1.5. Cartographic Communication Systems. Source: Mark S. Mon-
monier, *Maps, Distortion, and Meaning,* Resource Papers for College Geography no. 75-4 (Washington, D.C.: Association of American Geographers,
1977), p. 12, based on R. Jolliffe, "An Information Theory Approach to Cartography," *Cartography* 8 (1974), pp. 175–181. Reprinted by permission.

other models, can be highly subjective; thus they should be
carefully examined with regard to the purpose of the model
and any possible distortions or inaccuracies in the information presented.

A descriptive model is basically a stylistic description of
reality. The descriptive model can explain what is on the
landscape, whereas the static model essentially illustrates but
does not provide an explanation of the patterns on the land.
A normative model is used to predict what might be expected
to occur under certain stated conditions. For example, a
normative model could be used to estimate where people
will travel to shop or to estimate the flow of intercity moving.

A dynamic model deals fundamentally with motion or
change. For example, a dynamic model would be applicable
to the study of the spatial consequences of combining increased automobile ownership and road improvement with
increased per capita income and population growth. A
dynamic model that incorporates transportation, income, and
population variables might well help explain the movement

of people from the central cities to the suburbs.

The Importance of Scale

Scale is one of the most important concepts to keep in mind when using any model, and we have already noted the critical role scale plays in ecological analysis. Scale implies a relationship among items of different size and is a commonly used term. We often speak of large scale or small scale when, in effect, we are describing the level of generalization of our observation. The smaller our unit of observation, the more we can accurately describe phenomena and make valid assumptions. Larger units of observation present some problems in generalization, since a more numerous group almost certainly means a greater diversity of characteristics that must be entered into the analysis.

The Nature and Pattern of Spatial Distributions and Interaction

One definition of geography is that it is the science that deals with the study of the patterns found on the earth's surface. Geographical investigation focuses on the where, why, how, and future of patterns on the land. The patterns created by the human use of the earth include the patchwork-quilt appearance of agricultural land, urban roads and buildings, the land use patterns created by the slash-and-burn (swidden) agriculturalists, and the results of erosion. The list of topics for geographic inquiry is virtually endless.

Certain arrangements of activities, their spatial distributions, are basic to the study of geography. The spatial distribution of activities ranges from being random to highly structured in form and from appearing clustered to widely dispersed. For example, one model of the relationship of smaller cities to larger cities is based on a formal hexagonal pattern of locations; conversely, urban sprawl is much more random in spatial organization. Communities within a city may be clustered in unique neighborhoods or may be scattered throughout the urban area, as is the case with some ethnic or religious groups.

If we view the city as a vast mosaic of residential and commercial parts, the locations of the pieces of the mosaic have areal associations, which refers to the manner in which activities are grouped together and to the factors that cause such clustering. A high-income residential area may have an areal association (corresponding location) with an area in which local topography presents scenic views. For example, the Palos Verde area in Los Angeles County enables houses to have splendid views, but only at a very high price.

Spatial interactions involve flow, migration, linkages, and diffusion. Flow describes the amount of interaction between places, such as in the movement of people, goods, or ideas. For instance, the flow of blacks from the South to the North and to the West Coast following the Second World War was fairly significant (see Figure 1.6).

The actual movement of people between places is referred to as migration. The example of the black migrants illustrates interurban migration; a family moving across town represents an intraurban migration. A constant movement of people between and within cities is one of the essential components of the dynamic urban ecosystem.

Linkages are the routes of interaction between phenomena such as social groups or commercial establishments. The lines along which linkages occur are composed of communication and transportation systems. A person who moves to a new city, finds employment there, and then encourages his or her relatives to move to the same city has created a linkage path of interurban migration through communication.

Some industries find it advantageous to cluster groups of similar manufacturers. In this manner business organizations can share the costs of specialized goods and services sold by companies whose products are essential to the industries that are clustering together. Also distance, often the most expensive element in moving goods and services along a linkage path, can be minimized, thus holding costs down.

Diffusion is one of the more important aspects of spatial interaction. It is the process through which ideas and information spread over space and through time along specific channels of communication. Two general categories of diffusion can be identified: the spread of information that took

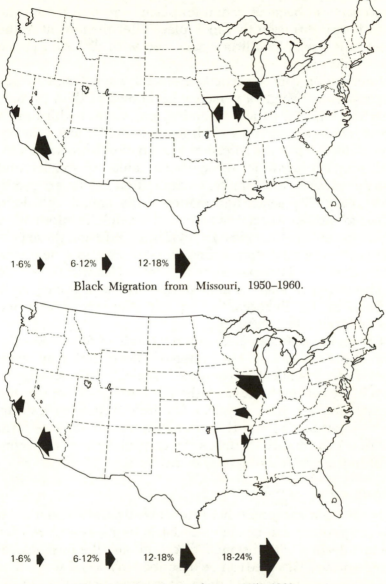

Black Migration from Missouri, 1950–1960.

Black Migration from Arkansas, 1950–1960.

FIGURE 1.6. Post–World War II Black Migration. Source: G. Davis and O. Donaldson, *Blacks in the United States: A Geographic Perspective* (Boston: Houghton Mifflin Company, 1975), p. 47.

place before the electronic age—when radio, television, and newspapers became commonplace in much of the world—and diffusion that took place after the advent of the electronic age. We will be concerned with diffusion in the electronic age.

Information can be carried in several ways. One involves expansion diffusion—a person who knows of the idea tells another, who tells another, and so on, so that with time a great many people know of the idea (Gould, 1969). Hierarchical diffusion is the spread of information from some central source downward through the ranks of smaller and smaller places. For example, a corporation headquartered in New York City sends information to its branch offices in Chicago and Los Angeles, which in turn send the information along to still smaller cities. In relocation diffusion those people who have the information actually move to a new area and carry the information with them. Historically ethnic communities in many American seaports have been greatly influenced by linkages to the Old Country established through relocation diffusion.

Barriers to diffusion exist in a multitude of forms. Restriction of the diffusion of innovation or information may be inspired by political, economic, social, intellectual, or psychological motivations. Although more important in the preelectronic world, physical features of the earth's surface—especially oceans, deserts, and mountain ranges—form barriers to diffusion. Diffusion is an especially important concept in the analysis of city systems.

Distance and Direction

It has been suggested that most investigations undertaken by geographers can be stated in basic terms as a search for factors dealing with distance, direction, and the linkages between places. Distance can be described in several ways. The most common measure of distance is some measure of linear distance, such as inches, feet, millimeters, or kilometers. However, and sometimes more important, distance may also be conceived of in terms of time. We often describe a journey in terms of an hour or two hours rather than in terms of miles.

A person's perception is also a measure by which earth space is described. The trip from one's home to work place might be perceived of as covering a great distance if stoplights are encountered at every intersection, but in reality, the trip may involve a very short linear distance. Again, time is an important element of our modern conception of distance, especially in urban areas.

Finally, distance is measured in terms of the monetary cost of travel. Americans of the late 1970s were made acutely aware of the cost of travel as fuel prices soared. In the summer of 1979 realtors reported that house buyers were becoming increasingly concerned with buying houses closer to their jobs.

Direction refers to the pattern of movement of people, goods, and services. Is the pattern of movement predictable, or is it so random that few conclusions about activity patterns can be drawn? The journey from home to work generally goes along some well-established corridor. A journey to visit friends, to shop, or to participate in a recreational activity probably does not follow a well-defined pattern. The direction people travel and the distance they are willing to cover are important elements in creating the circulation patterns found in cities. Commuting patterns are important elements in the urban ecosystem.

Location: Site and Situation

The site of a place is its fixed physical location. Site may be described in terms of a position of latitude and longitude or in terms of some fixed physical feature, such as a harbor. On the other hand, situation is the location of a place in relation to other places. The site of a city does not change, but its situation can change dramatically.

New Orleans has been referred to by some observers as the city that should never have been, mainly because it occupies a site that leaves much to be desired. Many parts of the city are built on natural levees only a few feet above sea level, whereas other parts are actually below sea level. Foundations for large buildings must be sunk seventy to one hundred feet or more in order to rest upon solid material. Built mainly within a major bend of the Mississippi River, the city has always lived with the threat of flood and the possibility that the river would again change its course, as it has done previously. The land beneath this charming city is sinking, and in some neighborhoods near Lake Pontchartrain, cracked brick fences and exposed secondary foundations are common. As if this list of site problems were not enough, the residents and officials of the city must also worry about hurricanes that often hit the Gulf Coast.

Why, we might wonder, has a million-plus metropolis grown up and persisted in such an unlikely location? The answer, of course, lies at least in part in the city's situation, in its relative location. The site of the original city, the French Quarter, was chosen by the French because a portage route from Bayou St. John intersected with the Mississippi River there. Today the site is still plagued with a host of problems, but the city thrives: As Peirce Lewis commented,

> One should not then feel too sorry for New Orleans, either in its early days or now, despite its appalling site. The very awfulness of that site gave the inhabitants a certain cheerful esprit de corps. They had conquered the swamp and were clearly pleased with themselves. This special feeling was not limited to the city, either, and New Orleans gained a reputation not merely as a city in the wilderness, but as a beacon which shone with special brilliance, and a prize most eagerly to be sought. Once that happened—only shortly after the founding of the city—no other place had any hope of competing with New Orleans for command of the Mississippi and what it represented. [Lewis, 1976, p. 30]

The site of the city of San Francisco is a peninsula surrounded by the Pacific Ocean to the west, the Golden Gate to the north, and San Francisco Bay to the east. At the time of its first European settlement the portion of the peninsula where San Francisco is located today was largely mud flats, hills, and sand dunes. In the later years of the 1840s San Francisco was a small and relatively quiet town. A decade later San Francisco had become one of the important cities in the United States. What brought about this metamorphosis?

The site of San Francisco had obviously not changed, but

its situation, or relative location, was altered remarkably when gold was discovered in the foothills of the Sierra Nevada in 1848. San Francisco became the gateway to the goldfields, and the town's population and economy grew by leaps and bounds. It became an "instant city" because of its location near the goldfields. The history of cities is also replete with examples of urban places that have gone from boom to bust as the importance of their location relative to other places has diminished.

The Concept of Region

Region is one of the most commonly used but least thought about words in the English language. An almost endless variety of regional patterns is found on the earth, and the regions are defined by applying different criteria to sets of physical and/or cultural phenomena. For example, we refer to the Ivy League, Corn Belt, Big Ten, Sunbelt, and Bible Belt as regions.

The determination of a region is based initially on the establishment of criteria by which phenomena will be grouped. If more than 50 percent of the residents in an area of a city are black and the criterion for inclusion in a particular region is that there be more than a 50 percent black population, then the area in question would be considered a region.

Once the criteria for a region have been established, the boundaries of the region are determined, as is its core or central area. Through this process groups of like people or types of commercial activities can be grouped together, and the space they occupy can be considered a region.

A formal region is much like the example of a region of black residents. A region that has formalized boundaries and specific quantitative criteria for membership is regarded as a formal region. In order to organize a city into a series of formal regions, one would obtain the population characteristics of a city and, using a strict numerical definition, would place every area that was, for example, more than 50 percent black in a particular ethnic region. (We are using 50 percent only for the sake of illustration; the actual criteria employed would be established by those creating the region.)

Suppose area A falls into such a region, and area B, which is directly across the street from A, has a 48 percent black population. Area B would not be a part of the region, even though it is close in both proximity and characteristics to the formal region. Formal regionalization frequently does not allow for transition zones as one moves past the boundaries of a region, because the boundaries of the reporting areas simply form the border of the region. Contemporary study of urban places often involves the creation of formal regions.

Functional regions are more flexible than formal regions. Once the criteria for regionalization have been determined, the boundaries of a functional region are determined by activity patterns. The areas from which commuters travel to work in the central city could be classified as composing a functional region. The boundaries of this "commuter shed" or zone of commute would be determined by the locations of those people who are involved in the activity rather than by some formal unit boundary such as a census tract.

Our approach to the study of cities is based on the application of fundamental concepts of geography to the methodology of urban ecosystem analysis and the process of urban development. We apply this framework to some of the more recent developments in the spatial evolution of cities, including new dimensions in urban planning and growth restriction in metropolitan areas.

THE U.S. CENSUS AND THE STUDY OF CITIES

One of the most important sources of information for urban investigations is the U.S. census. The need for, and importance of, an accurate and systematic method for gathering population data was recognized by the authors of the Constitution. The first U.S. census was taken in 1790 and was basically a count of the population, which numbered about 4 million. In 1810 Congress requested that a greater range of questions be asked by the census takers and that an industrial census be taken. By 1860 the census had become a sophisticated document. "Six separate census questionnaires carried 142 items covering population, health, mortality, literacy, pauperism, occupation, income, wealth, agriculture, manufactures, mining, fisheries, commerce, banking, insurance, transportation, schools, libraries, newspapers, crime, taxes, and religion. In effect, it asked for a complete inventory of national activity " (U.S. Department of Commerce, Bureau of the Census, 1974, p. 2).

At the beginning of the twentieth century, breakthroughs in the use of punchcards and mechanical tabulating equipment greatly improved census operations, and methods of obtaining and processing census data have continued to improve since 1900. The use of sampling techniques (1940) and computers (1950) led to the U.S. census becoming one of the finest nationwide sources of data in the world.

Urban researchers most often use three principal series of census reports: (1) the population census report, (2) the housing census report, and (3) the joint population and housing report. Census information is available for a variety of geographical scales. Frequently examined geographic areas are the standard metropolitan statistical area (SMSA), the census tract, and the block. An SMSA consists of a central city with a population of 50,000 or more and the surrounding metropolitan counties. A census tract is a small, relatively homogeneous area with an average population of 4,000. A block is the smallest unit of observation, having an average population of 100, and is identified in all urbanized areas (see Figure 1.7). The extent and variety of data decrease as the size of the area decreases.

Detailed information is collected for each of the geographic areas. If we were curious about the employment characteristics of a given part of a city, for example, we would first identify the census tract or tracts corresponding to that region (see Figure 1.8). Once the census tract number or numbers had been determined—for instance, census tract 1 located in the extreme northeast corner of the Great Falls SMSA map—then we would go to the data listed for that census tract or tracts (see Table 1.1). A detailed summary of the characteristics of any given location in an SMSA, or for the entirety of an SMSA, can be obtained in this manner.

Census data play a critical role in the study of cities. Infor-

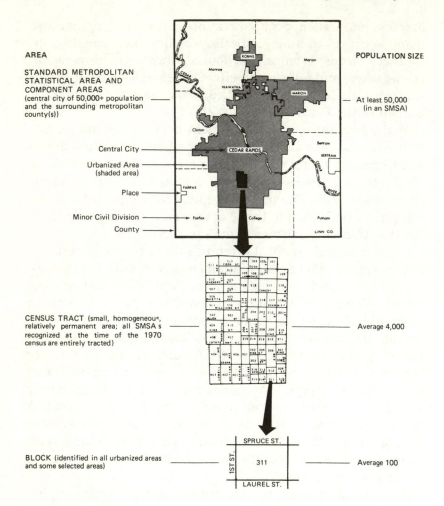

FIGURE 1.7. Geographic Areas in 1970 Census Reports. Source: U.S. Bureau of the Census, *Census Data for Community Action* (Washington, D.C., 1975).

mation from the census may be used by community groups desiring to influence land use decision making. Census data can aid in the task of defining urban areas, and as we continue with our consideration of the urban ecosystem other uses and the value of the U.S. census will become clear.

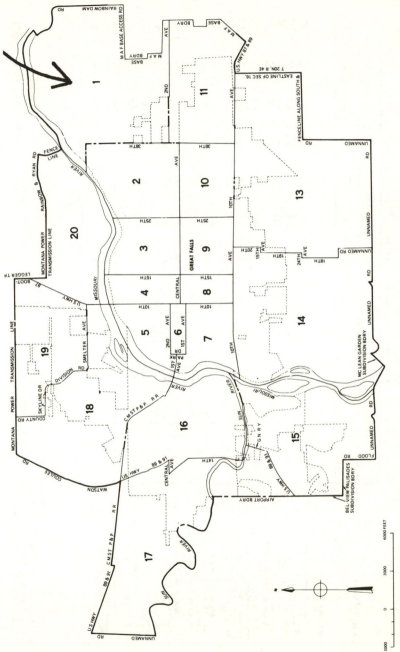

FIGURE 1.8. Census Tracts in the Great Falls, Montana, SMSA; Inset Map—Great Falls and Vicinity. Source: U.S. Bureau of the Census, *Census Tracts*, "Great Falls, Mont.," Final Report PHC(1)-81 (Washington, D.C., 1970).

TABLE 1.1. Labor Force Characteristics of the Population: 1970

[Data based on sample, see text. For minimum base for derived figures (percent, median, etc.) and meaning of symbols, see text][1]

Census Tracts	Cascade County			Great Falls								
	Total	Great Falls	Balance	Tract 0001	Tract 0002	Tract 0003	Tract 0004	Tract 0005	Tract 0006	Tract 0007	Tract 0008	Tract 0009
EMPLOYMENT STATUS												
Male, 16 years old and over	26 645	19 040	7 805	236	1 643	1 452	911	1 102	424	1 272	763	1 354
Labor force	21 796	15 073	6 723	205	1 244	1 136	671	803	280	833	550	1 037
Percent of total	81.2	79.2	86.1	86.9	75.7	78.2	73.7	72.9	66.0	65.5	72.1	76.6
Civilian labor force	17 160	13 677	3 483	169	1 120	957	612	623	255	700	461	994
Employed	16 232	12 928	3 304	153	1 095	902	569	601	193	604	437	900
Unemployed	928	749	179	16	25	55	43	22	62	96	24	94
Percent of civilian labor force	5.4	5.5	5.1	9.5	2.2	5.7	7.0	3.5	24.3	13.7	5.2	9.5
Not in labor force	5 049	3 967	1 082	31	399	316	240	299	144	439	213	317
Inmate of institution	169	162	7	—		11	18	4	—	17	7	7
Enrolled in school	1 443	1 146	297	21	151	69	67	34	11	41	20	111
Other under 65 years	1 202	904	298	5	79	62	35	68	59	158	64	75
Other 65 years and over	2 235	1 755	480	5	169	174	120	193	74	223	122	131
Male, 16 to 21 years old	4 321	2 705	1 616	32	243	253	152	190	31	155	93	286
Not enrolled in school	2 027	890	1 137	—	63	102	81	128	26	92	41	82
Not high school graduates	333	228	105	—	26	20	18	17	11	47	12	34
Unemployed or not in labor force	117	98	19	—	12	10	12	6	—	28	—	21
Female, 16 years old and over	27 377	21 333	6 044	218	1 846	1 746	1 088	1 386	422	1 241	925	1 741
Labor force	11 008	9 110	1 898	124	801	700	421	556	222	508	361	859
Percent of total	40.2	42.7	31.4	56.9	43.4	40.1	38.7	40.1	52.6	40.9	39.0	49.3
Civilian labor force	10 941	9 089	1 852	124	801	700	421	556	222	497	361	859
Employed	10 039	8 376	1 663	118	740	626	404	529	195	434	299	762
Unemployed	902	713	189	6	61	74	17	27	27	63	62	97
Percent of civilian labor force	8.2	7.8	10.2	4.8	7.6	10.6	4.0	4.9	12.2	12.7	17.2	11.3
Not in labor force	16 369	12 223	4 146	94	1 045	1 046	667	830	200	733	564	882
Married women, husband present	17 848	13 117	4 731	183	1 246	1 071	565	603	95	558	590	912
In labor force	6 869	5 410	1 459	103	479	394	197	149	55	231	206	445
With own children under 6 years	5 465	3 792	1 673	67	333	257	166	184	11	158	186	197
In labor force	1 572	1 199	373	30	99	61	28	30	6	54	64	85

[1] A dash "—" represents zero. Three dots "..." indicate that the data are being withheld to avoid disclosure of information for individual housing units, or that the base average, percentage, or ratio is too small for it to be shown.

GREAT FALLS, MONT., SMSA

THE CITY

What is a city? There is an immense amount of academic study that attempts to answer that question. A city may be defined much like a formal region, as an entity with definite political or legal boundaries. Encountering a city limits sign, a traveler becomes aware that one such formal boundary is about to be crossed. The city may also be defined in a functional sense.

We often use the terms urbanism, urbanization, urban, and city interchangeably. In reality each of these words describes a different facet of the phenomena associated with cities. Urbanism encompasses the conditions or characteristics of the way of life of those people who live in cities. Urbanization is the process that brings people into the cities. It may also describe the number of cities and the size of the urban population in a given area.

The definition of urban is more difficult. Population size is the principal factor used in defining cities in most nations. In the United States a place of more than 2,500 people is considered to be a city; in Canada a city must have a population of more than 1,000; in Switzerland, more than 10,000; and in Denmark, 250. We have seen that an SMSA in the United States is based on a city with a population of at least 50,000.

Specific needs often determine the definition of a city. A numerical definition is the most basic criterion from which to develop data to either support or refute a claim that a place is a city. In some nations, India for example, the definition of a city includes the factor that a certain percentage of the people living there not be involved in agriculture. Population density is a factor in other nations.

A number of philosophical issues need to be resolved to determine what constitutes a city. Suppose an American city has a population of 10,000 inhabitants but is simply a "bedroom community" of commuters who work in another city. If the bedroom community is only a collection of residences and has no real economic base, no cultural opportunities, and no social diversity, is that place a true city?

The questions and problems inherent in defining a city

have been the subject of considerable debate. For the purposes of this book, a strict definition of a city is not of critical importance, and we consider a place to be a city if it meets the criteria used by the particular nation in question. Most of our concern is with Western cities, especially North American cities.

REFERENCES

Chorley, R. J., and Haggett, P. 1967. *Models in Geography.* London: Methuen and Co.

Churchman, C. West. 1968. *The Systems Approach.* New York: Dell Publishing Co.

Clark, Kenneth. 1969. *Civilisation: A Personal View.* New York: Harper and Row, Publishers.

Dent, Borden, ed. 1976. *Census Data: Geographic Significance and Classroom Utility.* NCGE Pacesetter in Geography No. 2. Tualatin, Oreg.: Geographic and Area Study Publications.

Gould, Peter. 1969. *Spatial Diffusion.* Resource Paper No. 4. Washington, D.C.: Association of American Geographers.

Kain, John F. 1975. *Essays on Urban Spatial Structure.* Cambridge, Mass.: Ballinger Publishing Co.

Koestler, Arthur. 1978. *Janus: A Summing Up.* New York: Random House.

Lewis, Peirce F. 1976. *New Orleans—The Making of an Urban Landscape.* Cambridge, Mass.: Ballinger Publishing Co.

Palm, R., and Exline, C. 1976. "Electoral Geography and the Concept of Scale." In B. Dent, ed., *Census Data: Geographic Significance and Classroom Utility,* pp. 157–164. Tualatin, Oreg.: Geographic and Area Study Publications.

Stearns, F., and Montag, T., eds. 1974. *The Urban Ecosystem.* Stroudsburg, Pa.: Dowden, Hutchinson and Ross.

U.S., Department of Commerce, Bureau of the Census. 1974. *Census USA: A Thumbnail History of the Nation's Fact-finder.* Bureau of the Census Publication 1974-0-551-097. Washington, D.C.: U.S. Department of Commerce.

Vance, James E., Jr. 1966. "Focus on Downtown." *Community Planning Review* 16. Reprinted in L. Bourne, ed. 1971. *Internal Structure of the City,* pp. 112–120. New York: Oxford University Press.

2

The Physical Geography
of the City

Venice, once a flourishing center of commerce and the arts and still one of the world's most beautiful and romantic cities, is gradually sinking. The ancient city of Herculaneum was destroyed by an eruption of Mount Vesuvius in A.D. 79. In 1906 an earthquake on the San Andreas fault nearly demolished San Francisco. The list of cities ravaged by natural disasters goes on and on, yet only recently have urban geographers and planners begun to seriously consider the importance of the physical geography of cities.

Of course the importance of a city's physical environment is not limited to natural hazards such as earthquakes, landslides, and floods. For example, urban vegetation is significant, though not necessarily hazardous. Trees and shrubs provide shade and beauty, and they may also help to mitigate the harshness of urban noise.

Nowhere have people done more to alter the natural environment than they have in cities, yet the urban ecosystem cannot be isolated from the physical environment. Urban ecosystems are extremely complex, but we need to understand them as best we can, especially if we are going to adequately plan future environments and help solve some of today's vexing urban problems, from noise and traffic congestion to residential segregation and urban blight. Because cities are established in, depend on, and interact with their physical environments, we begin this study of cities with a look at their physical geography.

URBAN PROCESSES IN PERSPECTIVE

Human needs and wants, both biological and cultural, must be met. Growing cities have to continuously expand their use of technology in order to meet the needs of a growing population. With population growth and the expanded use of technology, along with a necessarily greater impact on the natural environment, urban ecosystems grow continuously more complex.

The urban ecosystem is an open system, and as such, it has various inputs and outputs, both cultural and physical. Ideas flow into and out of the city, as do people, technology, and water. Often outputs of the urban ecosystem are converted forms of inputs. For example, waste outputs are generated from food and material inputs. Air and water outputs come from inputs that have interacted with other elements of the urban ecosystem—as clean air, for example, interacts with automobile exhaust. People and their cities, of course, ultimately are dependent on the physical environment, a point often ignored by city dwellers. As Schmid has reminded us, "in the long run the preservation of man and the preservation of nature are one and the same, but in the short run there are always too many temptations to sacrifice the latter for the former" (Schmid, 1974, p. 240).

MAJOR PHYSICAL SUBSYSTEMS OF THE CITY

The urban ecosystem can be divided into two broad subsystems, one physical and the other cultural. In keeping with the holarchy concept, however, the physical subsystem can be further broken into smaller subsystems, including the following: geologic, climatic (or atmospheric), hydrologic, and biologic. Of course these subsystems are interdependent and interact among themselves in often complex ways.

Geology, Soils, and Topography of Cities

The physical site of a city is often far less important than other locational factors such as situation, but nonetheless it has an impact on the growth and development of the city once it has become established. Even in modern cities geologic structure, topography, and type of soil impose constraints on urban morphology, though many contraints can be overcome if cost is no obstacle (seldom the case). People can fill bays to build housing tracts, as they have done in San Francisco, or build houses on unstable hillsides, as they have done in Los Angeles, but often both the price and the attendant risks are high. In the case of Los Angeles, Eschman and Marcus have noted that "The city has become an impressive testimonial to man's technological ability to overwhelm his environment—but only if he blindly ignores the risks from landslides, earthquakes, and storms" (Eschman and Marcus, 1972, p. 32).

Hills and Slopes. Cities are especially suited to flat, open terrain. Transportation-system planners, for example, seek routes that have the fewest problems and the lowest cost. Hills and slopes create design problems for rails and streets, usually resulting in higher costs. Tunnels may be required, creating potential construction problems and traffic hazards. Even though hills and slopes create special problems, they may also give "character" to a city. Imagine, for example, San Francisco without Twin Peaks and Knob Hill or Boston without Beacon Hill.

Steep slopes are often barriers to urban expansion, because of high development costs and the risk of slope instability and landslides. Furthermore, developing slopes removes vegetation, which accelerates erosion and increases the rate of sedimentation downstream. Also, overland flow may be diverted into different drainage systems after urban development, changing the balance in local stream systems. In turn, increased sedimentation and aggradation downstream may harm biologic communities and hasten the silting up of reservoirs and estuaries.

The expansion of suburban residential growth onto steeper slopes is especially problematic, mainly because of the trade-off between risks and costs. Eschman and Marcus (1972) pointed out that people who venture to build on steep terrain in advance of planned housing developments represent two extremes with respect to income, rich and poor. They argued that

> families with high incomes can afford to clear and build on virgin terrain and to invest in expensive systems for water supply and sewerage. The advantages—privacy, a more natural landscape, perhaps scenic outlook, as well as avoidance of the environmental and social liabilities of the city—are considered worth the additional investment. Low-income families also move into these fringe areas as long as property values remain low . . . because they are willing to do with less elaborate utilities and provide their own construction. Thus, the edge of the city can present the incongruity of neighboring tarpaper shacks and elaborate homes. [Eschman and Marcus, 1972, p. 35]

Around Los Angeles, examples of expensive developments can be found in places in the Santa Monica Mountains and Malibu Canyon. The urban poor, however, more often live in crowded areas on steep slopes adjacent to cities in developing countries, such as in Brazilian *favelas* ("slums") and parts of Hong Kong. In places where slopes are a problem and motivation is sufficient, however, hills can be removed and the material used to fill in marshes or other low places, thus homogenizing the topography.

Cutting and Filling. Whether building interstate highways or suburban housing tracts, modern civilization finds it most convenient to level protruding surfaces and fill in low spots in an effort to provide level building sites. Anyone who has driven on Interstate 80 through Pennsylvania's beautiful "ridge and valley" landscape knows what we mean.

Most of Boston's many hills, mainly drumlins, have been leveled, or at least have had their tops removed, as urban expansion has required additional building space. Across the country, San Francisco has been filling in parts of the bay to provide additional space, and in Los Angeles hills are constantly being terraced to provide space for additional housing.

In and around many cities mining also leaves its mark.

Building construction requires sand and gravel for use in concrete, and these aggregates are likely to be obtained in close proximity to a city, mainly because of their low value per unit of weight. As urban sprawl continues, gravel pits become surrounded by housing tracts, and the new residents find the pits an eyesore. Aggregate producers then are forced further out of town, which means additional charges for increased transportation. Other mining activities occasionally affect cities also. For example, coal mine refuse piles still occupy prime urban land in Scranton and Wilkes-Barre in Pennsylvania's anthracite region.

Still, given people's desires and today's sophisticated technology, the topography of cities can be, and often is, rearranged to suit a city's perceived needs.

Earthquakes. Earthquakes are the result of movement along geologic faults, and they represent formidable geologic hazards. Because faults are unevenly distributed over the earth's surface, earthquakes are of considerable concern in some urban areas, such as Los Angeles and Tokyo, and of less concern in other cities. Major earthquake areas, such as the circum-Pacific belt, are located along the boundary zones between plates that move relative to each other. Stress builds up in the rocks along these zones, and when the strength of the rocks is exceeded, the rocks break along the faults.

The primary effects of earthquakes are those directly related to ground motion, including displacement of the land; destruction of buildings, bridges, and dams; and the uprooting of trees. During the 1906 San Francisco earthquake, for example, horizontal displacement along the San Andreas fault in some places was nearly five meters. The 1971 San Fernando earthquake damaged numerous homes and larger buildings, including the Olive View Hospital in Sylmar, a new building that had been built to conform with local standards for earthquake resistance. Yet that 1971 tremor was not a great one, measuring 6.6 on the Richter scale.

Earthquakes also produce a variety of secondary effects, such as flood, tsunami, and landslide, as well as such long-term effects as land subsidence or emergence and even fluctuations in groundwater levels. Fires burned for several days in San Francisco following the 1906 earthquake, for example, and numerous landslides and avalanches were produced by the 1964 Alaskan earthquake, which did considerable damage to Anchorage.

In addition to earthquakes, fault zones may create other problems in urban areas. For example, tectonic creep, or slow movement along a fault, may gradually damage roads, sidewalks, and even buildings.

Subsidence. Subsidence is a long-term consequence of earthquakes, but other causes of subsidence include underground mining, withdrawal of groundwater, and removal of petroleum. Subsidence can damage or destroy buildings, roads, and other artifacts rather easily, though generally gradually.

In Scranton, Pennsylvania, for example, abandoned coal mines have collapsed on several occasions, damaging homes and streets. Also, subsidence has occurred in parts of Long Beach, California, as a result of pumping oil from underneath the city (see Figure 2.1). Oil production began in 1936, and subsidence began shortly thereafter, averaging more than six inches per year. By 1962 parts of Long Beach had subsided as much as twenty-seven feet, and in order to maintain underground fluid pressure, water injection was begun. Although water injection halted subsidence for several years, new evidence in 1979 suggested that subsidence was again occurring in the harbor area.

The Climate of Cities

The climate of cities, affected by interactions between the atmosphere and various elements of the urban ecosystem, has been studied rather thoroughly in recent years, though we still have much to learn. City residents are often aware of variations in microclimate within a city. Downtown areas, for example, are often thought of as wind tunnels, and low areas are known to be colder because cold air drains into them, especially at night. Furthermore, urbanites are often aware that temperatures in suburban areas tend to be lower than the downtown temperatures. Climatologists and

FIGURE 2.1. Subsidence in Long Beach, California. Source: Long Beach Harbor Department.

meteorologists are seeking explanations for these and other phenomena of urban climates, and planners are beginning to take note of climatic effects of the urban ecosystem.

Urban Effects on Climate. Cities interact with the atmosphere in at least five significant ways to produce conditions that are different from those found in nearby rural areas (Oliver, 1979). In each case, as we shall see, the impact operates to warm the city in comparison to the surrounding countryside.

First, the city surface differs considerably from the rural surface, which changes the albedo rate (the percentage of radiant energy emitted back into space by a surface). Concrete, for example, absorbs and stores heat during the day, then releases it slowly during the night. Urban surfaces also generally have less vegetation than do rural surfaces, again increasing urban heat absorption. Overall, an urban area absorbs more heat during the day and releases stored heat more slowly at night when compared to the surrounding rural area.

Second, the city surface is usually rougher than the surface of the surrounding countryside. The multitude of vertical surfaces, presented by the sides of buildings and roofs pitched at various angles, acts to absorb low-angle solar radiation, which occurs during the early morning and late afternoon hours. Thus, the city's verticality increases its ability to absorb heat. Furthermore, the roughness attenuates surface wind velocities by as much as 25 percent, but it also increases both turbulence and the number of localized eddies (Bryson and Ross, 1972).

Third, the urban heat balance is affected by the impact of the urban ecosystem on surface water. Normally a certain amount of solar energy is utilized in the processes of evaporation and transpiration. However, as noted previously, urban areas usually have less vegetation than do rural areas, so urban areas also have less transpiration. Furthermore, considerable waterproofing occurs in urban surfaces as pavement and rooftops are substituted for open ground. The result, of course, is that precipitation runs off more quickly in the city, hence less moisture is on the surface and available for evaporation. As a result, the heat that would have been used for evaporation and transpiration is instead absorbed by the urban ecosystem.

Fourth, the city and its residents generate heat. As anyone who has been to a party in a crowded room can tell you, people radiate heat. According to Bryson and Ross, "a person produces about 100 watts at rest and about 200–300 watts while working" (Bryson and Ross, 1972, p. 56). Multiply those figures by millions of people, and you end up with a lot of heat in large cities.

The burning of fossil fuels also contributes to the heat production of cities. Manufacturing processes, home heating, and automobiles all produce heat that ends up in the urban atmosphere. According to Oliver, "In New York City . . . the amount of heat generated through the burning of fossil fuel in winter is two and one half times the amount of heat energy derived from the sun over the same period of time" (Oliver, 1979, p. 288). As energy prices soar and energy scarcities become more common during the 1980s, urban ecosystems are going to have to improve their ability to conserve energy.

Fifth, pollutants generated by the city have an impact on the atmosphere. Turbidity, the amount of particulates such as dust and smoke in the atmosphere, is higher over cities than over rural areas. Particulates have various effects on the urban climate. On the one hand, they reflect incoming solar radiation back into space, which decreases insolation in large cities by as much as 15 percent (Bryson and Ross, 1972). Indeed, some climatologists argue that increasing the particulate content of the atmosphere could lower global temperatures. On the other hand, some particulates are condensation nuclei. Lakshmanan and Chatterjee noted that

> increased amounts of condensation nuclei cause a higher frequency of fogs in cities than in their outlying areas. Fog incidence, dependent on the relative cleanliness of air, varies greatly among cities and among different decades in the same city. Cloudiness and precipitation increase because of increases in condensation nuclei, turbulence, and convection. Though considerable controversy still surrounds the issue on whether increased cloudiness causes increasing precipitation, studies show that several cities have higher rainfall than their environs. [Lakshmanan and Chatterjee, 1977, p. 13]

In turn, the increased cloud cover in the city increases the greenhouse effect, thus trapping more heat.

In summary, then, these five factors operate both independently and together to heat urban areas beyond the temperatures of the surrounding rural areas. Also, the warming of a city occurs both day and night, creating an urban heat island.

The Urban Heat Island. Just as an island is a body of land surrounded by water, the urban heat island is a city surrounded by a relatively cooler rural area. The heat-island phenomenon is found not only in the world's urban giants, such as London, Paris, or New York, but also in smaller towns, such as Corvallis, Oregon (Lowry, 1967). Bryson and Ross pointed out that "urban heating leads to increased buoyancy of the air over the city and to a city-induced wind field that dominates when regional weather patterns are too weak to displace the mass of urban air" (Bryson and Ross, 1972, p. 59).

Because of the heat-island effect, it is possible to identify a local circulation pattern. Warmer air in the city rises; it is then replaced by cooler air drawn in from the surrounding countryside. Of course, this localized pattern can be overridden by larger circulation systems.

Temperature variations from city to countryside may reach or exceed 10° F, and on one winter day in Madison, Wisconsin, the observed difference reached 37° F (Bryson and Ross, 1972). Also, busy streets tend to have higher temperatures than do quieter ones.

The Urban Dust Dome and Air Pollution. Because of the air circulation pattern just described, pollutants (Figure 2.2) are easily trapped within the warmer layer of urban air by a temperature inversion, which acts as a lid on the urban dust dome. Particulates and gases generated in the outer city are carried inward toward the urban center when the heat-island circulation pattern is present, further concentrating pollutants in the urban environment. Although a dust dome commonly develops when atmospheric conditions are calm, on windy days the contents of the dust dome are carried downwind, forming a dust plume. The plume may extend for several miles, carrying pollutants over suburbs and rural areas and even to downwind cities. For example, pollutants

FIGURE 2.2. Air Pollution in an Urban Area. Source: United Nations photo by John Orr.

from Chicago have been traced to Madison, Wisconsin, and pollutants from Canton, China, have been known to follow the Pearl River for seventy miles, ultimately affecting visibility and air quality in Hong Kong (Bryson and Ross, 1972).

In London in 1952 a severe smog episode was responsible for an estimated 4,000 deaths. Four years earlier a smog episode in Donora, Pennsylvania, had killed at least twenty people and made several thousand ill. Unfortunately, however, we are generally unable to distinguish the effect of air pollutants on morbidity and mortality in cities, though most observers would argue that pollutants have a significant impact.

We must not be misled into believing that air pollution is a twentieth-century phenomenon, however; early cave dwellers undoubtedly breathed pollutants generated by fires. But the Industrial Revolution certainly increased our ability to generate and distribute pollutants. Rudyard Kipling once commented that Chicago's air was nothing but dirt. Until recently, however, industry and progress have been synonymous, as is suggested by the following comment on late-nineteenth-century United States by Otto Bettmann.

> The smoke that billowed over the landscape was seen as a good omen; it meant prosperity. In the industrial communities it was considered a sign of feminine delicacy to complain about the bad air or to have a coughing spell. Mary Gilson, growing up in Pittsburgh in the 1890's, was reprimanded by her parents for complaining about the foul air: "We should be grateful for God's goodness in making work, which made smoke, which made prosperity." [Bettmann, 1974, p. 1]

If you draw a deep breath in almost any large city today, you are certain to treat your lungs to a wide array of substances other than just nitrogen and oxygen. Among them there is sure to be a variety of urban-generated pollutants, even if the term is limited only to substances that are considered harmful to plant and animal life.

Pollutants may be either substances that are added directly to the atmosphere or substances that have resulted from chemical reactions involving components of the air to varying degrees. Pollutants may be gases, liquids, or solids. Among the major urban pollutants are the following: particulates; oxides of carbon, nitrogen, and sulfur; hydrocarbons; and photochemical oxidants.

The urban atmosphere offers a variety of particulates, and many of them are the result of natural processes. Particulates occur in the atmosphere both as solids and as liquids. Common urban particulates are dust, smoke, metallic elements, pollen, and salts. As was noted earlier, particulates tend to reflect incoming solar radiation back into space.

Carbon monoxide (CO) and carbon dioxide (CO_2) are both colorless, odorless gases. Carbon monoxide is lethal and is produced by the burning of fossil fuels. According to Bach (1972), about 80 percent of the world's carbon monoxide is produced by automobiles. Carbon dioxide is not considered a pollutant; it occurs naturally and is essential to life. However, it is important for the earth's heat balance because it plays a major role in producing the greenhouse effect. The atmosphere's carbon dioxide content has been increasing as a result of the large-scale burning of fossil fuels, and many climatologists argue that the buildup of carbon dioxide may raise the earth's average temperature.

Nitrogen oxides (NO_x) of concern include nitric oxide (NO) and nitrogen dioxide (NO_2). Nature produces more nitrogen oxides than humans do, but human production concentrates these oxides in urban areas, which makes them more of a problem. Nitric oxide, produced by internal-combustion engines, reacts with oxygen or ozone to produce nitrogen dioxide. The latter is a pungent, yellowish brown gas that is harmful to plants and animals. Furthermore, nitrogen dioxide is essential for the formation of photochemical smog, which is created by chemical reactions initiated by the presence of sunlight.

Sulfur oxides (SO_x) are acrid, poisonous gases, mainly sulfur dioxide (SO_2) and sulfur trioxide (SO_3). Sulfur dioxide is produced from burning coal and oil, and it then reacts with oxygen to form sulfur trioxide. Of increasing concern to environmentalists is the impact of rainwater that contains sulfuric acid.

Hydrocarbons are derived primarily from the burning of wood and fossil fuels, as well as from the decomposition of vegetation. Although most hydrocarbons are produced by natural processes, they are concentrated by people in urban areas, and they are also ingredients of photochemical smog. Most hydrocarbons are not harmful in small quantities, but a few, such as benzopyrene, are known carcinogens (Bach, 1972).

Photochemical oxidants are produced by reactions between nitrogen oxides and hydrocarbons in the presence of sunlight. Among the most harmful of the photochemical oxidants are ozone, peroxyacetyl nitrate (PAN), and aldehydes. The latter two cause eye irritation, but ozone can be more dangerous to humans, especially when concentrations are high.

Table 2.1 shows both the relative amounts of various pollutants in the United States and the major contributors of pollutants. An inescapable conclusion, looking at either group, is that transportation is a major culprit in the pollution equation.

TABLE 2.1
Air Pollutants, Percentage by Weight, and Major Pollutant Sources

Pollutant	Percentage by Weight	Pollutant Source	Percentage
Carbon monoxide	47	transportation	42
Sulfur oxides	15	fuel combustion in stationary sources	21
Hydrocarbons	15	Industrial processes	14
Particulates	13	miscellaneous	10
Nitrogen oxides	10	forest fires	8
		solid waste disposal	5

Source: National Air Pollution Control Administration.

Water in the Urban Ecosystem

It has already been noted that the surface of the city has been greatly modified by humans, and many of the modifications affect the hydrology of urban areas. Urbanization increases runoff and the frequency of floods, pollutes streams, rearranges drainage patterns, and at times creates a seemingly insatiable thirst.

The Hydrologic Cycle. The hydrologic cycle is the initial model from which virtually all studies of water systems, urban or otherwise, are derived. It traces the many lines of water flows in all states, solid, liquid, and gas. The hydrologic cycle is a complex model, but it is often simplified somewhat as follows. Water evaporates from the oceans, condenses and falls as rain or snow on land surfaces, and then returns to the oceans either through surface streams or underground. Of course, some precipitation returns directly from the land to the atmosphere by means of evaporation and transpiration, and some evaporates even before it hits the earth's surface (see Figure 2.3).

Our concern is to see how urban areas affect the hydrologic cycle. Because of their abundance of condensation nuclei, cities tend to have more clouds and precipitation than do their surrounding countrysides, but they have other consequences as well, mainly because concrete and impervious rooftops have replaced natural soil and vegetation.

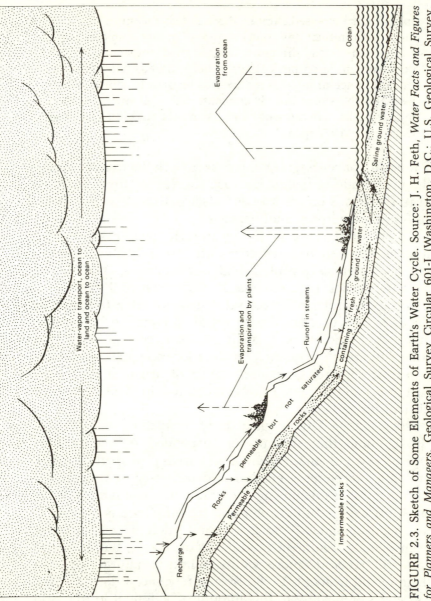

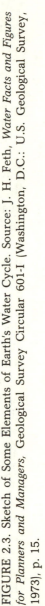

FIGURE 2.3. Sketch of Some Elements of Earth's Water Cycle. Source: J. H. Feth, *Water Facts and Figures for Planners and Managers*, Geological Survey Circular 601-I (Washington, D.C.: U.S. Geological Survey, 1973), p. 15.

Urban Runoff. As is noted in the following statement, runoff is modified by urbanization.

> In spite of increased rainfall there is less moisture in urban areas than in their environs because of greater run-off coefficients. The most dramatic hydrological impact of urban development is on peak flows, where the basic lag time (or time of concentration) is reduced as an area becomes urbanized and the storm flow is concentrated in sharper, shorter, higher peaks than those of natural run-offs. [Lakshmanan and Chatterjee, 1977, p. 11]

The result, of course, is an increase in both the frequency and the magnitude of floods, because shorter lag times increase peak flows (see Figure 2.4). Floods are discussed later in the section on environmental hazards.

Urban interference in the hydrologic cycle creates other problems related to increased runoff. Groundwater resources are not adequately replenished, for example. Also, urban stream channels require constant maintenance. Rains create drainage control problems, and streets are often temporarily flooded and occasionally enraged drivers sit in stalled automobiles. Solutions to such problems can be found, but the solutions are frequently costly. More adequate consideration of the hydrologic consequences of urbanization on the part of urban planners, however, could help to alleviate both difficulties and costs.

Sedimentation. One English study by Walling and Gregory (1970) found that amounts of suspended sediments were typically two to ten times greater in areas disturbed by urban building. Accelerated erosion and increased sedimentation are most noticeable during construction, when land surfaces are most exposed to erosion and runoff. Once construction has been completed and lawns and other vegetation have been planted, sediment production decreases, but an urban area still generates more sediment than a natural one does (Dunne and Leopold, 1978). Even a few vacant lots in a city can add significantly to the amount of sediment in the local drainage network.

Increased sediment loads also have significant downstream

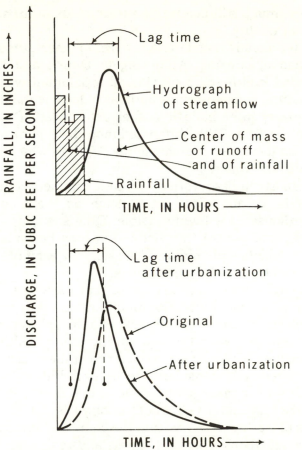

FIGURE 2.4. Hypothetical Unit Hydrographs Relating Runoff to Rainfall, with Definitions of Significant Parameters. Source: Luna B. Leopold, *Hydrology for Urban Land Planning—A Guidebook on the Hydrologic Effects of Urban Land Use,* Geological Survey Circular 554 (Washington, D.C.: U.S. Geological Survey, 1968), p. 3.

impacts. Sediment can wreak havoc with ecosystems by covering plants and animals in streambeds and by modifying the aquatic environment.

Urban Water Pollution. A variety of elements from urban areas enter local drainage systems, but it is not always clear whether an element should be considered a pollutant. Furthermore, much still needs to be learned about urbanization and water quality.

We have already noted that urbanization increases the sediment load of streams. According to Dunne and Leopold, "suspended load may be considered a pollutant when it exceeds natural concentrations and has a detrimental effect on water quality in its biologic and esthetic sense" (Dunne and Leopold, 1978, p. 714). When sediment load increases, turbidity also increases, decreasing the depth to which sunlight penetrates the water.

An almost endless variety of industrial effluents enter streams in urban areas. Some, such as the blood from slaughterhouses, are highly visible. Others, such as minute asbestos particles, are less visible but may be far more injurious to plants and animals. Asbestos, for example, is generally considered to be a carcinogen.

Combined sewage systems, those that carry both sewage and runoff, are major contributors to urban water pollution. Such sewage treatment plants can't handle high water flows, so raw sewage passes through during storms. Although it would be possible to detain and later treat the overflows, the costs are generally considered to be prohibitive. However, some cities have managed to move in that direction. For example, the Minneapolis–St. Paul Sanitary District has devised a means of storing wastes within the combined system by using inflatable dams, automatic gates, and remote sensors.

Finally, the thermal pollution of streams is becoming a serious problem and an especially troublesome one because the major sources of thermal pollution are power plants, along with other industrial plants. Power plants are important because they are relatively inefficient, are increasing in number, and are already sources of public debate in the conflict between economic growth and environmental protection.

Noting that the United States would have a power-generating capacity of at least 570,000 megawatts by 1980, Dunne and Leopold commented that

the cooling-water requirements of these plants will exceed

750 million cubic meters per day, or about one-sixth of the average daily runoff from the 48 conterminous states. Cooling water can, of course, be re-used many times, so the problem is not as bad as it seems at first glance. On the other hand, these requirements represent about one-third of the average dry-season runoff of the country and an even larger proportion of the low flow of streams in subhumid areas. [Dunne and Leopold, 1978, p. 716]

Furthermore, nuclear power plants present a potential not only for thermal pollution but for radioactive pollution as well.

In the United States water pollution and water quality have long been a concern of the government, of course. The Refuse Act of 1899 made it unlawful to place refuse from any source into navigable waterways. The National Environmental Policy Act of 1969 (NEPA) sought a wide variety of ways to prevent environmental degradation, including water pollution. The Water Quality Act of 1970 provided a comprehensive water pollution control law, mainly by expanding powers that had been granted by the Federal Water and Pollution Control Act of 1956.

Urban Vegetation

Urban vegetation is of interest for several reasons. It plays a role in transpiration, alters microclimates, and adds an aesthetic touch to the urban ecosystem. However, the study of urban vegetation is a somewhat different challenge than the study of natural vegetation. Furthermore, urban vegetation has not been thoroughly studied.

The distribution of vegetation in urban areas varies considerably from city to city. Generally, the amount of urban vegetation decreases as we move from rural to suburban to central city to central business district, though exceptions are common. Parks such as New York's Central Park in Manhattan are examples of such exceptions.

Schmid noted that

both native and cultivated plants suffer displacement or land use intensifies and rents increase upon the arrival of urban commercial or residential activity. Native *ecosystems,* whether involving grassland, desert flora, or forest-understory shrubs and herbs, virtually never survive into modern American landscapes – with the exception of sacrosanct forest preserves, watersheds, or tiny residual bits of land between plots in outer suburbia, all frequently characterized by some environmental hazard. [Schmid, 1974, p. 227]

Trees, however, do survive as parts of the urban ecosystem in many cases, though their life span is probably reduced because of their altered environment. In orchard-growing regions urban encroachment on farmland sometimes preserves parts of the orchards in residential developments. In Chico, California, for example, suburban housing tracts built on sites previously occupied by almond orchards have preserved numerous almond trees. Although the almond trees appear to be randomly distributed through the housing developments, aerial photographs show that the trees form parts of neat rows. Good use is sometimes made of natural forests as well – as in the community of Reston, Virginia, for example. However, all too often the developers seem to prefer beginning with a "clean slate"; thus they expose bare surfaces to erosion and build treeless tracts of houses.

In considering urban vegetation Detwyler (1972) proposed the following four types: (1) the interstitial forest, (2) parks and green space, (3) gardens, and (4) lawns.

The Interstitial Forest. Despite the 300 million years that trees have been on earth and the several thousand years that people have lived in cities, trees and cities were not consciously and intentionally joined together until about two centuries ago (Zube, 1973). Trees are common now in urban areas, and they have a place in most people's conceptions of an ideal urban environment.

According to Detwyler (1972) the interstitial forest is typical of older residential and commercial areas. Such a forest consists of trees scattered among various urban creations – e.g., buildings – and it often forms an overhead canopy. It consists mainly of shade trees, either natural or planted. Newer suburbs are often unshaded and contrast

FIGURE 2.5. New Suburban Area in Southern California. Source: Gary Peters.

sharply with older residential areas (Figure 2.5).

Parks and Green Space. Most people, if asked about their perceptions of urban vegetation, would probably first think of parks and other green spaces, such as golf courses, as being examples of urban vegetation. Those green areas are places of solace where urbanites can seek refuge and feel closer to nature, though unfortunately they also are scenes of increasing crime and violence. Central Park, for example, quickly conjures up images of muggers and rapists as well as images of grass, shrubs, and trees (Figure 2.6).

Greenbelts, basically circular parks that separate residential areas from industrial zones, are common around London and some of its surrounding towns. Visitors to Hong Kong's newly created Ocean Park, a 170-acre park between Aberdeen Harbour and Repulse Bay, are able to enjoy an almost natural setting of woods, lakes, flowers, and even a bird sanctuary.

Gardens. Urban gardens are not recent innovations – they existed in Babylon and in ancient Egypt, for example. Both

FIGURE 2.6. Central Park in New York City. Source: United Nations photo by J. Isaac.

public and private gardens have aesthetic settings that provide some closeness to nature. Gardens vary considerably
among different cultures, but gardens everywhere appeal to
people in similar ways. As Shepard commented, "The garden
is the perfect human habitat. So far as there is one paradise
for all men, all gardens in all times and places are alike; their
peculiarities measure the unique experiences of each society
as it confronts nature" (Shepard, 1967, p. 114).

Gardens vary from those that are starkly geometric and obviously planted by man to those that recreate nature as carefully as possible. The Japanese garden, designed to create a sense of tranquillity, is an example of the latter. Its essential ingredients are stones, plants, wood, and water, all arranged in a natural harmonious style. Space is carefully utilized, and often the Japanese garden creates an illusion of being larger than it really is; even the smallest home gardens have a feeling of spaciousness. Japanese garden paths are almost never straight, bamboos and pines are preferred to flowering plants, and contemplation is encouraged. By contrast, the classic Italian garden is strongly geometric, with straight paved paths and rectangular ponds.

Home gardens often satisfy needs other than our need to feel close to nature. For many people a home garden is a form of recreation that provides both exercise and a sense of accomplishment. Furthermore, gardens often supply fresh fruits and vegetables as well as flowers. Given the high food prices and the rather poor quality of some supermarket produce, people in American cities are growing more of their own food than at any time since the "victory gardens" of the Second World War.

Lawns. It is possible that lawns originated in England's parks, but nowhere are they more uniformly accepted than in the American suburbs, where ideally they are richly green and require almost constant attention. A suburbanite who fails to maintain a lawn violates an unwritten law and may be confronted or chastised by neighbors, or at least viewed with a mixture of suspicion and contempt. Detwyler nicely captured the suburban experience in the following statement.

Today through our suburban lawns we may try to assert our role as "lord of the estate." In reality, however, the present role of the suburbanite in relation to his lawn is pathetic. With his power mower he artificially assumes the cropping function of domestic animals that have long since disappeared. The primary pay off from this activity is maintaining social "appearances" in the neighborhood and property value. [Detwyler, 1972, p. 236]

Lawns are major consumers of the urban water supply and of chemical fertilizers, and a great deal of money and countless hours of labor are spent on them each year. What justifies these efforts? According to Jackson (1951) the front yard satisfies a person's love of beauty. Whatever the reason, front yards and lawns seem destined to survive.

THE CITY AS HUMAN HABITAT

Despite smog, congestion, noise, and exposure to a variety of environmental risks, cities are assumed to be habitats for humans. However, most people have viewed cities more as functional systems designed to efficiently produce an abundance of material goods than as desirable residential areas. Whenever able, people have escaped to the suburbs and beyond, seeking a cleaner and more peaceful environment. Services and industries, however, have often followed, creating cities within cities or what some now refer to as "outer cities." For now, we need to look at some of the consequences for humans caused by physical subsystems within the urban ecosystem.

Pollution and Health

Major episodes of air pollution have been directly responsible for increased mortality and morbidity, as in the specific examples of London and Donora. However, it is considerably more difficult to *prove* that continued exposure to lower levels of air pollution are deleterious to human health, though intuitively one would argue that it is. Considerable work needs to be done by the medical profession in order to identify the detrimental effects of the common pollutants, both individually and interdependently. The latter is necessary because pollutants that may be relatively harmless by themselves may react in combination to create more-potent pollutants, as in the formation of photochemical smog (Figure 2.7).

Despite the attention given to major pollution episodes, it is far more important that we understand the long-term effects of living in polluted urban ecosystems. The very young, the

FIGURE 2.7. Air Pollution, New York City. Source: HUD.

elderly, and the chronically ill are especially susceptible to
pollution. Although all the evidence is not in on all the effects
of pollutants, we do know some of the effects of some of
them. Carbon monoxide, for example, combines more efficiently than oxygen with hemoglobin in the blood, displacing
needed oxygen. The heart and lungs must then work harder
to supply oxygen, which creates problems for people with
heart and lung diseases.

Ozone, a major photochemical oxidant produced in the Los
Angeles type of smog, causes throat and nose irritation, even
at rather low levels (below one part per million). Prolonged
exposure to ozone produces headaches, impairs athletic ability, and creates breathing difficulties for people with lung
diseases, especially for those with emphysema.

Like carbon monoxide, nitrogen dioxide, a pungent gas that
produces that familiar brownish haze, reduces the oxygen-

carrying capacity of the blood. It also causes eye irritation and lung problems, including acute pulmonary edema (Lynn, 1976).

Sulfur dioxide by itself is not known to be harmful, but the synergistic effect of sulfur dioxide and suspended particulates causes an increase in bronchitis and emphysema. This synergistic effect is assumed to have been the major cause of increased mortality during the 1952 smog episode in London (Bach, 1972).

Environmental Hazards and the Urban Ecosystem

Before ending this discussion of the physical environment, we need to briefly examine some of the problems that are related to living with natural hazards in the urban ecosystem. Examples of natural hazards that have affected cities include floods, tornadoes, earthquakes, and volcanoes. By concentrating people, buildings, and economic activities in cities we have increased the probability of having major losses of life as well as major economic losses. As Baumann and Kates phrased it, "The natural hazardousness of cities arises from the impact of natural events on an urban structure that at best is only partly designed to absorb, buffer, or reflect such events, and that at worst exacerbates them" (Baumann and Kates, 1972, p. 169).

According to Burton and Kates, natural hazards are "those elements in the physical environment harmful to man and caused by forces extraneous to him" (Burton and Kates, 1964, p. 413). How people prepare for or react to natural hazards depends on how much people think about their natural environment. Catastrophic natural events occur only infrequently in a given location, so people, preoccupied with daily activities, are prone to give little if any thought to environmental hazards until after some natural disaster has occurred. However, once a disaster has occurred, people tend to remember it for some time, as was the case with the 1906 earthquake in San Francisco. Real concern, however, tends to diminish as people return to their regular lives following an earthquake, a flood, or some other catastrophic event.

Floods. Urbanization decreases runoff lag times and increases the frequency of floods of a given magnitude. To further complicate matters, cities are often built on floodplains, with little thought about why geologists call them that. According to Baumann and Kates, "people's perception of the associated hazard and adjustment to floods relates to the probable frequency of these events" (Baumann and Kates, 1972, p. 176). In other words, people are least aware of floods in areas where they occur infrequently and most aware of the hazard in areas where they are relatively frequent events.

Overall, despite the threat of flood, floodplains and other flood-prone areas such as lake fronts and beaches are attractive for human settlement for a variety of reasons. Such areas provide flat land for urban development, corridors for transportation, and fertile soil for agriculture. Among the floodplain occupants, farmers seem to be more sensitive to flood hazards than are urbanites. Flood control systems, though hardly fail-safe, ease the minds of many people who live in flood-prone areas, and flood insurance perhaps eases the financial risk of inhabiting a flood zone.

Given the attraction of many flood-prone areas, people often are willing to accept a trade-off between risks and benefits. Also, land developers may fail to clearly state the risks of living on a floodplain, in a new suburban housing tract, for instance. Furthermore, people find ways of adapting to flood hazards.

Flood losses can be minimized in various ways. Local site elevations can be raised, either by a landfill or by building on stilts as is common in parts of Asia. Buildings can be made floodproof or at least flood resistant. Levees and dams can be built to protect against floods, and river channels can be improved by deepening them and keeping them clear of debris. However, complacency about floods may be a by-product of flood control attempts, and such attempts may fail. For example, Teton Dam, an earthfill dam in Idaho, collapsed on June 5, 1976, leaving in its wake human deaths, thousands of dead livestock, and a billion dollars worth of property damage.

Tornadoes. Tornadoes are highly localized, savage storms that can quickly destroy buildings and raze entire city blocks (Figure 2.8). About 90 percent of the world's tornadoes occur in the United States. Within the United States, tornadoes occur most frequently on the Great Plains, especially along a

FIGURE 2.8. Aftermath of a Tornado. Source: HUD.

band that stretches across the Texas panhandle, through most of Oklahoma, on across central and northeastern Kansas, and into the northwestern tip of Missouri. Although the conditions that spawn tornadoes can be predicted with some degree of accuracy, it is impossible to predict either exact locations where tornadoes might originate or their likely paths.

The National Weather Service has developed a tornado warning system that has helped decrease the loss of life caused by such storms. However, the effectiveness of the tornado warning system varies somewhat, depending on how much of an environmental hazard people in a particular region consider tornadoes to be (Baumann and Kates, 1972).

Earthquakes. Tens of thousands of earthquakes occur annually, but most are imperceptibly small tremors. However, a few earthquakes each year are large enough to cause moderate to substantial damage. As is true with other natural hazards, we are mostly made aware of damage when earthquakes occur in populated areas.

In a matter of seconds an earthquake nearly destroyed

Managua, the capital of Nicaragua, on December 22, 1975; two months later, 23,000 people died in another earthquake in nearby Guatemala; and in July 1976, an estimated 600,000 Chinese died in the Tangshan earthquake. Large cities such as Los Angeles, Tokyo, and Peking are located in earthquake-prone areas, and sooner or later devastating earthquakes are likely. Those cities have experienced earthquakes before, of course, but then they had smaller populations. For example, on September 1, 1923, Tokyo was rocked by the Kanto Plain earthquake, which has been estimated at a magnitude of 7.9 on the Richter scale, about the same as the 1906 San Francisco earthquake. Nearly 150,000 lives were lost in and around Tokyo out of a population of about 2 million; in 1981, the population of Tokyo was about 9 million.

Progress is being made in predicting earthquakes and developing warning systems, but adequate prediction is still a long way off. Scientists in Japan, China, Russia, and the United States are involved in various research projects related to earthquake prediction. Current research focuses on rapid or anomalous changes in rates of uplift or subsidence, changes in the velocity of primary seismic waves, gaps along known active fault zones, and changes in the amount of radon gas in deep wells. However, much needs to be learned before earthquake prediction is reliable. One recent disappointment was an earthquake that shook San Francisco on August 6, 1979. Even though it measured 5.7 on the Richter scale, it occurred without any observed warning signals.

People have adapted their settlements to earthquake hazards to some degree and in some places. Earthquake-proof structures have been built in San Francisco, Los Angeles, Tokyo, and elsewhere, though for the most part new high-rise structures remain untested. Television ads in Los Angeles and Tokyo provide information on what to do if an earthquake strikes. In Tokyo city parks have been designated as refugee centers, nearby warehouses are stocked with food, blankets, and clothing, and earthquake drills are held in Tokyo schools.

Volcanoes. Cities are not generally located adjacent to active volcanoes, but some are, and some of those, such as Pompeii, have paid the price. One of the most violent volcanic eruptions in recent decades was that of Mt. Bezy, in a virtually uninhabited area of Kamchatka in Soviet Russia. Among the volcanic eruptions that have taken lives and destroyed property during the twentieth century are the following examples: Mt. Pelée on Martinique erupted in 1902, killing an estimated 30,000 people in a matter of minutes; an eruption of Mt. Lamington killed 6,000 on Papua in 1951; and more recently, more than 5,000 people were driven from their homes in Vestmannaeyjar, Iceland, by an eruption of Mt. Helgafell.

In the spring of 1980 residents of the northwestern United States were greeted with the news that majestic Mount St. Helens in southwestern Washington State was rumbling and stirring to life. At first small eruptions of steam and dust attracted both professional geologists and tourists; newswriters and television cameras converged on the mountain and on such tiny nearby towns as Cougar, Washington.

On May 18, 1980, an explosive eruption rocked Mount St. Helens, blowing approximately 1,300 feet off the top of the mountain and spewing forth a cloud of volcanic ash that began moving northeastward. As the ash settled, fields and trees, cities and towns, were turned gray. By August of 1980 the volcano had erupted five more times, though not as spectacularly as the first time, and residents of the Pacific Northwest were adjusting to life in the shadow of an active volcano.

Of the nearby cities, the largest one to be significantly affected by the first volcanic eruption of Mount St. Helens was Spokane, Washington, where ash fell in considerable quantities. Television news crews filmed local citizens trying to clean up the city, fighting blowing ash, and wearing surgical masks. A June eruption affected Portland, Oregon. Some airline services were temporarily disrupted, low visibility slowed automobile traffic to a crawl, and surgical masks again became part of the necessary attire. Dust pollution was at unhealthful levels for several days, and in some cases drinking water had to come from alternate sources because ash had dropped into the local reservoirs.

The major adjustment to volcanic activity is rapid evacuation. The prediction of volcanic activity is generally inadequate and poorly developed; but in some areas, such as Hawaii, careful monitoring along with well-established volcano behavior patterns may make prediction feasible.

REFERENCES

Bach, Wilfred. 1972. *Atmospheric Pollution.* New York: McGraw-Hill Book Company.

Baumann, Duane D., and Kates, Robert W. 1972. "Risk from Nature in the City." In Thomas R. Detwyler and Melvin G. Marcus, eds., *Urbanization and Environment: The Physical Geography of the City,* pp. 169–194. Belmont, Calif.: Duxbury Press.

Bettmann, Otto L. 1974. *The Good Old Days—They Were Terrible.* New York: Random House.

Bryson, Reid A., and Ross, John E. 1972. "The Climate of the City." In Thomas R. Detwyler and Melvin G. Marcus, eds., *Urbanization and Environment: The Physical Geography of the City,* pp. 51–68. Belmont, Calif.: Duxbury Press.

Burton, Ian, and Kates, Robert. 1964. "The Perception of Natural Hazards in Resource Management." *Natural Resources Journal* 3: 412–441.

Detwyler, Thomas R. 1972. "Vegetation of the City." In Thomas R. Detwyler and Melvin G. Marcus, eds., *Urbanization and Environment: The Physical Geography of the City,* pp. 229–259. Belmont, Calif.: Duxbury Press.

Detwyler, Thomas R., ed. 1971. *Man's Impact on Environment.* New York: McGraw-Hill Book Company.

Detwyler, Thomas R., and Marcus, Melvin G., eds. 1972. *Urbanization and Environment: The Physical Geography of the City.* Belmont, Calif.: Duxbury Press.

Dunne, Thomas, and Leopold, Luna B. 1978. *Water in Environmental Planning.* San Francisco: W. H. Freeman and Company.

Ehrlich, Paul R.; Ehrlich, Anne H.; and Holdren, John P. 1977. *Ecoscience: Population, Resources, Environment.* San Francisco: W. H. Freeman and Company.

Eschman, Donald F., and Marcus, Melvin G. 1972. "The Geologic and Topographic Setting of Cities." In Thomas R. Detwyler and Melvin G. Marcus, eds., *Urbanization and Environment: The Physical Geography of the City,* pp. 27–50. Belmont, Calif.: Duxbury Press.

Fabos, Julius Gy. 1979. *Planning the Total Landscape: A Guide to Intelligent Land Use.* Boulder, Colo.: Westview Press.

Feth, J. H. 1973. *Water Facts and Figures for Planners and Managers.*
Geological Survey Circular 601-I. Washington, D.C.: U.S.
Geological Survey.

Flawn, Peter T. 1970. *Environmental Geology: Conservation, Land-
Use Planning, and Resource Management.* New York: Harper and
Row, Publishers.

Foin, Theodore C., Jr. 1976. *Ecological Systems and the Environment.* Boston: Houghton Mifflin Company.

Grandjean, E., and Gilgen, A. 1976. *Environmental Factors in Urban
Planning.* English translation by Harold Oldroyd. London: Taylor
and Francis. Originally published in 1973 by Ott Verlag Thun
under the title *Umwelthygiene in der Raumplanung.*

Hasegawa, T., and Inoue, K., eds. 1978. *Urban, Regional, and National Planning (UNRENAP): Environmental Aspects.* Oxford: Pergamon Press for the International Federation of Automatic Control.

Jackson, John B. 1951. "Ghosts at the Door." *Landscape* 1: 3–9.

Lakshmanan, T. R., and Chatterjee, Lata R. 1977. *Urbanization and
Environmental Quality.* Resource Papers for College Geography
No. 77-1. Washington, D.C.: Association of American Geo-
graphers.

Legget, Robert F. 1973. *Cities and Geology.* New York: McGraw-
Hill Book Company.

Leopold, Luna B. 1968. *Hydrology for Urban Land Planning—A
Guidebook on the Hydrologic Effects of Urban Land Use.* Geological
Survey Circular 554. Washington, D.C.: U.S. Geological Survey.

Lowry, W. P. 1967. "The Climate of Cities." *Scientific American* 226:
15–23.

Lynn, D. A. 1976. *Air Pollution: Threat and Response.* Reading,
Mass.: Addison-Wesley.

Keller, Edward A. 1976. *Environmental Geology.* Columbus, Ohio:
Charles E. Merrill Publishing Company.

Manners, Ian R., and Mikesell, Marvin W., eds. 1974. *Perspectives
on Environment.* Washington, D.C.: Association of American
Geographers.

Mrowka, Jack P. 1974. "Man's Impact on Stream Regimen and
Quality." In Ian R. Manners and Marvin W. Mikesell, eds.,
Perspectives on Environment, pp. 79–104. Washington, D.C.:
Association of American Geographers.

Oliver, John E. 1979. *Physical Geography: Principles and Applications.* North Scituate, Mass.: Duxbury Press.

Schmid, James A. 1974. "The Environmental Impact of Urbanization." In Ian R. Manners and Marvin W. Mikesell, eds., *Perspectives on Environment*, pp. 213-251. Washington, D.C.: Association of American Geographers.

Shepard, Paul. 1967. *Man in the Landscape: A Historic View of the Esthetics of Nature.* New York: Ballantine Books.

South Coast Air Quality Management District. 1976. *Air Quality and Meteorology: 1976 Annual Report.* Los Angeles: South Coast Air Quality Management District.

Walling, D. E., and Gregory, K. J. 1970. "The Measurement of the Effects of Building Construction on Drainage Basin Dynamics." *Journal of Hydrology* 11: 129-144.

Zube, Ervin H. 1973. "The Natural History of Urban Trees." *Natural History Magazine* 82: 48-51.

3

THE HUMAN MOSAIC

Many types of mosaics exist. Setting small pieces of colored tile in mortar to form a picture is what most people imagine when they hear the word *mosaic*. A virus creates light and dark areas on the leaves of plants that are also referred to as a mosaic, as are overlapping aerial photographs that are fitted together to form a single photograph. What do these definitions have in common? A single entity composed of parts arranged or created by a systematic process seems to be the common theme. Recall our definition of a system, a collection of parts and the relationship between those parts. A mosaic of any type is therefore somewhat like a system.

The human mosaic of a city is that element of the urban environment that is composed of the arrangements and distributions of people. We have used the term *mosaic* because the way in which social groups are distributed does not come about because of a chance series of events but as the result of fairly well-defined systematic processes. Just as the artist's mosaic can be seen either as individual pieces of color or as colors blurred together to form a picture, we may look at the city as a collection of discrete homogeneous subareas, or we may blend the subareas together to form broad general patterns. This chapter concentrates on the individual elements of the human mosaic within a city—the communities—and specifically on what types of communities exist in cities and the manner in which those social areas have evolved.

DIVISIONS OF SOCIETY

The way people view the social composition of cities is

largely the result of images or perceptions of people and places. We have a number of social identifiers, or descriptive words, that evoke an impression of the residents of a place.

As a word of caution, in most cases we deal with generalizations or stereotypes in our view of urban society, and assumptions about human behavior and many other characteristics form the basis of the stereotypes. It should be noted that conceptions commonly held about a group may not reflect fact and do not allow for the possibility that individual members of a group may not share the assumed values and norms of the whole group. For example, many people believe certain stereotypes about college students and may assume that any college student encountered has the characteristics of the much larger group. This is obviously a very weak assumption, for the perceived behavior of the group may be much different than the actual behavior and beliefs of the individual. Conversely, if a person only knows one college student and assumes that all college students are like the one-student sample, a great potential for erroneous assumptions exists. We must remember, therefore, that when considering the social-spatial organization of a city, there is a possibility of error inherent in generalizing or stereotyping. This is especially true when we deal with social identifiers.

What types of people are found in cities? Take a moment to answer this question. Your answers most probably involve three broad categories of social identifiers. In all likelihood, the different types of people found in cities are said to be old, young, rich, poor, blue-collar, white-collar, professional, those with much education and those with little formal education, black, white, brown, yellow, Italian, Irish, Polish, and so on. The list could virtually be without end.

What three broad categories are found in the list? First, people of different ages are mentioned. Second, income, type of employment, and education come into play – characteristics that are reflective of socioeconomic status (SES). The ethnic nature of urban populations makes up the third major category. Age, socioeconomic status, and ethnicity are thus the main categories of city social identifiers (Figure 3.1).

Stereotypes are wedded to these various social identifiers.

FIGURE 3.1A. Ethnic Market. Source: Hud.

FIGURE 3.1B. Young People at Shopping Mall. Source: HUD.

If a description of a blue-collar worker includes the terms *aged black person* or *middle-aged white*, certain images about those types of people, in terms of their life-styles and perhaps even physical characteristics, will probably come to mind. It may also be that some places in the city are immediately pictured when one discusses blue-collar workers or blacks. Most urban residents have mental images of their city, including spatial images or mental maps.

Places or areas that have become synonymous with certain social groups, to the point where a mention of a place name produces an image of the residents, are said to be geographic identifiers, descriptive of the social characteristics of the residents. For decades Harlem was identified as the place of residence for blacks in New York City, and mention of the word Harlem was sufficient for most people to have a mental image of that place. Harlem also serves as an example of how places change in social composition, for now we often refer to Spanish Harlem because of the influx of Puerto Ricans into that area.

In Los Angeles, Watts is a geographic identifier for a black community, whereas the names Bel Air and Beverly Hills trigger images of upper-income areas. Chinatown in San Francisco is obviously an Asian area (Figure 3.2), whereas "the Hill" in St. Louis was a region inhabited predominantly by those of Italian descent.

In discussing social identifiers and geographic identifiers, we are linking distinct social groups to particular places. The question at this point is, How did particular groups come to occupy a unique place in the human mosaic of the city?

Community Formation and Development

The concept of community is far more complex than may first appear. Does a community have to be a discrete spatial entity in which all members are adjacent to each other, much like a formal region? Or can a community be composed of members widely scattered throughout the city but united through some common interest, thereby forming a type of functional region? Reviewing the academic studies that deal with these questions, we find arguments in favor of both

FIGURE 3.2. Chinatown, San Francisco. Source: HUD.

types of communities. Throughout this chapter we consider communities as discrete spatial units that have a relatively homogeneous population and occupy a unique social space within the city.

In a curious way community formation and development parallel many of the factors that urban scholars say brought people together in cities some 6,000 years ago. If we were to place theories of the origin of urban places into broad categories, then the most likely reasons for people first clustering in cities would be religious practice, economics, technological change, population pressure, defense, or environmental factors. Each of these considerations has also affected where people have settled in cities in the United States.

Ethnic Communities. We often think of the major U.S. cities as having core areas of Italians, blacks, Irish, Polish, and so forth. During the time of the great immigration of people into the United States in the nineteenth and early twentieth centuries, those core areas were established and expanded, especially in the coastal cities. Over time those ethnic communities grew and became firmly established parts of the urban scene.

One way to visualize the origin of such communities would be to imagine the plight of a Chinese immigrant entering the United States. Having left a country where he or she was most probably not much different from anyone else in dress, language, and custom, the immigrant was suddenly thrust into a new culture, one in which he or she was a member of a minority group. It is little wonder that this person would seek the shelter offered by other people with the same cultural background. Attraction to an ethnic community, therefore, is partially for reasons of defense from the economic and social pressures of the new culture. Additionally, the direct move to an ethnic community offers some stability during the period of transition and adjustment to a new culture.

At times, occupational specialization has been the factor that pulled people to a specific place in the city. For example, if the person's trade in his or her native land has been in the garment industry, then there is every likelihood that the immigrant might settle in a place where such an industry exists in the new country.

Immigrant groups have generally offered a source of relatively cheap labor, owing to a lack of skills in the language or to outright discrimination, which keeps them from higher-paying jobs. In the past one can see this pattern in the percentage of certain ethnic groups in certain occupations. Historically, the stereotypes of the Irish policeman or fireman, the Polish or German mill worker in Chicago, and the Italian construction worker in northern California were largely true, partially because these groups were restricted from other occupations. In today's world one needs only to look at the various industries found in the Asian areas of West Coast cities to see the same pattern in operation.

A chain migration pattern often developed as immigrants living in the United States described the place in which they lived and their occupation to people in their homeland, which led some of those people to also immigrate to the United States. Often the newer immigrants would be linked (hence chain migration) to the same area and very often would become involved in the same occupational categories as their predecessors. This pattern also helped reinforce occupational stereotypes and strengthen ethnic areas within cities.

We can generalize by saying that members of ethnic groups that have moved into cities in the United States have generally concentrated in some centralized area. Some groups rapidly disperse, becoming assimilated into the main part of the society and leaving the core ethnic area behind. This has been particularly true of groups that are close in physical characteristics to the Anglo and that arrived in relatively small numbers. Other groups, such as urban blacks, have remained more segregated in distinct social areas.

The Life Cycle: Age and Family Status. Social scientists have long been concerned with the degree to which life-style and family status contribute to the social areas of cities. Bell (1958) suggested that in an economically developed country three life-styles existed. First in Bell's scheme was "familism," in which the raising of children was the dominant factor in people's life-style. Second, "careerism" was seen as the life-style in which participants were working toward the goal of upward social mobility. Third, Bell suggested that some would opt for a life-style centered around the pursuit of the materially good life, which was referred to as "consumerism."

Traditionally, stages of the life cycle were held to be more important than life-style in influencing behavior. A number of stages in the life cycle following marriage have been described: prechild, child bearing, child rearing, child launching, postchild, and widowhood (Foote, Abu-Lughod, Foley, and Winnick, 1960). Many changes in social behavior have occurred since the development of that model, and some contemporary social trends indicate these changes. For example, more women are now involved in the work force than in 1960, the age at which a woman bears her first child has risen dramatically, and there has been a significant increase in the

number of single-parent households. Although the traditional
stages in the life cycle may seem less than relevant to some
people in today's world, those stages are still an important
consideration in that a vast number of people continue to
follow the general pattern.

Why are these social constructs—the three general types of
life-style and the stages in the life cycle—important to the urban scientist and especially the urban geographer? Basically,
each type of behavior or choice of activity pattern has implications for the type of dwelling unit and place of residential
location that people will select in a city. Familism, for instance, would probably require people to live in a larger
house, whereas people with a careerism life-style would in all
probability have fewer children, and there would be an associated reduction in dwelling space. During the child-bearing
and child-rearing years in the life cycle, one might find people selecting a suburban residence because of the requirement for space, but in the postchild stage, a smaller residence
such as a townhouse, condominium, or mobile home might
be preferred. In the widowhood period, a community highly
populated by older persons may be the desired location.

Age and behavioral patterns influence the spatial distribution of people within the city and therefore form one of the
three broad categories in the study of the location of people
within the city. The third and final factor is that of
socioeconomic status (SES).

Socioeconomic Status. In most societies there is a social
hierarchy. When measuring characteristics of social status in
American cities, information on occupation, income, level of
education, and the value of the home or the amount of rent
paid is used to describe social status. For example, one column from the U.S. census shows an ordering or a type of
ranking of occupational groups (see Table 3.1). Sociologists
have devised rating scales based on the status of particular
job categories, which we will investigate in a later chapter.

The variables used to describe socioeconomic status are
assumed to be interrelated. More schooling, for example,
may lead to a higher-paying job, which in turn makes possible a prestige factor such as an expensive house. Again, our

Table 3.1
Occupation Categories

Occupation

Professional, technical, and kindred workers
   Health Workers
   Teachers, elementary and secondary schools
Managers and administrators, except farm
   Salaried
   Self-employed in retail trade

Sales Workers
   Retail trade
Clerical and kindred workers
Craftsmen, foremen, and kindred workers
   Construction craftsmen
   Mechanics and repairmen
Operatives, except transport
Transport equipment operatives

Laborers, except farm
Farm workers
Service workers
   Cleaning and food service workers
   Protective service workers
   Personal and health service workers
Private household workers

Source: United States Census of Population, 1970

caveat about generalizations and stereotypes should be kept in mind.

Diverse socioeconomic groups have an obvious part in the spatial organization of the city. One of the most fundamental models of urban locations, that proposed by Hoyt (1939), suggests that all urban spatial organization is determined by the location of high-status groups, and we often perceive urban areas as being primarily composed of communities of varying socioeconomic status.

Social and geographic identifiers focus on urban society as being divided into ethnic groups, stages in the life cycle, and a variety of SES categories. Mapping the locations of these diverse groups does not present the picture of the human mosaic, however, because mapping does not provide a sense of the processes that led to the patterns of human groups one finds in cities. Urban scientists have attempted to model those processes.

Models of Urban Social Structure

Much of the study of the human mosaic in cities was, and to some extent still is, based upon the underlying principles of three models of urban spatial structure. These models, which focus upon the socioeconomic patterns found in cities, have direct applications to life cycle patterns and ethnic communities.

The Concentric Zone Model. The first of the models was developed in the 1920s by E. W. Burgess in collaboration with R. E. Park. Burgess sought to understand the city in relation to human behavior and commented that "we were very impressed with the great difference between the various neighborhoods of the city, and one of our earliest goals was to try and find a pattern of this patchwork of differences, and to make sense of it. Mapping was the method which seemed most appropriate for such a problem" (Burgess and Bogue, 1967, p. 6).

After reviewing a large number of maps of the social areas of the city of Chicago, Burgess concluded that five zones of urban structure could be determined. These zones have been renamed several times, but they first appeared (Burgess, 1924) as

1. Central business district (CBD)
2. Zone in transition
3. Zone of independent workingmen's homes
4. Zone of better residences
5. Commuter zone

A later version of the Burgess model has zone three listed as a zone of second-generation immigrants; zone four, as middle-class residential district; and zone five, as high-class residential district. Regardless of the terminology attached to each zone, Burgess found a concentric ring pattern in the social structure of cities (see Figure 3.3).

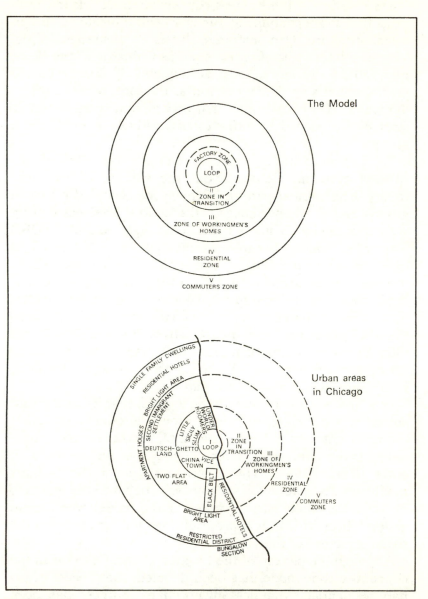

The Model

Urban areas
in Chicago

FIGURE 3.3. Concentric Theory of Urban Structure. Reprinted from *The City* by R. Park, E. Burgess, and R. McKenzie (Chicago: University of Chicago Press, 1925), pp. 51, 55, by permission of the University of Chicago Press.

Examination of the Burgess concentric model clearly indicates that socioeconomic status is a valid indicator of urban
social structure. Demonstrated also is an awareness of the
various ethnic areas of cities, such as Chinatown, the Black
Belt, Little Sicily, and so forth (see Figure 3.3). Burgess placed
great emphasis on the city center as the focal point of urban
dynamics. He also assumed that urban population growth is
strongly influenced by influxes of relatively low-SES alien
groups.

Publication of the concentric zone model was followed by a
spirited academic debate about the validity of Burgess's
theory. The circular pattern of the space occupied by social
groups and the importance of the central business district
were questioned. Critics of the model suggested that the CBD
was not necessarily the sole commercial center of a city, and
in fact it may be more logical to search the outskirts of the urban area for industrial activity. On the periphery of the city,
land is less expensive and transportation is probably better
than in the center of the city, hence the edge is a better location than the center for many industries. It was observed that
industries and commercial land uses may be located along
linear features such as rail lines, roads, or water features,
thus distorting the concentric pattern.

Low-SES housing is likely to be located near industrial and
commercial activities, therefore it might also be linear rather
than concentric in pattern. Several of Burgess's critics maintained that no universal pattern in housing could be found in
cities (Davie, 1938). The arguments against the Burgess
model were countered by scholars who believed the model to
be accurate. Their basic defense of the model was that in
general it provided an appropriate method for studying the
social structure of the city.

Although the pattern of the location of social groups in the
concentric zone model has been debated, the process of urban residential dynamics suggested by Burgess has been
almost universally accepted. He maintained that the city was
much like a biological ecosystem. Ecological analogies – wed-
ding processes found in the natural environment to processes
found in the urban setting – were used to describe, and in

some cases to explain, the dynamics of residential change in the city. Burgess visualized population movements as occurring from the center toward the edge of the city. Immigrants to the urban area come to the center of the city if they are in low-SES groups and push outward into the surrounding zones, a process referred to as succession.

The first step in succession is the "invasion" of an area by a particular group. The residents of the area may react to the presence of the new group in a variety of ways; however, if the influx of newcomers is sufficient, the residents may decide to leave the area. The void left by this abandonment is then filled by members of the invading group. This process can be long and subtle or brief and rather violent. The process occurs in nature, for example, when an alpine marsh becomes, over time, a coniferous forest. The grasses and aquatic plants of the marsh are replaced by soils and shallow-rooted grasses and shrubs. Given time, the shrubs may be displaced by deciduous trees, which in turn are invaded and overcome by conifers. When an equilibrium has been achieved, a state of "climax" is said to have been achieved.

The swamp-to-forest ecosystem change occurs because of stimulus, response, and interaction among variables such as climate, soil, sunlight, moisture availability, and changes in biotic communities. The urban dynamic is the result of factors such as economics, politics, history, and social forces. Burgess maintained that the ecological process provides a method of study for the examination of the social changes within cities.

The residential element of cities is always in a state of flux. Individuals are constantly changing their residence, so the larger social areas tend to expand and contract with time through processes of growth and change. Although some of the generalities in the Burgess model cannot be defended in all places and in all time frameworks, it was through his ecological perspective on the formation, establishment, and growth of diverse social areas of the city that Burgess made his most important contribution to our understanding of the urban ecosystem.

The Sector Model. In 1939 an alternative to the Burgess

model was presented by Homer Hoyt (Hoyt, 1939). Hoyt's model was originally designed to be an analytical tool for research on real estate markets in the United States. His criticisms of the Burgess model were similar to those already discussed. In order to remedy perceived deficiencies in the Burgess model, Hoyt determined that a pattern of sectors, rather than concentric circles, best illustrates the organization of urban social space.

Hoyt examined the rental patterns in nearly 150 cities and determined that the highest rental, or home value, areas are in one or more sectors on the edge of the city. He then theorized that the location of such sectors is dynamic in nature (see Figure 3.4). Adjacent to the high-rent sectors are, most often, sectors of slightly lower rental, or home value, housing. A gradation exists as one moves away from the high-rent sectors, which eliminates, for the most part, the potential for the very rich living next to the very poor.

Hoyt discussed the dynamics of land use in his model by first hypothesizing that high-rent areas expand along established lines of travel and favor amenity areas such as high ground or shorelines. Once established in outlying areas, high-rent residential areas become entrenched and dictate the use of the surrounding land.

One of the more interesting aspects of the Hoyt model is in his contention that a "filtering" of housing stock occurs as the rich move outward. Filtering refers to the process by which dwelling units change hands between socioeconomic groups. A large single-family house occupied by a rich family near the city center may be subdivided into a multifamily unit if the rich move outward. In that manner, housing stock undergoes a physical transformation and becomes occupied by new socioeconomic groups. There are many factors that could trigger the filtering process, but Hoyt based his assumptions on the belief that housing stock deterioration is the basic cause of the process. Filtering is an important element in Hoyt's urban social dynamic. He assumed that social groups follow the rich and that filtering provides a more or less continuous supply of housing for groups in the lower social and economic ranks.

Hoyt's sector model provides an interesting insight into ur-

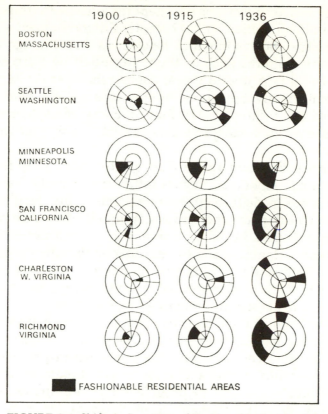

FIGURE 3.4. Shifts in Location of Fashionable Residential Areas. Source: H. Hoyt, *The Structure and Growth of Residential Neighborhoods in American Cities* (Washington, D.C.: Federal Housing Administration, 1939), p. 115.

ban structure. The suggestion that high-SES groups dominate land use patterns is generally what reviewers focus upon when citing the contributions of Hoyt to the understanding of the city. The importance of transportation routes and the linear patterns formed by social groups and economic activities were also proposed by Hoyt. In addition, an emphasis on the role of land at the edge of the city is part of the Hoyt model. We believe that Hoyt's contribution to urban science was in his consideration of transportation and the importance of the urban periphery.

Burgess and Hoyt have both been criticized for their use of

economic determinism as the agent responsible for the spatial organization of cities. In 1947 Walter Firey produced a study of the city of Boston in which he claimed that although vague geometric patterns such as those suggested by Burgess and Hoyt could be found in cities, choices made as the result of economic motivation were not necessarily the reason for such patterns (Firey, 1947). Firey found a great diversity of land use within sectors of zones and asked why that was the case.

Urban patterns were, in Firey's estimation, the result of cultural and emotional factors rather than simply the result of decisions made through economic rationality. Sentimental attachment to place and strong community ties were said to be major factors in the determination of land use patterns. The Boston Common and the number of churches in an area of very high land value, plus the prestige of living on Beacon Hill, were cited as examples of sentimental and symbolic attachment to place as influencing urban land use (Firey, 1947).

Firey's criticism, which goes beyond the scope of this brief discussion, is well founded. It is important to remember, however, that each attempt to explain urban patterns produces new information and lends tools to the urban scientist but is highly unlikely to provide the entire answer to the question. With this thought in mind, we can appreciate the germane aspects of a number of theories and retrieve those parts of each theory that aid in problem solving. We may do this without the burden of having to accept all parts of any single theory. Thus, Burgess, Hoyt, and Firey all contribute in unique ways to our understanding of the city.

In the decade of the 1940s, Burgess and Hoyt came under attack for reasons other than those presented by Firey. At issue was the relevance of the concentric and sector models in the age of the automobile.

The Multiple Nuclei Model. In 1945 Edward Ullman and Chauncy Harris created an explanation of urban structure based on the city having more than one focal point (Harris and Ullman, 1945). Harris and Ullman theorized that cities have more than one dominant nucleus for several reasons. For example, many types of economic activity demand large amounts of space and cannot absorb the high costs of locating near the city center–automobile dealerships fall into this category. Industrial or office complexes often cluster in districts in order to minimize costs and maximize the sharing of resources. Noxious industries and similar types of land use are often detrimental to many other activities, such as expensive housing, so areas of such less-desirable activities may develop. Finally, many types of land use require unique facilities–port activities and the easy accessibility needed for shopping malls may serve as examples.

The central business district of a city simply cannot fulfill all needs, so many centers of activity evolve within cities (see Figure 3.5), especially in cities that have undergone their greatest growth during the age of the automobile. These various centers tend to influence use of the surrounding land. Light manufacturing, such as in the electronics industry, will attract similar industries, for instance. Using the multiple

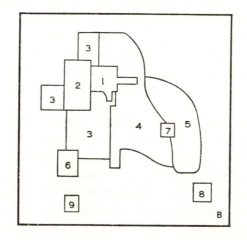

1 Central Business District	6 Heavy Manufacturing
2 Wholesale Light Manufacturing	7 Outlying Business District
3 Low-class Residential	8 Residential Suburb
4 Medium-class Residential	9 Industrial Suburb
5 High-class Residential	

FIGURE 3.5. Multiple Nuclei Theory. Reprinted from "The Nature of Cities," by C. Harris and E. Ullman in vol. 242 of *The Annals of the American Academy of Political and Social Science* (1945), p. 13.

nuclei model, we find a number of points from which urban social and economic structures develop.

Factorial Ecology. Returning to the human aspect of the urban mosaic, we find that complex statistical techniques are used to describe the social structure of contemporary cities. The term factorial ecology is used to describe the method of analysis of urban-spatial structure that employs as a major technique either factor analysis or principal components analysis. Factorial ecology is one of the contemporary methods of urban study.

In a factorial ecology the organizational procedures are much the same regardless of which technique – factor analysis or principal components analysis – is used. Although major computational differences exist between factor analysis and principal components analysis, the most pertinent difference for our consideration is that principal components analysis is more general and deterministic in approach, because all variation in a given population is assumed to be contained within the variables that define that population. Factor analysis is based on the assumption that only a part of the variation in a given population is contained within the variables used to define that population, therefore factor analysis can be used in a much more flexible and experimental context.

The principal use of factorial ecology is to determine subareas of a city or suburb by identifying the main dimensions of urban social structure – stage in the life cycle, ethnicity, and socioeconomic status. This summarizing device operates from a set of input variables chosen to cover a wide range of demographic, economic, racial, and housing characteristics. The following input variables from the 1970 U.S. census are typical of the kinds of variables used in factorial ecology studies.

1. Socioeconomic status variables: home value, average rent, percentage of professional workers, percentage of managerial workers, percentage of sales workers, percentage of blue-collar workers, percentage of service workers, high school education (ED1), college education (ED2), median income

2. Ethnicity variables: Spanish language, percentage black, percentage other
3. Stage in the life cycle: percentage under eighteen years of age, median age, percentage age sixty and over

The data sources for the input variables used are generally the U.S. census and other federal, state, and local surveys. The initial areal unit of consideration is usually the individual census tract. In order to best summarize input variables as they relate to census tracts, a series of "diagnostic input factors" are statistically derived to account for the measurable amounts of initial variance within the data. The nature of these factors is identifiable by their association with the original variables. This means that a factor that is strongly identifiable with original variables that deal with socioeconomic status is a summation device indicative of either some high or some low characteristics of socioeconomic status for the units of input, the census tracts.

In Table 3.2, the lefthand column lists the input variables that we want to analyze. Again, we are mainly concerned with the three major dimensions of urban social structure. Information regarding each of these variables from the census tracts that compose our study area is input for our analysis. Four factors are generated that together summarize the variables. The numerical range of the factor scores can run from +.999 to 0 to −.999. The higher the positive number, the stronger the relationship between the factor and the variables. Conversely, the strength of the negative number indicates the degree to which the variable is negatively related to the factor. In Table 3.2, factor one is strongly related to high home value (+.879), professional workers (+.751), and high income (+.791). There is a negative relationship between factor one and blue-collar workers (−.612). We would assume that factor one is descriptive of high socioeconomic status.

Once the characteristics of the factors have been determined and all possible random association between variables and factors has been eliminated, it is necessary to group or cluster the units of input, the census tracts. Tracts having similar characteristics, as indicated by the factors, are

TABLE 3.2
Varimax Rotation Factor Pattern

Variables	Factors 1	2	3	4
Home Value	.879	.471	-.316	-.629
Average Rent	.813	.510	-.412	-.610
Professional Workers	.751	.432	-.260	-.117
Managerial Workers	.422	.361		
Sales Workers		.138	.173	
Blue-collar Workers	-.612	-.350	.577	.683
Service Workers	-.183	-.212	.461	.721
High School Education	.381	.441		
College Education	.542	.433		-.170
Median Income	.791	.561	-.117	-.675
Spanish Language			.170	.115
Percent Black				.881
Percent Other				
Percent Under 18 Years	-.133	-.117		
Median Age	.436	.890		

Source: Factorial ecology using 1970 United States census data.
Developed by authors.

grouped into homogeneous units with respect to any of the three dimensions of social structure. The remaining task is simply to transfer the statistical information generated by factor type and related cluster group to the map in order to delimit that particular social area.

The data in Table 3.3 are used to produce a map that shows the results of the study. The four factors are included, as are the five cluster groups. The cluster groups are actually lists of census tracts; for instance, cluster group one may contain tracts 20, 21, 36, 41, and 50, which are grouped together because they share similar characteristics.

Again, the higher the positive number, the stronger the relationship between factor and cluster group. Notice that there is a very strong relationship between factor one, which we know to be indicative of high socioeconomic status, and cluster group five. We would assume that all the census tracts

TABLE 3.3
Distance Between Cluster Group and Factor Means

| Cluster Group | Factors | | | |
	1	2	3	4
1	-17.4	-11.7	7.0	31.4
2	- 4.0	- 6.8	15.8	10.1
3	2.5	22.2	- 3.0	-17.3
4	3.1	6.8	1.0	- 6.2
5	28.2	7.5	-16.0	-14.7

Distance is measured in standard deviations from the mean based on a unit mean of 50 with a unit standard deviation of 10. For example, a value of 28.8 would represent 2.8 standard deviations above the mean. Unless indicated values are positive.

Source: Factorial ecology from 1970 United States census data. Developed by authors.

listed in group five are high in SES attributes, and we would indicate that fact on a map. Cluster group one has a negative relationship with factor one, thus we would assume that the census tracts listed in group one are low in SES characteristics. Thus, by knowing how the variables relate to the factors and how the factors relate to the cluster groups, we can produce a map of the social areas of a city.

This method of delimiting social space has several positive qualities. It has the advantage of providing a means by which large quantities of data can be handled efficiently. There is also the advantage of utilizing a technique that can be applied in a variety of cultural and economic contexts, both Western and non-Western.

In any technique that has such a wide range of application, problems exist — in this case, for example, there are problems of data comparability and the fact that studies seem to indicate that non-Western cities have only two social dimensions, socioeconomic status and stage in the life cycle. If we exclude cross-cultural studies and focus solely on the technique itself, there are several important considerations to be made. There must be an input of quality data with a meaningful balance of variables and the use of adequate territorial units if a factorial ecology is to produce accurate and useful data.

IMAGES OF THE CITY

Critics contend that factorial ecology and other methods of statistical analysis are not sufficient by themselves to provide an understanding of what goes on in the urban ecosystem. They argue that indices of poverty and poor housing, for example, cannot convey the reality of life in New York's South Bronx with its crumbling tenements, rubble-strewn streets, and rat-infested apartments. Although dry statistics may accurately reflect a place's characteristics, residents and visitors may perceive that place in a variety of ways. Thus, we need to consider the more-subjective images of cities that people have developed as a result of their impressions. That such images exist is undeniable. To mention Soho to a Londoner, the Left Bank to a Parisian, or Brooklyn to a New Yorker, for example, immediately activates a set of impressions. However, no two New Yorkers, Parisians, or Londoners are likely to have identical sets of impressions.

Our perceptions of places are influenced by numerous variables such as the degree of familiarity that we have with a place, the amount of time that we have spent learning about it, the interest we have in it, and even the mood that we sensed in it. Our perceptions of places depend also on their nature and size. Perceptions of a small neighborhood—our own or another—are quite different from perceptions we might have of an entire city. Similarly, perceptions of our own city are formed differently from those we have of more-distant cities. Although you may not have been there, consider for a moment the impressions you have of Beijing (Peking), Hong Kong, or Calcutta.

Furthermore, the way we perceive a city varies considerably depending on our age, sex, race or ethnic group, income, occupation, and educational level. Blacks and whites, for example, aren't likely to have the same image of Detroit or Chicago; whites and Chicanos don't share the same image of Los Angeles; nor do blacks and Puerto Ricans see New York

City in identical ways. Yet the way that each of us sees our city, the mental map that we have of it, affects our behavior in it. The places that we choose to frequent or avoid and the routes that we use to get from place to place are selected on the basis of the images that we have, so the geography of the urban ecosystem is affected by and in turn affects the way we perceive the urban milieu.

Kevin Lynch was one of the first people to become interested in people's mental maps of cities (Lynch, 1960). Using samples of residents in Boston, Newark, and Los Angeles, he studied various components of city images and the ways that people perceived their cities in an attempt to discern how people develop and utilize mental maps of cities. What he found was that certain spatial components are especially important in the formation of urban images—namely, edges, districts, landmarks, nodes, and paths.

Edges are pronounced linear elements in the urban landscape, examples of which range from seashores to freeways and railroads. Districts are areas within a city, bounded by edges and paths, that have a definite identity for people, especially for those who live or work within them. Landmarks are features of the cityscape that are used as reference points, and they are usually special or unique features within the urban ecosystem. Nodes are major points of origin or destination for individuals, including home, school, office, and shopping and recreation areas, and they serve as major orientation points for people's mental maps. Paths are the normal channels of movement used by individuals within the urban area and serve as major elements in the urban image. These elements combine, Lynch found, to produce an urban image, or mental map, that an individual develops as a necessary guide for life in the city.

Following Lynch's original work, researchers have used samples of urban residents to compile mental maps of numerous cities in a number of different countries, from Cambridge, England, to Melbourne, Australia. Such work, despite the usual limitations of small samples, at least allows a general assessment of how people perceive their city and what they think about its appearance. Such information may in turn be useful to urban and regional planners, who are increasingly interested in creating livable environments. Places are more than just collections of human and material artifacts, they are meaningful symbols in the human experience, as many novelists have been able to tell us.

Sense of Place

Whereas factorial ecology uses statistical methods and census data to help us understand the spatial structure of urban ecosystems, many observers are quick to point out that such statistical manipulations fail to convey many things about cities. However objective the use of collected data and its analysis may seem, occasionally we need to peer beneath the outer layer of data to ask about the actual nature of living in the urban ecosystem. Cities are composites of expressions of hopes and fears, places where lives gain or lose meaning. Cities are not always easy to know, whether we approach them objectively or subjectively, yet in either case looking for meaning in the urban mosaic will reward us if we are patient.

Although geographers speak of place in terms of location, place may connote much more. As Prince once commented, "We cannot know a place until we discover its literature, its arts and its sciences; nor, conversely, can we understand literature or art or science without some knowledge of geography. A knowledge of places is an indispensable link in the chain of knowledge" (Prince, 1961, p. 22). In the same essay, Prince suggested that "Both regions and writers, place and person, are unique, and it is in their distinctive qualities that we may find their essential character" (Prince, 1961, p. 24). It is this essential character of places that composes the central theme in studies of "the sense of place." Admittedly subjective and always elusive, a sense of place is palpable and real, and understanding it helps us to elucidate the urban experience.

The personalities of places are likely to be complex and multifaceted, and they certainly are perceived differently by different observers, as we have already noted. Thus, there is not one Philadelphia nor one London but many, just as there is not one Italian cuisine but many, from that of the Piedmont to that of Rome. As Hurst aptly observed,

> Every place has a special character for its residents, its visitors, and those who "know" it only second-hand. Each place has a personality of its own, buried perhaps beneath prejudice and emotion, derived not just from buildings, but also from contours, street patterns, drama, color, surprises, smells, noises, and so on. [Hurst, 1975, p. 41]

Thus, the sense of place derives not only from the characteristics of a place, but also from the ways that that place is perceived by various individuals and groups. Values and experiences affect the way people perceive cities, and in turn the nature of cities affects what people do in them. Our experience of a place ranges from fleeting impressions to careful studies on a highly abstract and theoretical level.

Studying the sense of place requires a different approach from that used in studying the spatial structure of places. According to Relph, "Place and sense of place do not lend themselves to scientific analysis for they are inextricably bound up with all the hopes, frustrations, and confusions of life, and possibly because of this social sciences have avoided these topics" (Relph, 1976, Preface). In his book *Place and Placelessness,* Relph pursued the following four themes: (1) relationships between space and place; (2) components and intensities of place experience; (3) the nature of the identity of places and of people within places; and (4) the ways in which attachments to place, and the sense of place, are involved in the making of places. His approach to understanding places is phenomenological rather than scientific.

> Whether place is understood and experienced as landscape in the direct and obvious sense that visual features provide tangible evidence of some concentration of human activities, or in a more subtle sense as reflecting human values and intentions, appearance is an important feature of all places. But it is hardly possible to understand all place experiences as landscape experiences. [Relph, 1976, p. 31]

Relph was also concerned with placelessness, the diminishing differences between places, and the effect of what he referred to as "other-directed architecture." Undoubtedly industrialization and commercialization have carried with them a tendency to homogenize societies, to create landscapes strewn with Kentucky Fried Chicken, golden arches, "31 flavors," and pizza palaces. Howard Johnsons and Holiday Inns line our freeways from coast to coast, creating a sameness that somehow appeals to the weary traveler.

Yet despite the pressures that are pushing cities toward an increasing placelessness, differences still remain. You can't wake up in Santa Fe and be unaware of how different it is from Boston, for example, nor can you easily confuse Seattle with Topeka or Houston. However, you may have to remain observant if you want to find differences rather than similarities from place to place. Too often ugliness persists in industrial and commercial landscapes, in spite of the best efforts of critics who point out that ugliness has a detrimental effect on humans. Both beauty and ugliness of course contribute to the sense of place. Both the ridiculous and the sublime affect our impressions.

Places are destined to remain important, whether or not we can precisely calculate their contribution to our well-being. Artists, poets, and novelists continue to offer us images of ourselves and our landscapes, but social scientists have been slow to accept and consider subjective contributions, opting instead for a more rigorous scientific approach grounded in logical positivism. However, any consideration of the sense of place in such activities as urban and regional planning requires an acceptance of subjective feelings about places, not as a replacement for other planning considerations but as an additional element.

Reflections on South Chicago, by Thomas J. Napierkowski

During my youth in Chicago, some thirty years ago, growing up "ethnic" was the rule, not the exception. Then, as now,

---

"Reflections on South Chicago" was written especially for this book by Professor Thomas J. Napierkowski of the University of Colorado, Colorado Springs.

Chicago consisted largely of a vast network of various national, racial, and cultural neighborhoods; and my section of the city was one such district.

The son of a steelworker, I was born and raised in an area of the city called South Chicago. Unlike communities that are today regarded as essential to the good life, South Chicago had a very haphazard beginning. About the turn of the century, Eastern European immigrants, mainly Poles, who had been lured to the area to accept work as unskilled steel laborers, built their modest homes in the shadows of the mills. In most respects South Chicago is a typical northern, industrial, urban community. The residential sections of the community, for example, display old frame bungalows and two-family structures along narrow, one-way streets. Although these homes are well maintained and shelter carefully nurtured gardens in the rear, there is clear evidence of the pollution, congestion, and political neglect that plague the area. The city has provided a few parks and playgrounds, but these are inadequate in number and poorly staffed. Most children prefer to regard the neighborhood's sidewalks and alleys as long narrow playgrounds (a ball hit into a background was an automatic out, and the batter had to get the ball himself). The public schools in the area are crowded, understaffed, and old, and the parochial schools, mainly Catholic, provide a better education but demand financial sacrifices beyond the means of many families. Recently cocaine has become a major problem, and most residents no longer feel safe sending their children to the corner grocery store or neighborhood bakery after dark.

With this in mind, it amazes even me to realize that there were, and are, advantages to raising children and growing up in such places. These advantages revolve about the three cornerstones of all such ethnic neighborhoods: family, parish, and sense of community. These support systems provide tremendous assistance, which are lost in many model communities, to individuals and groups alike. Not the least of these advantages for minority groups is the protection such a ghetto life furnishes for ethnic or racial identity, especially during childhood. America's attitudes toward immigrant groups have been almost as violent as the hostility toward blacks, and even more insidious because the country has generally refused to recognize this reality. In very subtle ways, which I have since realized were profound, South Chicago nurtured my identity; and although that identity has exposed me to moments of intense pain and bitter anger toward American society, it has also furnished some of the most rewarding aspects of my life.

The center of everyone's life in South Chicago was the family—both the nuclear and the extended family. The atmosphere of most homes was distinctly ethnic. The foods we ate, the sounds we heard, and the rituals we observed were heavily, but not exclusively, Polish; indeed, I occasionally rebelled at not getting enough "American" food like chili and pizza. These rebellions were sometimes ignored, infrequently indulged, but most often squelched. My parents' experience led them to insist upon such virtues as obedience, self-control, respect for authority, and determination; and strict discipline was maintained in the home. Traditions such as the Polish Christmas Eve dinner (*Wigilia*), consisting of meatless dishes, and the Easter morning breakfast, which after the gloom of Lent, gloriously reintroduced us to the tastes of ham, sausage, and baked goods, were observed by virtually the entire neighborhood. Finally, although my parents spoke Polish, the language most commonly employed was English. Circumstances dictating the use of Polish ranged from visits of relatives, an almost daily occurrence, to attempts at concealing something from the children. Despite the fact that children were generally not taught Polish, most learned to get along in the language from its frequent use in the house and in the neighborhood's stores and churches.

As I grew up, I don't think I ever heard the phrase "extended family," but I certainly lived the phenomenon. No matter what drugstore I visited to buy cigarettes or what bar I braved to buy beer, I was invariably confronted by an aunt or uncle who reported my business to my parents. On the other hand, no matter where in the community I might be, I could be certain that help, if needed, was no more than a few doors away. South Chicago seemed a patchwork of grandparents, uncles, aunts, cousins, and in-laws. Not infrequently, nuclear families included at least one additional adult relative who shared bed and board, privileges and duties along with the parents and children. The extended family, then, provided support for each of the component nuclear families, parents and children alike. Someone was always there to share joys and to alleviate grief. Advice, loans, baby-sitting, a buyer for raffle tickets—you name it—the family supplied it. The great American virtue of "self-reliance" was alien to most residents of my neighborhood.

My formal education, and a great deal of my informal education, began at St. Mary Magdalene Church and the parish grade school. A genuine benefit of attending the parish school was that the attitude of the teachers and the general atmosphere of the classroom reinforced those of the home. I was, therefore, spared the trauma, not uncommon among ethnic children, of having the values and norms taught at home attacked in school. There my identity was nurtured, both by direct and subtle means.

Our texts, like all those of more than a generation ago, reflected exclusively the Anglo-Saxon experience. The Polish nuns who taught us, however, filled the gap in our education by providing details about the minority and immigrant history of millions of Americans. In other more subtle ways, I was also put at ease about my identity. My name, for example, was not a source of curiosity or ridicule (as it has often been for my children), and it was even pronounced correctly. Furthermore, there was little economic rivalry among the children, since we all came from similar backgrounds.

Liturgically, every canonical service in which the Catholic Church authorized the use of the vernacular was available in both Polish and English. Most often, in fact, Polish was the preferred language; sermons at four of the seven Masses at our church were in Polish. In addition, our liturgy catered to the feasts, rites, and hymns special to Polish Catholicism, which attempts to touch the heart and appeal to the senses as well as to satisfy the intellect.

Like so many immigrant churches, our parish was also the center of our social life outside the home. And there again, the ethnic factor was always at play. Holy Name dances admitted current times; but *obereks* and polkas were commonly heard. Parish bazaars and carnivals featured Polish dishes. Even athletic teams frequently had national names. In short, the parish, like the home, both contributed to and cushioned the discrepancy between my life and the usual image of American life presented in the media, textbooks, and political speeches.

Briefly, a final hallmark of life in South Chicago is a genuine sense of community. Common problems, shared values, and mutual aid cut across ethnic and racial lines to foster a genuine sense of unity among the residents of the area. In addition to family ties and parish loyalties, fraternal organizations and the locals of national labor unions provide a common bond to all. This bond is reflected in the leisure habits of the community. Residents spend most of their free time with relatives, but social life outside the family centers around local churches, taverns, union halls, and ward political organizations. A sense of turf, roots, a common lot – call it what you will – it contributes a valuable dimension to the identity of all residents.

Sociologists define a neighborhood as "a network of nuclear families locked together through mutual participation in activities and social life and by residence in a specific geographic area." Such an academic definition does not begin to identify the benefits I reaped by growing up in an ethnic community. The value is better indicated by the fact that I regret that my children miss so many advantages of the experience.

People in Cities

Professor Napierkowski's excellent essay reminds us that although urban scientists often view the city as a laboratory for statistical analysis, we must not separate humanism from urban analysis and our perceptions of the city. The questions to pose regarding social areas of cities include, Where are these places? What factors brought them into being? What does the future hold in store? and How do they function as an environment for people? In this chapter we have presented some of the methodologies, past and present, that attempt to answer these questions. The task now is to consider some of the other interrelated elements of the urban ecosystem.

REFERENCES

Bell, W. 1958. "Social Choice, Life Styles, and Suburban Residence." In W. Dobriner, ed., *The Suburban Community*, pp. 225–247. New York: G. P. Putnam's Sons.

Berry, B., and Kasarba, J. 1977. *Contemporary Urban Ecology.* New York: Macmillan.

Burgess, E. W. 1924. "The Growth of the City: An Introduction to a Research Project." *Publications* (American Sociological Society) 18: 85–97.

Burgess, E. W., and Bogue, D. J., eds. 1967. *Urban Sociology.* Chicago: University of Chicago Press.

Davie, M. R. 1938. "The Pattern of Urban Growth." In G. Murdoch, ed., *Studies in the Science of Society.* New Haven: Yale University Press.

Firey, Walter. 1947. *Land Use in Central Boston.* Cambridge: Harvard University Press.

Foote, N. N.; Abu-Lughod, J.; Foley, M. M.; and Winnick, L. 1960. *Housing Choices and Constraints.* New York: McGraw-Hill Book Company.

Harris, C. D., and Ullman, E. L. 1945. "The Nature of Cities." *Annals of the American Academy of Political Science* 242: 7–17.

Hoyt, Homer. 1939. *The Structure and Growth of Residential Neighborhoods in American Cities.* Washington, D.C.: Federal Housing Administration.

Hurst, M. E. Eliot, ed. 1975. *I Came to the City: Essays and Comments on the Urban Scene.* Boston: Houghton Mifflin Company.

Johnstone, R. J. 1971. *Urban Residential Patterns.* New York: Praeger Publishers.

Lynch, Kevin. 1960. *The Image of the City.* Cambridge: Technology Press and Harvard University Press.

Peters, Gary L. 1980. "Geography and the Sense of Place." In R. B. Mandal and V. N. P. Sinha, eds., *Recent Trends and Concepts in Geography*, vol. 1, pp. 75–94. New Delhi: Concept Publishing Company.

Prince, Hugh C. 1961. "The Geographical Imagination." *Landscape* 11: 22–25.

Relph, E. 1976. *Place and Placelessness.* London: Pion Limited.

Rummel, R. J. 1970. *Applied Factor Analysis.* Evanston, Ill.: Northwestern University Press.

Timms, D. 1971. *The Urban Mosaic.* Cambridge: Cambridge University Press.

Ward, D. 1971. *Cities and Immigrants.* New York: Oxford University Press.

4

THe Economic Basis
of THe City

Not all modern cities are dominated by manufacturing, but almost all are offspring of the Industrial Revolution. Put a different way, urbanization is closely tied to industrialization, and the life of cities in modern nations is closely related to manufacturing. Large-scale manufacturing is spatially concentrated, requires a nearby labor force, and creates jobs both directly and via multiplier effects both within and beyond the urban ecosystem. For example, the manufacturing population requires services of all sorts, from retail stores for groceries and clothes to barbershops and hospitals.

Cities are centers of research activities and innovations, both of which are essential to industrial societies if they are to maintain their economic competitiveness. Furthermore, as centers cities exert control over the lives and livelihoods of people virtually everywhere. The products of mines and farms, for example, are channeled toward the cities where the products are processed, transformed, and consumed. Cities occupy only a small portion of a nation's land, but their economic importance is reflected in the monetary value of their real estate. Look around any large city and try to imagine the cost of an acre of downtown land. Typically we're talking about values in excess of a million dollars! By those standards even "expensive" farmland is dirt cheap.

THE ECONOMIC ORGANIZATION OF THE CITY

Although land values are high in urban areas, they are not

uniformly so. They tend to be highest in the center of the city and to decrease as one moves outward. As one can well imagine, the spatial pattern of land uses within the city is going to be related to land values, though the location of specific economic activities may be affected by numerous other factors as well.

Before considering the internal arrangement of economic activities within the urban ecosystem, we should mention a broader view of the location of economic activities, specifically, industrial location within the national urban system. Not all manufacturing activities are found in all cities, nor for that matter are all services. For example, not all cities have steel mills or stock markets.

The location of industry is a two-step process. First, an industry seeks a profitable location within the national context, that is, an industry chooses cities or regions where it can operate a plant at a profit. The locational choice is based on costs and revenues at alternate locations. Among the major costs, of course, are the following: (1) procurement costs for raw materials; (2) production costs, including the costs of labor, management, capital, and energy; and (3) distribution costs. By comparing these costs at different locations, firms can decide where to locate. Some types of manufacturing can locate in almost any city – soda pop bottlers and bakeries, for example – whereas only a few locations would be profitable for others – steel production and automobile manufacturing, for example.

Second, once a firm knows what city it is going to locate in, it must choose a site within that city. This choice, like the first one, must involve a consideration of costs and revenues, of course, but the firm must also be concerned with site and neighborhood characteristics as well as with local zoning ordinances, taxes, and even public attitudes. It is this second stage in the locational process, the choice of site within the city, that we are concerned with in this chapter.

Models of Land Use Competition

The geographic arrangement of economic activities within a city at a given time is the result of numerous private and public decisions made over a long period of time within the context of constantly changing conditions both within the city and in its relationship to other cities. The pattern of economic activities within the city is neither a rigid one, repeated in identical fashion in city after city, nor a chaotic one about which no generalizations can be made. Rather, we can identify many variations on a general theme, the major chords of which are access and land rent. Recognizable features of American cities related to this general theme include a downtown area, segregated industrial zones, and in larger cities at least, outlying shopping centers and industrial parks. Variations on the central theme are nearly infinite, reflecting a city's historical evolution and its attractiveness for particular types of economic activities as well as the competition that exists for land within it. Thus, some cities are noted for particular economic activities—Detroit for automobiles or Pittsburgh for steel—and other cities, such as Chicago, are known only as major manufacturing centers. We shall examine mainly the central themes, recognizing, however, that the character of a city is often determined by its unique manufacturing specializations. According to Boyce (1978, p. 302), "the composite land use pattern of a city is a compromise among a number of opposing forces, some tending to pull functions to outlying areas (centrifugal forces), and others tending to attract certain activities to a more central position (centripetal forces)."

Access. Because of both markets and input needs many businesses locate in close proximity to each other. Businesses are also concerned with access to their markets as well as to their suppliers, so they are concerned about where they locate in the urban ecosystem. In turn, their locational choices help to shape the urban ecosystem and to determine patterns of spatial interaction within it. For example, the commuting patterns between residential areas and jobs are conditioned in part by the location of businesses, as are people's residential choices. What businesses seek, of course, are locations that have good connections with other places within the city, thus maximizing the potential for interaction with other businesses and with consumers. Because access is also a function of distance, the most accessible location would be the one that could be reached by all a city's population in the shortest total distance traveled, or what is often referred to as the minimum aggregate travel point. Typically in North American cities, this point will be in the central business district where major transportation routes converge. Thus, the structure of cities is conditioned by accessibility to the CBD, though suburbanization has often drawn businesses and people away from the central city, creating problems of decay in many CBDs across the country. Also, highways have often distorted the centrality of the CBD and given rise to new economic growth along highway corridors.

Although centrality has been an important determinant of business locations, it has also given rise to some dilemmas. For example, businesses need employees, and workers need access to their places of work. As cities have expanded, however, people are often faced with a difficult trade-off between residence and commuting distance. New housing developments are being built further out from the CBD, so those working in the CBD who want new houses are forced to commute longer distances, a particularly unhealthy pattern for what promises to be an energy-deficient decade, the 1980s. One alternative, mentioned previously, is for businesses to move to where new suburban housing is available – as has occurred in Orange County, California, throughout the 1970s and into the 1980s. Another alternative is to make housing near the CBD more attractive, as is occurring in Chicago and Philadelphia, for example. However, restoring inner-city housing often creates another problem; steeply rising housing costs displace the poor, the elderly, and many racial and ethnic groups, which often leads to conflicts. Thus, a change in one area of the urban ecosystem is likely to have repercussions in other areas, often in unpredictable ways.

The Bid-Rent Function. The importance of accessibility and its relationship to economic rent was clearly recognized over fifty years ago.

> When it was noted that it was not the most fertile lands that were first occupied but rather those nearest new settlements, accessibility or proximity to cities was recognized as an im-

portant factor in creating agricultural ground rent. In cities, economic rent is based on superiority of location only, the sole function of city land being to furnish area on which to erect buildings. [Hurd, 1924, p. 1]

Of course, buildings are not the only things that occupy urban land. Today, streets and parking lots are large consumers of land, as are parks and airports. But the importance of economic rent in determining land use in the city is still recognized, and that importance can most easily be understood by considering a theoretical bid-rent curve.

Although all types of urban land users bid for land, we will begin by simplifying our discussion to a consideration of commercial land users, who are the highest bidders for urban land and thus occupy most of the very central locations. Furthermore, we will assume that the bid-rent function is linear, whereas in reality it is most likely to be curvilinear.

For a given firm both costs and revenues vary from place to place, and maximum profit may be made at several different sites, mainly because of variations in access costs. All else being equal, the firm's revenue will be maximized at the center, so the firm would be willing to pay a high rent to attain the most central location. Away from the most central location, rents are lower, as is shown graphically in Figure 4.1, which shows rent on the vertical axis and distance from the most central location (in the CBD) on the horizontal axis. What this simplified bid-rent curve illustrates is that the further a location is from the point of maximum access, the less it is worth to prospective users. According to Emerson and Lamphear,

Generally, the amount of rent a firm is willing to bid for an off-center site just offsets any difference in total revenue and production costs between the off-center site and the urban center. In such a case, the maximum profit for the off-center site is the same as for the urban center. Since more than one maximum-profit site exists, a firm can indifferently choose any one of the maximum-profit sites. [Emerson and Lamphear, 1975, p. 201]

So far we have considered a single firm in a single industry

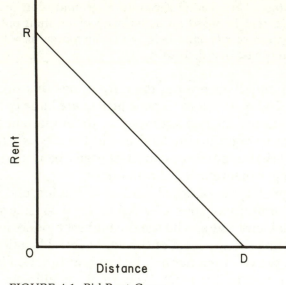

FIGURE 4.1. Bid-Rent Curve.

bidding to occupy a particular location, producing a single bid-rent curve. If other industries and firms enter into the bidding process, then a bid-rent curve can be developed for each industry, and a theoretical pattern of land use emerges. Experience tells us that some businesses are more successful than others, that input requirements vary among different industry groups, and that the intensity with which land is employed as a factor of production varies among various industries. Thus, different businesses will have different capacities to pay rent for accessible locations, and those most able to pay will occupy the most central locations. We can view competing bid-rent curves graphically (see Figure 4.2), still assuming simple linear bid-rent functions. The bid-rent gradient—the rate at which rent declines as we travel away from the most central location, 0—differs for different industries. In the example, industry 1 has a much steeper bid-rent gradient than does industry 2, indicating that industry 1 places a higher importance on centrality and is more able to pay for it.

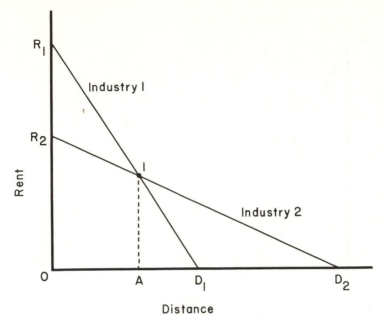

Distance

FIGURE 4.2. Bid-Rent Curves for Two Industries. Note that land uses would be determined by the composite bid-rent curve R_1ID_2.

Between the central location, 0, and point A, industry 1 is able to outbid industry 2, whereas beyond point A, industry 2 is able to outbid industry 1. Thus, if there were only two industries in a hypothetical city, then firms in industry 1 would all locate between the center and point A, firms in industry 2 would locate between A and D_2, and beyond D_2 nothing would be located. The city would have a concentric pattern of land use described about the city center. Other industries' bid-rent curves could be added, and the concentric pattern of land use would simply become more complicated.

Also, we could begin to consider, in similar fashion, other types of land use, including residential uses. If we consider three major categories of land use—business, industrial and residential—then we would find the general bid-rent curves to be somewhat like those shown in Figure 4.3. In our hypothetical city, three concentric land use zones would ap-

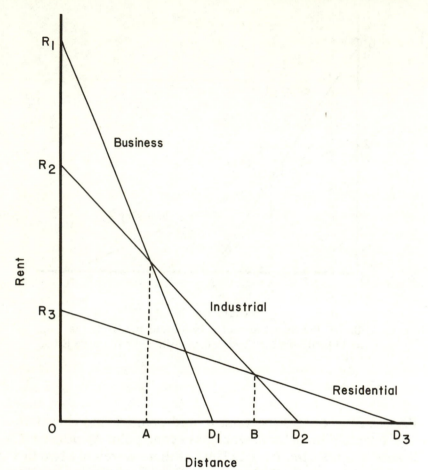

FIGURE 4.3. Bid-Rent Curves for Three General Categories of Land Use.

pear. Businesses would occupy the innermost zone (the CBD) between 0 and point A, industry would occupy the zone between points A and B, and residential uses would be found between points B and D_3. In this generalized picture, business users are most in need of accessibility, residential users least, and industrial users in between. Of course, patterns of land use in the urban ecosystem are much more complex than what has been mentioned so far, but the principle of the bid-rent curve is one significant factor influencing the arrangement of land uses.

Competition, Linkage, and the
Distribution of Economic Activities

Competitive bidding for urban locations is not the only determinant of the intraurban location of economic activities; the linkages, or lack of them, among firms are also important. The location of one business, in other words, may well be linked to the locations of other businesses, especially if those businesses are suppliers of or markets for the first business. It is the various linkages within the urban web that begin to alter our simplified concentric pattern of land use, and few economic activities are so independent as to stand above the effects of linkage. What we see, then, is that similar types of land use are more clustered than bid-rent functions alone would lead us to expect. Used car dealers, for example, are not usually distributed randomly throughout a specified concentric land use zone. Rather, they often tend to congregate together. Long Beach Boulevard in Long Beach, California, for example, is often referred to as "auto row," and such areas are common throughout all cities in the United States (Figure 4.4). More often than not similar land use types are attracted to each other in urban areas, and dissimilar land uses find separate locations.

One reason why businesses cluster together is because they share, or compete for, the same set of consumers. In a suburban shopping center, for example, numerous stores are located together, not because of ties to each other, but because they are competing for the same set of potential customers (Figure 4.5). Likewise, service stations are often found on all four corners of a busy intersection, linked not to each other but to the potential market.

Whereas competitive forces generate a clustered distribution of many businesses, other businesses locate near each other for complementary reasons. That is, they cluster together because they sell different, but complementary,

FIGURE 4.4. Auto Row, Long Beach, California. Source: Gary Peters.

FIGURE 4.5. Suburban Shopping Center. Source: Gary Peters.

items to the same set of consumers. A jewelry store, for example, may want to be located near stores that sell high-fashion women's clothing.

Earlier in this century, commercial activities typically clustered in the CBD. However, as changes occurred in the urban ecosystem a new pattern emerged. As the location of people spread outward, for example, access to consumers, especially those with medium to high incomes, could best be had by moving businesses to the suburbs. Thus, the suburban shopping mall became a fixture in urban America during the decades following 1950. The CBD remained, but it ran into increasing financial difficulties. In most cities, however, the CBD is still at the top of the hierarchy of commercial centers, which runs the gamut from large regional shopping centers to neighborhood shopping centers that are composed of perhaps a supermarket, a drugstore, and a variety market of some sort.

Manufacturing activities also tend to be clustered together within the urban ecosystem, partly for the same economic reasons that influence the spatial arrangement of commercial activities. Industrial firms choose locations not only because of land rents but also, and varying from industry to industry, because of available transportation, local taxes, availability of land suited for industrial use, access to labor, access to inputs, and water supplies. Some industries are severely restricted in their locational choices by pollution restrictions, neighborhood attitudes, and zoning ordinances. High-income residential neighborhoods, for example, don't want noisy or dirty industrial neighbors.

Linkages again play an important role in causing industries to cluster together. For example, firms may cluster together because they manufacture different parts required for the manufacture of some final product, such as transistors, capacitors, and resistors that are assembled into radios, television sets, and stereos. Clustering is also encouraged now in many metropolitan areas by the package deals offered by industrial parks, many of which are found in suburban or peripheral locations (Figure 4.6). Rising urban land costs and the changing distribution of the labor force are likely to con-

FIGURE 4.6. Industrial Park. Source: HUD.

tinue to lure manufacturing activities away from central locations, toward both suburban and nonmetropolitan sites.
Stricter pollution controls would also tend to discourage central locations. Furthermore, many European nations, including England, the Netherlands, and France, have policies
that are designed to decentralize the location of economic activities and to distribute them more equitably throughout the
nation.

Economic Space in the Urban Ecosystem

So far we have been looking at the location of economic activities in intraurban space as being influenced by competing
abilities to pay rent for urban space and by linkages that
serve to concentrate commercial and industrial uses into
clusters. Thus, the bid-rent curve has acted as the dominant

theme in determining land use, and clustering has been the major variation on that theme. However, we need to briefly consider three other variations as well—zoning, local taxation, and transportation.

Zoning. The primary purpose of zoning is to control and reduce negative elements that arise from uncontrolled land development (Emerson and Lamphear, 1975). Zoning provides a means whereby an urban area is divided into zones of different land use types, theoretically diminishing conflicts between incompatible land uses. Without zoning, the argument goes, we might end up with children going to schools that are located directly under airport flight paths, with quiet residential areas sprouting smokestacks as manufacturers settle next door, and with endless blight. Other people argue that zoning is ineffective, that it only interferes with the market system's ability to allocate resources to their best and most effective use (even when that operation might mean replacing a fine example of local architecture with a service station or a fast-food restaurant).

The actual practice of zoning varies widely among American cities, with some, such as Houston, Texas, avoiding it entirely. Most cities, however, do have some zoning. As we have already observed, change is constantly occurring within the urban ecosystem, so zoning decisions need to be flexible. Zoning must be closely tied to planning efforts in order to secure zoning decisions that are compatible with long-term growth projections; otherwise a city may constantly be bombarded with requests for changes in land use within zoned areas. Rezoning is often difficult.

Within a particular land use zone, of course, both firms and individuals are free to make locational choices. Manufacturing zones are especially important because both homeowners and businessmen often think of industries as undesirable neighbors. Certainly many heavy industries produce noxious odors, have belching smokestacks, and create landscapes that look like an earthly version of hell. But not all industrial landscapes are so unsightly. For example, many of the new industrial parks are quiet, attractively landscaped, and pleasant to work in.

The impact of zoning on the location of economic activities, then, is that it tends to reinforce the clustering of similar types of activities. Furthermore, over a period of time industries that need central city land may be forced into suburban locations in cities where too little of the central area was originally zoned for industrial purposes.

Local Taxation. Local taxes on land, buildings, and profits may affect the location of economic activities, though their impact is likely to be slight in most cases. For most industries, local taxes are only a relatively small part of the total production cost, and the other costs are more likely to influence most locational choices. As a generalization, taxes are higher in the central city and lower in suburbs, so when taxes do affect locational decisions, their impact is in the direction of decentralizing economic activities.

Local taxes may also be used to help control pollution since they can be used to discourage polluting industries from locating in already polluted areas. Some localities may, on the other hand, offer tax incentives to induce new industries to locate within them rather than elsewhere. Such incentives have been used, for example, to attract chemical industries to locate in certain parts of the southeastern United States. Such incentives may include reduced property taxes, reduced taxes on profits, and deferred tax payments.

Transportation. Transportation networks weave together the patterns of locations and interactions that make up the urban ecosystem. As such, transportation networks are discussed in detail elsewhere in this book, but here we do want to point out their rather obvious effects on the spatial distribution of urban economic activities. Access, of course, is the key that opens the door to understanding how and why the shape of the transport system shapes the pattern of economic activities.

Perhaps the most obvious observation we can make is that the CBD is usually centered on converging transportation corridors. Economic development also concentrates along selected major corridors, such as along Wilshire Boulevard in Los Angeles. Ports also serve as a focus for economic activities, including oil refining and petrochemicals, and similarly, industrial zones are common around most metropolitan air-

FIGURE 4.7. Port Activities at Long Beach, California. Source: Gary Peters.

ports. Around both ports and airports, we are likely to find industries that have specialized transportation needs (Figure 4.7).

THE CITY AS AN ECONOMIC SYSTEM

The modern urban ecosystem is a complex economic system that functions as part of a dynamic national system of cities and often as part of the international system as well. In this section our concern is with the city as an economic system; systems of cities are dealt with in another chapter.

City Types and Functions

In order to understand cities, it is necessary to consider how they can be classified. Classification is an essential step in the process of scientific inquiry, allowing us in this case to generalize about various types of cities and their associated economic functions.

Harris and Ullman (1945) suggested that a general urban

classification system could be composed of three types of cities: (1) central places, (2) transportation cities, and (3) specialized-function cities. Central places provide a set of diversified services for the hinterlands, transportation cities are often related to break-of-bulk points or other transportation features related to larger regions, and specialized-function cities are often tied to national and international markets. Examples of the last include cities dominated by manufacturing, mining, or recreational activities.

Classifying cities according to their functions is not quite as easy as it first appears. For example, how are we to determine the degree to which a city must engage in a particular function in order to be so classified? Many cities have residents employed in mining, but not all of those places would be considered mining towns. Furthermore, we must decide whether a given city can have one and only one classification, or whether a recreation town, for example, could also be classified as a mining town or a manufacturing town.

In one attempt at a functional classification of cities, Harris (1943) classified 605 American cities, mainly on the basis of employment profiles. Each city was assigned to one of the following ten classes: (1) manufacturing cities, M^1 subtype, (2) manufacturing cities, M subtype, (3) wholesale cities, (4) transportation cities, (5) resort-retirement cities, (6) retail cities, (7) diversified cities, (8) mining cities, (9) university cities, and (10) political cities. Harris found that more than 80 percent of all cities were one of three types – manufacturing, diversified, or retail. Manufacturing cities were by far the most numerous, over 40 percent of all cities.

The Harris classification has been criticized, especially because of the subjective way in which he established levels of employment needed for specialization. However, most recent urban classification schemes have been variations on Harris's general theme, though there has been an attempt to make the later schemes more objective in the way cities are assigned to various categories.

Basic/Nonbasic Operations

Regardless of why a city may have originally been established, its continued existence is mainly dependent on its economic functions. Thompson (1965) suggested a sequence of stages of urban growth: (1) export specialization, (2) the export complex, (3) economic maturation, (4) regional metropolis, and (5) technical-professional virtuosity. The last, he suggested, could come before or after the stage of regional metropolis. In this sequence of urban development, narrow export specialization gives way to more-diverse export production, which in turn leads to imports being replaced by local goods and finally to a regional center that is integrated with other cities and exports services. The stage of technical-professional virtuosity comes about when the city rises to national prominence for some specific productive endeavor. Note that in each case urban growth depends on exporting goods and/or services – that is, selling them outside of the city – which brings income into the city. Conversely, items brought in from outside the city represent a drain on the city's income, hence the early interest in substituting locally produced goods for imports.

The division of a city's economic activities into basic and nonbasic activities is related to Thompson's view of the process of urban growth. According to Bendavid, "The heart of economic base theory is the proposition that the rate and direction of growth of a region or city is determined by its function as an exporter to the rest of the world" (Bendavid, 1974, p. 103). In other words, a city's growth depends on bringing in money from the outside, either by exporting goods and services or by selling them locally to outsiders such as tourists. Those industries that bring money in from outside the city are basic industries. On the other hand, industries that provide goods and services to residents within the city are nonbasic industries. Examples of basic industries include steel and aluminum plants, whereas examples of nonbasic activities would include supermarkets and bakeries. Thus, the economic base theory explains urban economic growth as being related to an outside demand for a city's goods and services.

Notice that a linkage exists between the basic and nonbasic sectors of a city's employment. If outside demand increases, then basic employment must increase to satisfy that demand. However, an increase in basic employment in turn increases the demand for nonbasic goods and services, hence an increase in nonbasic employment also occurs. Consider a simple example. Suppose that a town has a steel mill as one of its basic industries. Suppose also that an increase in the demand for steel creates new jobs at the mill. Let's assume that 100 new jobs are created and filled by people who move into the town, a total of, say, 275 people when family members are included. These new residents, then, would increase the local demand for groceries, haircuts, and many other nonbasic items so that expansion would also occur in the nonbasic sector. Thus, both sectors are linked to external demand, and that linkage is through the basic sector.

If we count a city's employment in each sector, then we can calculate a base ratio, expressed as the number of basic employees to the number of nonbasic employees. (We could also, by the way, measure both sectors in terms of income rather than employment!) If we found that two workers were employed in basic industries for every three employed in nonbasic activities, then we would have a base ratio of 2:3, or 1:1.5. We can then calculate a base multiplier as follows:

$$\text{base multiplier} = \frac{\text{total employment}}{\text{basic employment}}$$

With a basic employment of 2 and a nonbasic employment of 3, total employment is 5, so the base multiplier is 5/2 or 2.5. This multiplier can help us know the actual total impact of a change in basic employment. If we go back to the steel mill example, there was an increase in basic employment of 100, but that would not be the total employment impact because of the increased demand for nonbasic items. We find the total employment impact of a change in basic employment as follows:

$$\text{total employment impact} = \text{base multiplier} \times \text{change in basic employment}$$

In the example, then, with a base multiplier of 2.5 and a basic employment change of 100, the total employment impact would be 250. Thus, the base multiplier provides a useful means of estimating the impact of a new or expanding industry in an urban area. However, there are problems associated with putting the economic base model into operation.

Two problems arise immediately when we try to employ the basic/nonbasic concept. First, we need to decide on a suitable measurement of economic activity, usually either employment or income. Because the latter is more difficult to ascertain, employment is most frequently used. Second, we need to find a way to distinguish between basic and nonbasic activities. At first this appears quite simple, but a closer look reveals the nature of the difficulties. Factories, for example, may produce items that are consumed both locally and outside the city, in which case some of their employment is nonbasic, and the remainder is basic. The same situation occurs in many wholesale activities, especially in larger regional cities.

Among the various approaches to determining whether employment is basic or nonbasic are (1) the assumptions approach, (2) the location quotient approach, and (3) the minimum requirements approach. Because of numerous inadequacies associated with the first two approaches, only the minimum requirements approach is discussed here, but it, also, has its critics.

Discussed by Tiebout (1962) and employed by Ullman, Dacey, and Brodsky (1969), the minimum requirements approach involves a comparative technique in which the levels of employment in various economic activities are used to calculate the minimum requirements for those activities for any specified city size. For each industry in each city of a given size, in other words, we would calculate the percentage of the labor force the industry employed. The lowest percentage for each industry in that city-size category would represent the minimum requirements for that industry. Thus, we could develop a profile of minimum requirements for all economic activities for any given city size. As Bendavid noted, "The assumption underlying this approach is that the region in which an industry represents the smallest proportion of the total from among the selected regions contains the minimum requirement in that industry necessary to service local needs" (Bendavid, 1974, p. 110). Once the minimum requirements for an industry are established, of course, we can then assume that all employment in that industry in excess of the minimum requirements is basic employment.

We should note, also, that the more a city's employment exceeds the minimum requirements in a given sector, the more specialized that city is in that particular activity. In turn, we could argue that the more that city specializes in that particular activity and the more a city specializes in one industrial sector, the more vulnerable that city is to the fortunes and misfortunes of ripples in the national and international economic systems. For example, Boeing's aerospace employment in Seattle provided a major problem in the past. In 1968 Boeing employed over 100,000 people in Seattle, but by 1971 employment fell to less than 40,000. Tens of thousands of people left the city, and a local billboard read, "Will the last person leaving Seattle please turn out the lights?" With cities, as with other ecosystems, diversity is the key to stability.

REFERENCES

Bendavid, Avrom. 1974. *Regional Economic Analysis for Practitioners.* Rev. ed. New York: Praeger Publishers.

Boyce, Ronald R. 1978. *The Bases of Economic Geography.* 2d ed. New York: Holt, Rinehart and Winston.

Emerson, M. Jarvin, and Lamphear, F. Charles. 1975. *Urban and Regional Economics: Structure and Change.* Boston: Allyn and Bacon.

Harris, C. D. 1943. "A Functional Classification of Cities in the United States." *Geographical Review* 33: 86–99.

Harris, C. D., and Ullman, E. L. 1945. "The Nature of Cities." *Annals of the American Academy of Political and Social Science* 242: 7–17.

Hurd, Richard M. 1924. *Principles of City Land Values.* New York: Record and Guide.

Northam, Ray M. 1979. *Urban Geography.* 2d ed. New York: John Wiley and Sons.

Thompson, Wilbur R. 1965. *A Preface to Urban Economics.* Baltimore: Johns Hopkins Press published for Resources for the Future.

Tiebout, Charles M. 1962. *The Community Economic Base Study.* Supplementary Paper No. 16. New York: Committee for Economic Development.

Ullman, E. L.; Dacey, M. F.; and Brodsky, H. 1969. *The Economic Base of American Cities.* Seattle: University of Washington Press.

Vance, James E., Jr. 1966. "Focus on Downtown." *Community Planning Review* 16: 9–15.

Yeates, Maurice, and Garner, Barry. 1976. *The North American City.* 2d ed. New York: Harper and Row, Publishers.

5

Transportation, Land Use, and Urban Form

Most analysts of the current urban situation agree that something is severely amiss with the transportation systems in cities and metropolitan areas. We have all confronted, at one time or another, our own personal transportation "problem." The problem could take the form of a bus that is not on schedule or waiting in a long line of cars in a traffic jam on a freeway. The problems are complex, and the solutions are just as complex. In this chapter we outline the nature of the transportation network in cities and discuss the problems associated with that network.

URBAN CONGESTION IN HISTORICAL PERSPECTIVE

The problems of traffic and congestion are not new; they have been confounding the experts for centuries. The great cities of all advanced civilizations have had to cope with traffic problems. The Romans tried to solve their problems by building a network of permanent stone highways. During the Renaissance, the port of Milan experienced congestion because of its rapid growth, and a solution to the problem was proposed by Leonardo da Vinci. His solution was to develop underground thoroughfares that would be used for commercial traffic, leaving the streets for strollers and light traffic. Unfortunately, the people of Milan rejected the idea, and in the 400 years since then traffic congestion has been synonymous with urban living everywhere (Fischler, 1979, p. 35).

The subway eventually made its debut. On January 10, 1863, the first subway was opened in London, and by the end of that year more than 1.5 million passengers had traveled on its subterranean rails. As the population of London increased to over 4 million inhabitants by the turn of the century, the poorer inhabitants of the city were forced out of the central area, because of high land values, to the outlying regions. Those people became the first commuters, or journeymen as they were called at the time. According to C. H. Holden's study of London at that time, congestion was even experienced by those on foot, with the daily "streams of walkers two, three and four miles long, converging on the city" (Holden, 1951, p. 166). By the early 1890s, over 1 million passengers were carried each year on a thousand London horse buses. Also, the rail system brought over 400,000 commuters per day into the city.

During the same time period, people in American cities were constructing subways and elevated railroads in an effort to relieve their congestion problems. In the early twentieth century, rush hour congestion was the primary problem of large cities in the United States; this congestion was due to the crowding of horses, people, and street cars. Thus, even before the widespread use of motor vehicles, congestion was a major urban problem. The basic causes of the problem then, as today, were the concentration of people and economic activity in small land areas and the lack of proper planning to accommodate changing urban functions.

Cities have simply grown too fast, particularly in the past several decades. Transport systems are responsible for this rapid growth, yet on the other hand urban areas have now grown to the point where they, according to Wilfred Owen, "threaten to strangle the transportation that made them possible" (Owen, 1966, p. 1). Older cities that developed their physical characteristics during less-mobile times have not been able to cope with modern transportation developments.

STAGES OF URBAN MOBILITY

The urban transportation problem is not limited to the

United States. Nations throughout the world are changing from agricultural societies to urban industrial societies, and that transformation presents all cities with similar problems of achieving acceptable standards of urban mobility. Even in cities where the automobile is not paramount, other modes of transport, like the truck, bus, and even the bicycle, can create severe problems.

The evolution of urban transportation systems has been identified as a four-stage process (Owen, 1972, pp. 128–131). The first stage, particularly in low-income countries, involves a great deal of pedestrian and bicycle traffic. There are few automobiles, and they are primarily owned by the wealthy. The private automobile is thought to have negative economic and social effects, especially where there are no automobile support industries. In this stage, there is some reliance on the commuter railway and bus systems.

During the second stage economic takeoff occurs, with a concomitant increase in automobile use and production. Automobile production provides employment opportunities, and the availability of automobiles at relatively low cost can have favorable political and social implications.

Most of the world's cities are now in the third stage of transport evolution. During this stage congestion, with its associated environmental and social problems, becomes a major obstacle to urban development. The congestion is primarily the result of high levels of car ownership. Large numbers of automobiles and their associated problems induce the search for rapid transit substitutes. The subway appears to be the primary rapid transit alternative, particularly in the center city areas. However, because city governments cannot control automobile use and have little effective control over the density and spatial arrangements of the city, they quickly find that subways are not the answer to the problem.

The frustration with mass transit solutions leads to the fourth stage of development. During this stage all mass transit solutions to urban transportation problems are questioned by city officials, and the focus is shifted to the spatial structure of the city and the need for planned development. This stage involves a parallel advancement in both the means of transportation and the spatial design of communities. According to Wilfred Owen, the major efforts will be to "minimize unnecessary movement, to control the automobile to safeguard the urban environment, to invent acceptable substitutes for the automobile, and to meet the transport needs of the nondriving population" (Owen, 1972, p. 131).

THE CAR AND THE CITY

On December 30, 1940, Culbert Olson, then governor of California, officially dedicated the first freeway in the United States. It was called "the miracle boulevard," and little did the on-lookers realize that the six-mile stretch of highway would be a model for urban transportation in the United States for the next half century or more (Figure 5.1).

The Subsidized Highway

During the two decades after the Second World War, the concept of "freeway" gained enormous popular support. The idea of multilane, limited-access thoroughfares criss-crossing the nation was accepted by almost everyone, especially road builders, politicians, and state and federal highway officials, trucking interests, and most important, the millions of automobile owners. By the mid-fifties most public figures were in favor of superhighways both as links between cities and as avenues for commuter travel within cities (Davies, 1975, p. 4).

In response to this massive public support for faster and safer highways, and also to the need to ease traffic congestion in urban areas, the President's Advisory Committee on a National Highway Program held public hearings on October 7–8, 1954. An analysis of the groups that testified before the committee points out the wide diversity of interest groups that supported more highway construction. Testimony included presentations by the American Farm Bureau Federation, U.S. Chamber of Commerce, U.S. Conference of Mayors, American Road Builders Association, National Association of County Officials, Automotive Safety Founda-

FIGURE 5.1. Interstate Highway Through an Urban Area. Source: HUD.

tion, American Automobile Association, American Petroleum Institute, American Trucking Association, and various other organizations ("Summary . . . 1954"). In response to this public outcry of support, the National System of Interstate and Defense Highways was created by Congress in 1956.

The network would include 41,000 miles of freeways, including 7,000 miles within metropolitan areas (Figure 5.2). Included in the system would be almost all cities with populations over 50,000. Completion for this original system was to be in 1972, at a total cost of approximately $26 billion. An additional 1,500 miles were added by Congress in 1968, and because changes were made for a variety of reasons, the completion date was extended to the 1980s. Because of inflation and rising costs, the final total for construction costs is expected to be over $100 billion.

The interstate system was hailed by almost everyone, and even during the Eisenhower administration, a heyday of fiscal conservatism, there were few challenges to the cost of the program. Even the archconservative George M. Humphrey, secretary of the treasury, approved of it, stating that "America lives on wheels, and we have to provide the highways to keep America living on wheels and keep the kind and form of life we want" (Rose, 1973, p. 215). According to Richard O. Davies in his study of the automobile and the freeway,

> Enthusiasm soared. . . . City planners hailed the new system as a means of uniting the city by making it possible for suburban residents to commute swiftly to their jobs in the central business district; furthermore, the highways would blend neatly into the planners' ambitious plans for slum clearance and urban renewal in the blighted areas of the central city. Local politicos, hard pressed to pay the rapidly rising costs of government, joyously received the financing formula that would have the federal government paying ninety percent of the urban freeway costs, leaving the state government the remainder. It is not every day that a financially troubled city can get a spanking new transportation system virtually for free. [Davies, 1975, p. 4]

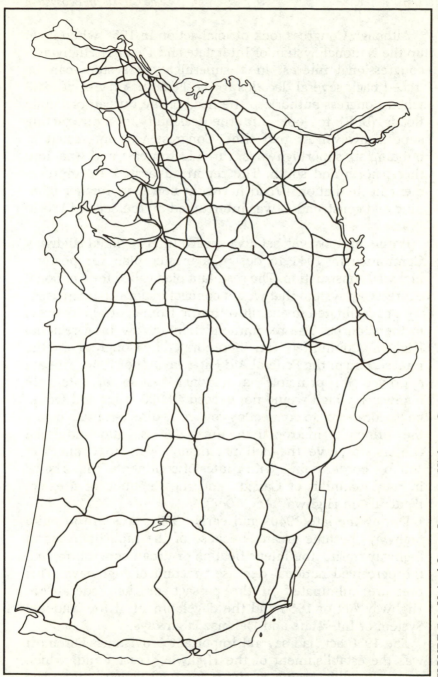

FIGURE 5.2. United States Interstate Highway System.

Although Congress took official action in 1956 when it set up the National System of Interstate and Defense Highways, congressional interest in a superhighway system can be traced back several decades to the Federal Aid Act of 1938 when Congress authorized the head of the Bureau of Public Roads (BPR) to look into the feasibility of constructing superhighways. At that time Congress was interested in building six superhighways, three to run east and west and three, north and south. The report advocated an improvement in the national road network; however, further planning and construction was interrupted by the Second World War.

President Roosevelt set up a special Inter-regional Highway Committee in 1941 to design a master plan for postwar highway construction. The resultant plan called for a national expressway system that would connect major urban areas, as well as facilitate movement of traffic from central city areas to the suburbs. The recommendations of the Inter-regional Highway Committee were incorporated by Congress into the final section of the Federal Aid Highway Act of 1944. This act approved "in principle" a national system of interstate highways, which would not exceed 40,000 miles and would be "so located as to connect by routes, as direct as practicable, the principle metropolitan areas, cities, and industrial centers, to serve the national defense and to connect at suitable border points with routes of continental importance in the Dominion of Canada and the Republic of Mexico" (Federal Aid Highway Act, 1944).

During the late 1940s and early 1950s, pressure to build highways became greater because of the rapid increase in highway traffic, the intensification of urban congestion, and the perceived national defense function of highways. This pressure culminated in the passage of the Federal Aid Highway Act of 1956 and the development of the National System of Interstate and Defense Highways.

The 1956 act had several important provisions. Foremost was the establishment of the Highway Trust Fund, which was to provide grants to states for road construction. The source of money for these grants was from federal taxes on oil and gasoline, as well as from other highway-related taxes. A second important aspect of the 1956 act was the provision that 90 percent of the cost of the interstate system would come from federal revenues, with the remaining 10 percent from state sources.

Because most of the early construction of the interstate system took place in rural areas, little criticism appeared during the early years of construction. Some early opposition by environmentalists was heard, but most protests erupted only later when construction began in urban areas. The most notable of the earlier prophetic voices, however, was that of Lewis Mumford, who said a few months after the Federal Aid Highway Act passed that

> the most charitable thing to assume about this is that they hadn't the faintest notion of what they were doing. . . . Within the next fifteen years they will doubtless find out; but by that time it will be too late to correct all the damage to our cities and our countryside, to say nothing of all the inefficient organization of industry and transportation, that this ill-conceived and absurdly unbalanced program will have wrought. [Mumford, 1963, p. 234]

The Impact of the Automobile

The development of the automobile as the principal method of transportation has had a tremendous impact on the nature and structure of urban areas. It has increased the radius of travel for urban dwellers and, consequently, the size of urbanized areas. Many distance and time limitations that previously restricted the location of residences and business enterprises were altered considerably because of the automobile. The constraints that forced urban growth at the center and along railway networks leading to the center were overcome, and urban growth spread in every direction along the roads that are now the giant skeleton of the modern metropolis (Owen, 1966, p. 26).

The automobile is the major means of personal transportation in cities today, and it accounts for a large percentage of the expenditures for transportation (Figure 5.3). Over 80 percent of American families have at least one automobile, and in some cities the proportion of automobile owners is even higher. Our reliance on the automobile has had an enormous effect on the physical characteristics of the city. In the days prior to the automobile and railroads, the average commuting distance, by horse or foot travel, was between two and three miles, and the size of most cities was limited to approxi-

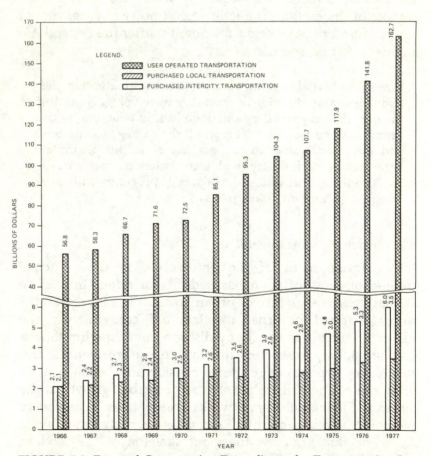

FIGURE 5.3. Personal Consumption Expenditures by Transportation Sector, 1966–1977. Source: U.S. Department of Transportation, "National Transportation Statistics," *Annual Report,* September (Washington, D.C.: Government Printing Office, 1978), p. 63.

mately twenty square miles. With the advent of the railroad, streetcar, and other forms of rapid transit, the radius of commuter movement was increased to five miles, and the area of most cities grew to about seventy-nine square miles (Bartholomew, 1952, p. 1). The addition of large numbers of automobiles to the urban scene greatly expanded both commuting distances and areas of cities. It is not uncommon for some cities to have a commuting radius of over forty miles and an urban area that covers several thousand square miles. Consider Los Angeles, for example, where people commonly commute an hour or more to and from work.

Although the automobile is the most common method of transportation and although it does offer many advantages in terms of comfort, privacy, and freedom, it also has its drawbacks. For example, automobiles make considerable demands on limited urban space. A large proportion of the land in cities is now devoted to parking lots, streets, freeways, and huge cloverleaf freeway interchanges. The result, according to Wilfred Owen, is that

> where all-out efforts have been made to accommodate the car, the streets are still congested, commuting is increasingly difficult, urban aesthetics have suffered, and the quality of life has been eroded. In an automotive age, cities have become the negation of communities—a setting for machines instead of people. The automobile has taken over, motorist and nonmotorist alike are caught up in the congestion, and everyone is a victim of the damaging effects of the conflict between the car and the community. The automobile is an irresistible force that may become an immovable object, and in the process destroy the city. [Owen, 1972, p. 1]

The idea of the city as a place for machines (automobiles) and not for people was further developed by the geographer Ronald Horvath with his concept of "machine space." Horvath believed that the automobile may prove to be the single most significant cultural innovation in the United States in the twentieth century. He defined "machine space" as automobile territory—territory that includes any area that is devoted to the movement, servicing, or storage of automobiles. This definition would therefore include streets, alleys, parking lots, driveways, garages, gasoline stations, car washes, and so on.

The amount of automobile territory has been mapped for several areas of Detroit and East Lansing, Michigan, and Figure 5.4 illustrates the distribution of automobile territory in the central business district of Detroit. It is obvious that much of the urban landscape is devoted to the automobile (Figure 5.5). Are cities "a setting for machines instead of people"? In answer to that question Horvath said:

> Machines, quite obviously, by definition. Consider a hypothetical situation of a group of children who are playing baseball in an empty municipal parking lot. If someone decides to park his car in the middle of the lot, the children must discontinue their game. The individual could be a

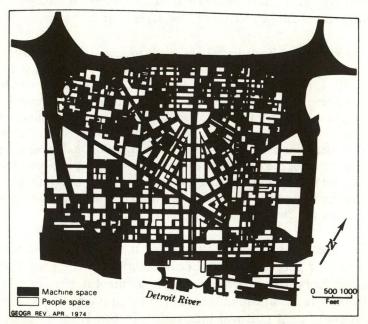

FIGURE 5.4. Automobile Territory in the CBD of Detroit, Michigan. Reprinted from Ronald J. Horvath, "Machine Space," *Geographical Review* 64:2 (April 1974), p. 171, by permission of the American Geographical Society.

stranger, indeed, not even a local taxpayer (whereas the children are the sons and daughters of the taxpayers who financed the parking lot), but his right to use the lot supersedes the rights of the children because he came in a machine. [Horvath, 1974, p. 179]

In addition to the amount of space the automobile uses in a city, the automobile is also a large consumer of both materials and energy. A great deal of the U.S. outputs of iron, steel, plastic, and rubber go into automobile production. Also, the voracious appetite of the United States for energy is primarily a result of an automobile-centered society.

One of the original purposes of developing the interstate system was to ease traffic congestion in metropolitan areas, but much to the chagrin of traffic planners the freeways did not necessarily reduce the congestion. As critic John Jerome observed:

FIGURE 5.5. Play Space in the City. Source: HUD.

Freeways make congestion. . . . Freeways funnel local traffic, in search of convenience, into the streams of long-haul through traffic for which the freeways were originally planned . . . traffic is, in the end, simply dumped . . . six lanes into two, the bottleneck sending waves of congestion rippling back out the freeway to close off the very freeness for which it was created. [Jerome, 1972, p. 107]

The increase in traffic, particularly in the central business district, brought about another problem: where to put all the cars. Parking space became scarce, and consequently, high-rise parking garages have become a common feature of downtown areas of cities. It has been estimated that approximately one-third of the land in the downtown areas of most American cities is devoted to parking space (Davies, 1975, p. 30).

There is little doubt that urban freeways have had a negative impact on the urban poor. Most of the urban poor live in the central city where low-cost housing is available. However, when highway planners designated routes for highway construction, it was common to route a highway directly through a low-cost housing neighborhood. In this respect, the historian Sam Bass Warner, Jr., observed that

by an unhappy convergence of history, the interstate highway program passed Congress in an era of political reaction, so that the seizure of poor urban neighborhoods coincided with a cutback in public housing. Since the location of roads just outside the urban center was implicit in the wheel strategy of the highway engineer, the cry of "blight" urged on him the merits of taking as much of the land as he wished. Thus to rip out the houses of the poor was a transportation principle that became a public contribution rather than an act of social irresponsibility. [Warner, 1972, pp. 47–48]

The expansion of the highway system certainly had an impact on the central city, but perhaps even more significant was the impact of highways on the suburbanization process. The development of superhighways greatly accelerated the movement of people to suburban areas, and expressway interchanges became the focus for both residential and commercial development. Easy access to an interchange became an attractive feature for home buyers, and subsequently, new shopping centers and office complexes were built. Eventually, even manufacturers were attracted to the suburbs because of relatively low land values and easy access. Rapid suburbanization had a negative impact by drawing resources away from the central city, thus leading to the decline of central city businesses.

We have seen the tremendous impact the automobile, and the highways built in conjunction with the increase in the number of automobiles, have had on the urban landscape. Another important impact of the automobile has been its effect on the quality of air within urban areas. The air pollution index is commonly reported by most weather people on the radio or television in metropolitan areas. The atmospheric pollution associated with motor vehicles is considered by many to be a threat to the health and welfare of the population, although there is little agreement on the seriousness of the threat or its long-term implications. The actual effects of automotive pollutants depends upon the length of exposure to them as well as upon the extent of the pollutant concentrations in the atmosphere. Those concentrations are primarily the result of climate, topography, emissions per vehicle, and traffic density. Because climate and topography are relatively constant, the best means of controlling air pollution is by reducing the average emission per vehicle and/or by decreasing the traffic density.

A variety of measures have been proposed and implemented in various places in an attempt to control air pollution caused by motor vehicles. One highly effective method is to exclude cars from certain streets. Experiments in a number of countries have shown that carbon monoxide concentrations can be reduced by as much as two-thirds in that way, and perhaps the most convincing evidence of the effectiveness and public acceptance of traffic-free areas is their recent growth, both in extent and number. Over one hundred cities have banned traffic from portions of their central districts (Gakenheimer, 1978, p. 385).

Other methods of reducing pollution include incentives to encourage car pooling, the rerouting of through traffic (particularly heavy trucks), allowing the employees of large industrial, commercial, or governmental organizations to stagger their working hours, and encouraging greater use of rapid transit systems. In the long term, automobile pollution could be controlled by more rational urban and land use planning. Also, the design of motor vehicles could be improved, and technological advances could produce a pollution-free automobile.

PUBLIC TRANSPORTATION IN THE CITY

There is currently a great deal of research on developing answers to the problems of urban transit. Some of this research is concerned with new, and perhaps exotic, methods of transportation, and more than a hundred new transit systems are in various stages of conceptualization or experimentation. Other research is concerned with upgrading conventional methods of transportation to provide greater speed, economy, and comfort.

Standard Rapid Transit

The standard rapid transit or subway system is a relatively old form of mass transit dating back to when the first rapid transit lines were opened in London in 1863 and New York City in 1867. The original source of power for these trains was steam, but the introduction of electricity before the turn of the century allowed the rapid transit system to expand greatly. In 1940 there were 930 miles of track in operation in eighteen major cities in the world. Between 1940 and 1960 route construction slowed down, but since 1960 there has been a great increase. By 1975 rapid transit systems totaled 1,890 miles in fifty-one cities throughout the world (see Figure 5.6).

The subway, or metro, is considered by many people to be the most effective method of dealing with the problems of urban congestion. This form of rapid transit – particularly the new subway systems that have been developed (Figure

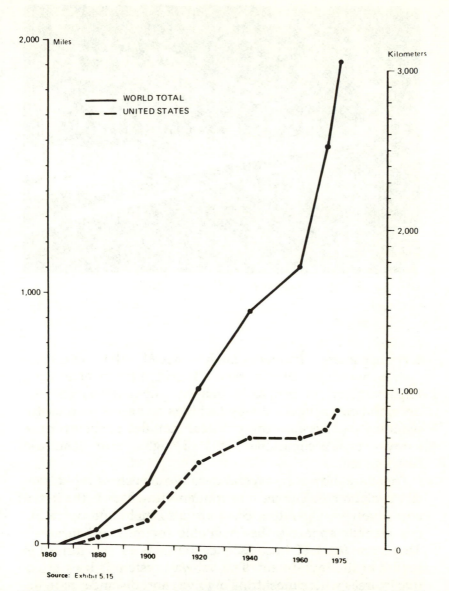

Source: Exhibit 5.15

FIGURE 5.6. Route Miles of Rail Rapid Transit Systems, U.S. and World Total, 1863–1975. From *Public Transportation and Land Use Policy* by Boris S. Pushkarev and Jeffrey M. Zupan (Bloomington: Indiana University Press, 1977), p. 170. Reprinted by permission of the publisher.

FIGURE 5.7. Metro, Washington, D.C. Source: HUD.

5.7) – has many advantages such as speed, safety, and comfort. Subways are also a very efficient method of moving large numbers of people in densely populated areas. The development of new subway facilities can serve as a useful planning tool because the physical facilities needed for the subway can become the focus of high-density land use development.

There are, however, several negative aspects of rapid transit development. The most prominent drawback is the initial cost involved. Operating costs are also high, and operating cost deficits appear to be inevitable for most urban areas. There are fears of obsolescence because of the inflexible nature of the investment. The subway system is least effective in areas where most trips involve short distances or in urban areas that are not densely populated, as in southern California.

Commuter Rail Transit

Commuter rail transit is a train service between the central business district and outlying suburban areas. These trains run less frequently than standard rapid transit service and have a definite time schedule to follow. Passengers on commuter rail transit ride for longer distances, between fifteen and twenty-six miles, and therefore there is more concern for passenger comfort.

Light Rail Transit

Light rail transit is commonly called a streetcar or tramway system. This mode of urban transit was much more common in the past than it is now. Before 1920 there were over 50,000 miles of track in urban areas devoted to this type of transit, but today less than 2 percent of that track remains. Light rail vehicles commonly run singly or in short trains and operate in mixed traffic. Because they run on a fixed track, their route is much more permanent than that of a bus.

Light Guideway Transit

Light guideway transit is a term used to describe a number of relatively new transit systems that have been developed in the past two decades. These systems are also called by a number of acronyms and trade names like ACT (automatically controlled transport), AGT (automatic guideway transit), ICT (intermediate capacity transit), and skytrain. These systems are primarily used in centers of activity like airports or amusement centers. A good example is the system at the Dallas–Fort Worth Airport. Light guideway transit systems represent a response to three basic shortcomings of traditional public transport systems: "(1) the inability to provide very frequent all-day service without incurring huge labor costs, (2) the need to delay all passengers by stopping for others, and (3) the high cost of building fully grade-separated guideways to achieve high speed with large conventional transit vehicles" (Pushkarev and Zupan, 1977, p. 70).

Most light guideway transit systems operate automatically, use relatively small vehicles (twenty to twenty-five passengers), and have no attendants on board. These systems are much more flexible than larger systems, and every vehicle does not have to stop at every station. Also, the number of vehicles can be geared to specific demand patterns.

Although light guideway systems have several advantages,

they also have several shortcomings. One major problem is that of reliability. Such systems require a considerable amount of maintenance because of their mechanical and electronic complexity. It was originally thought that building costs for these systems would be considerably less than for standard systems; however, actual costs show that they are not much cheaper to build than the standard systems.

Local or Express Bus

Local and express buses are the most commonly used form of mass transportation in urban areas today. They operate along specified routes, and each carries from thirty-five to fifty passengers. The cost of bus transportation is relatively low when compared with other methods of mass transit; however, the rider pays for that lower cost in several ways. The rider must commonly wait outdoors for the bus, an inconvenience in many areas. In addition to having to walk to the bus stop and possibly having to change buses if the bus does not go near the rider's destination, the bus can be very slow, particularly if it makes many stops or gets into heavy traffic. Although bus travel is cheap, it is also slow and perhaps uncomfortable.

The systems described above are the major forms of mass transit. Each mode has advantages and disadvantages, and whether a particular mode is successful in a particular city depends on a variety of factors. Some of those factors relate to the commuter, and others are the result of spatial urban patterns.

THE URBAN COMMUTER

As the problems associated with the automobile and urban traffic have become more pronounced, public attention has turned to mass transit as the panacea. Corridors associated with mass transit are as important to the modern city as the urban expressway is, but the mass transit alternative is not without its problems. All mass transit systems have similar peaking patterns, and the times of peak demand last for only short time periods (see Figure 5.8).

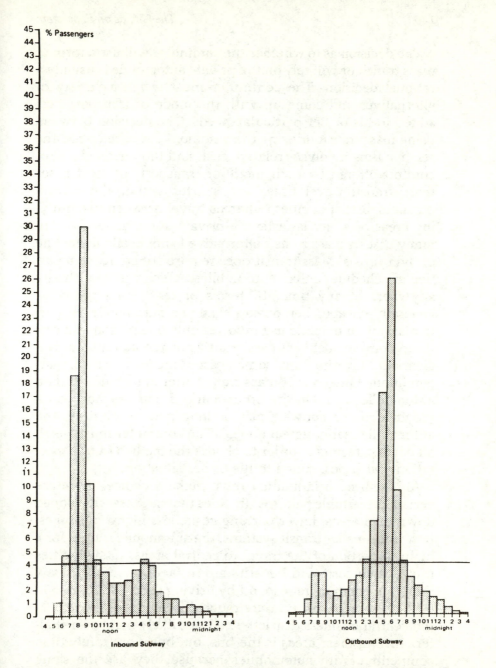

FIGURE 5.8. Subway Peaking Patterns. Source: Tri-State Regional Planning Commission, *Suburban Commuter Parking and Inter-Modal Transfer Study,* ITR 4270-2108, 5203 (Washington, D.C., 1970).

The decision as to whether the commuter will use a form of mass transit or will rely on the private automobile is usually a rational decision. The commuter must weigh a variety of alternatives and come up with the mode of transport best suited to his or her particular needs. The decision between using mass transit or using the automobile is based upon the relative time involved, relative cost, and the relative level of comfort offered by each mode of transport. In most cases mass transit travel times are shorter within the central business district of cities, whereas travel between two outlying areas of a city is faster by private automobile. Also, in many cases a mass transit alternative is not available for the outlying areas. Mass transit does require adherence to a particular schedule, unlike automobiles, which can go virtually anywhere at any time. In terms of cost, mass transit is generally cheaper per person than the automobile is, particularly if automobile use involves only one person in a car. As to comfort, neither mass transit nor the automobile is a clear-cut favorite. In some cases modern, clean, air-conditioned methods of mass transit offer more comfort than automobiles can. On the other hand, if one has stood on a moving bus or subway car for long periods of time, the automobile seat has great appeal. The commuter must weigh all of these factors in order to choose the method of transportation that is best suited to his or her situation.

Although each individual must make a choice, there are certain discernible patterns. In cities that have less-developed downtown areas, lower parking costs, less highway congestion, and smaller transit systems, the automobile is used for a high proportion of the travel to central areas. In such cities the relative costs and benefits are in favor of the highway, therefore commuters respond by driving (Lisco, 1970, p. 55).

The commuter patterns are much different in areas outside the central business district. The most likely mass transit alternative in these areas is the bus, but buses are rarely time competitive with automobiles because they use the same highway network and must make frequent stops. In terms of cost, the bus is also not as competitive. Because parking is readily available and is usually free outside of the central business district, automobile costs usually involve only operating costs. These costs are close to those of mass transportation.

URBAN TRANSPORTATION PLANNING PACKAGES

It is apparent that urban transportation problems are going to exist in the foreseeable future and that transportation planning at all levels in the urban ecosystem must receive considerable attention during the 1980s and beyond. Planning in turn requires adequate data and a careful analysis of current transportation systems. In the United States the Bureau of the Census collects a considerable volume of useful data that we should know about.

An Urban Transportation Planning Package (UTPP) is a special tabulation of census data for an individual standard metropolitan statistical area in a geographic region that is of particular interest to urban and regional transportation planners. The UTPPs were first produced by the Census Bureau after the 1970 census. In order to initiate these special tabulations, local planning organizations must submit specifications to the Census Bureau describing the geographic detail that they require for their SMSA. The Census Bureau then produces a standard set of tabulations for those planning areas on a reimbursable basis. UTPPs based on the 1980 census are, or soon will be, available.

In 1980 the Census Bureau, using funds provided by the Department of Transportation, was developing computer programs for the UTPPs. By spring of 1981 cost estimates for UTPPs were to be available for SMSAs, and the Census Bureau planned to begin actual production on the packages by late 1981.

The 1980 UTPPs consist of six parts with varying content and geography.

PART	CONTENT	GEOGRAPHY
1.	Characteristics of households, persons, and workers	Census tract or block group of residence

2.	Characteristics of households and workers	Large geographic areas of residence
3.	Characteristics of workers	Census tract of work
4.	Characteristics of workers	Census tract of residence by census tract of work
5.	Characteristics of workers	Block group of work
6.	Characteristics of workers	County of residence by county of work

Beyond the detailed cross-tabulations of data for the resident population, the major advantage of the UTPPs is that they provide place-of-work data tabulated on geographic levels that are much finer than any shown on the standard Summary Tape Files. Detailed and extensive resource lists, such as companies, businesses, buildings, shopping centers, and various institutions, have been put together for each SMSA and geocoded to census tracts and blocks, thus allowing the Census Bureau to code incomplete place-of-work responses.

Clearly, the Census Bureau, in coordination with the Department of Transportation, is working to help fill the perceived needs of urban and regional transportation planners. It is to be hoped that these and other data will allow better planning of future urban transportation systems because, as we have already seen, transportation is a major connecting element in the web of activities that compose the twentieth-century urban ecosystem.

REFERENCES

Bartholomew, Harland. 1952. "Planning for Metropolitan Transportation." *Planning and Civic Content* 18, September.

Davies, Richard O. 1975. *The Age of Asphalt: The Automobile, the Freeway, and the Condition of Metropolitan America.* New York: J. B. Lippincott Company.

Fischler, Stanley I. 1979. *Moving Millions: An Inside Look at Mass*

Transit. New York: Harper and Row, Publishers.

Gakenheimer, Ralph, ed. 1978. *The Automobile and the Environment.* Cambridge, Mass.: M.I.T. Press.

Holden, C. H. 1951. *The City of London: A Record of Destruction and Survival.* London: Architectural Press.

Horvath, Ronald J. 1974. "Machine Space." *Geographical Review* 64: 167–188.

Jerome, John. 1972. *The Death of the Automobile.* New York: W. W. Norton.

Lisco, Thomas E. 1970. "The Cinderella of the Cities: Urban Mass Transit." *Public Interest* 18: 52–74.

Mumford, Lewis. 1963. *The Highway and the City.* New York: Harcourt, Brace and World.

Owen, Wilfred. 1966. *The Metropolitan Transportation Problem.* Washington, D.C.: Brookings Institution.

———. 1972. *The Accessible City.* Washington, D.C.: Brookings Institution.

Pushkarev, Boris S., and Zupan, Jeffrey M. 1977. *Public Transportation and Land Use Policy.* Bloomington: Indiana University Press.

Rose, Mark Howard. 1973. "Express Highway Politics, 1939–1956." Ph.D. dissertation, Ohio State University.

"Summary of Clay Committee Hearings – Oct. 7-8, 1954." John S. Bragdon Files, Eisenhower Library, Abilene, Kansas.

U.S. 1944. Federal Aid Highway Act. 58 Stat. 838, sec. 7.

U.S., Department of Transportation. 1978. "National Transportation Statistics." *Annual Report, Sept. 1978.* Washington, D.C.: Government Printing Office.

Warner, Sam Bass, Jr. 1972. *The Urban Wilderness.* New York: Harper and Row, Publishers.

6

Circulation: The Movement of People Within and Between Cities

Circulation, in this case the movement of people, is an essential component of the urban ecosystem. Changes in residences have various causes and consequences and represent a major adjustment mechanism. According to Weinberg and Atkinson,

> As a result of residential mobility, the social, political, and economic fabric of metropolitan areas changes—sometimes slowly, sometimes rapidly. Houses and apartments change hands, and prices and rents rise or fall in response to the relative balance of supply and demand. Understanding mobility and the search for housing that must precede any move is thus an important element in understanding urban change and is consequently critical to the development of a sensitive and sensible urban policy. [Weinberg and Atkinson, 1979, p. 22]

So important a process certainly deserves our attention, especially because change and adaptation are necessary in the urban ecosystem. In keeping with the overall approach used in this book, residential change, or migration, is viewed first within the city and then between cities. In either case, however, we must be concerned with the decision-making process that is related to migration.

MIGRATION AND THE DECISION-MAKING PROCESS

At first glance migration seems simple and straightforward; defining a "migrant" should be easy. However, definitional problems do appear. For example, suppose we define a migrant as someone who "moves." First, we need to agree upon what constitutes a move. Should the move be permanent, or should we also count transients and vacationers as migrants? Second, we might consider distance as a factor in deciding who is or is not a migrant. For example, is a person who moves to a house across the street to be considered as much a migrant as someone who moves from Seattle to Miami? No one definition of a migrant satisfies everyone or solves all the problems associated with the study of migration. However, we can find some agreement on definitions because our conceptual ideas of migration are often limited by pragmatic considerations, including the ways that data are collected and published and the ways that geographic space has been divided into various administrative units. According to Thomlinson,

> Demographers thus define persons as migrants if they change their place of normal habitation for a substantial period of time, crossing a political boundary. Demographers distinguish between moves and migrants according to a single criterion. Movers are persons who change their place of residence; migrants, those whose change of residence takes them into a new political unit. . . . thus all migrants are movers, but some movers are not migrants. [Thomlinson, 1976, pp. 267–268]

In the United States the Bureau of the Census follows the demographic definition, defining movers as those who change residence during some time period and migrants as those who, in the process of changing residence, cross a county boundary.

The causes and consequences of residential change are numerous, vary in both time and space, and affect different people in different ways. Despite a plethora of migration studies, no definitive theory of migration yet exists. However, some generalities about migration and spatial mobility are worth consideration at this point.

One useful theory of migration decision making is the simple push-pull explanation. A potential migrant living in a particular location may consider moving because he or she is not satisfied with present conditions. For example, the house or the neighborhood may be deteriorating, or employment opportunities may be too limited. These would be push factors in the sense that they are "pushing" the potential migrant to another location. Similarly, the potential migrant may perceive that more-attractive conditions and better opportunities can be found elsewhere. Rural residents, for example, may think the "bright lights" of the city represent greater opportunities for employment and social interaction. Thus, opportunities elsewhere "pull" the migrant toward them. Most often both push and pull factors probably affect the decision to migrate, a decision that for most people is not easy to make. Such a decision is likely to be made when someone either is dissatisfied with a present location or thinks that the benefits of moving outweigh the costs. Of course, numerous events are likely to generate a move. Examples include losing a job, getting married or divorced, or having the house burn down.

Similar to the simple push-pull theory of migration is a more recent analysis, complete with a set of hypotheses about the volume, streams, and characteristics of migrants, proposed by Lee (1966). He began by separating the elements that influence migration into (1) factors associated with a migrant's origin, (2) factors associated with possible destinations, (3) obstacles between origin and destination that the migrant must overcome, referred to as intervening obstacles, and (4) personal factors. Thus, Lee added to the push-pull model the complications of intervening obstacles and personal factors.

People may move because of conditions where they are currently living, conditions at their destination, or some combination of the two. Not everyone in a given area perceives conditions in that area in the same way; thus in-

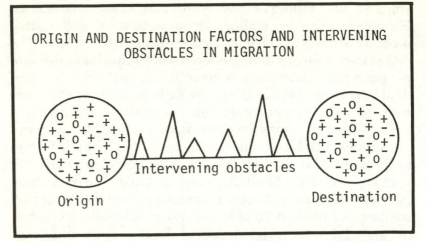

FIGURE 6.1. Origin and Destination Factors and Intervening Obstacles in Migration. Source: Everett S. Lee, "A Theory of Migration," *Demography* 3:1 (1966), p. 50.

dividuals respond differently to the same set of stimuli. Lee summarized his ideas with the schema shown in Figure 6.1. The circles representing the places of origin and destination have pluses, zeros, and minuses. The pluses indicate elements to which potential migrants respond favorably, whereas the minuses are elements to which they react negatively. Zeros stand for elements toward which potential migrants are indifferent.

A potential migrant adds up the pluses and minuses for both origin and possible destination, then decides whether to move or stay. If the decision is to stay, then that person may still become a migrant at a later time if his or her perception of the pluses and minuses changes. Before a migrant decides to move, however, another set of circumstances still needs to be considered—namely, Lee's intervening obstacles. Among them are the actual cost of making the move, which is obviously related to distance, and psychological costs, such as the necessity of breaking ties with family, friends, and community, especially when long distances are involved.

Beyond the considerations discussed so far, many personal

factors may also influence a migration decision. Among them are health, age, marital status, and number of children. Thus, a person's decision to migrate depends upon many varied considerations. Because the process of residential mobility is complex, its study is often divided into studies of intraurban mobility and migration, though the boundaries between the two approaches are not always clearly defined. Quite often a major difference between the two types of movement is whether or not the residential change also involves a job change. People often move within the urban ecosystem without changing jobs, mainly to change neighborhoods or to have a house that is deemed necessary to meet family requirements. However, when people move to another city or state it is usually associated with a job change, which can mean retirement or job loss as well as transfer or shift from one job to another.

INTRAURBAN MIGRATION

The movement of people within the urban ecosystem is an important determinant of change in urban residential structure. In turn, residential structure influences residential mobility. For example, aging neighborhoods may push people toward newer housing, as we have seen so frequently in twentieth-century urban America. However, as one group of people leaves a neighborhood, another group of people is likely to move in, altering both the structure and the composition of the neighborhood's population. Any attempt to understand, explain, and predict intraurban migration must begin by focusing on the household as a decision-making unit.

Migration and Behavior

Among geographers, Wolpert (1965) was one of the first to approach the study of migration by concentrating on individual behavior rather than on aggregate data. He argued that understanding and explaining migration patterns is dependent on sorting out constants in migration behavior, ultimately identifying the following three central concepts of migration behavior: (1) place utility, (2) field theory approach to search behavior, and (3) life cycle approach to threshold formation.

According to Wolpert, place utility "refers to the net composite of utilities which are derived from the individual's integration at some position in space" (Wolpert, 1965, p. 162). Therefore, dissatisfaction with one's current location acts as the major stimulus to begin searching for another location. Place utility may be either positive or negative, depending on how an individual perceives his or her location. Of considerable importance, then, is how the individual perceives the utility of his or her current place in relation to the perceived utility of other places. As viewed by Wolpert, "The utility with respect to these alternative sites consists largely of anticipated utility and optimism which lacks the reinforcement of past rewards. This is precisely why the stream of information is so important in long-distance migration – information about prospects must somehow compensate for the absence of personal experience" (Wolpert, 1965, p. 162).

In a subsequent paper Wolpert (1966) suggested that residential mobility should be viewed in terms of stresses in the current place of origin and the potential migrant's threshold for stress. Thus, the decision to move is dependent on both the alternatives available at a given time and the potential mover's ability to cope with stress. Somewhat earlier Rossi (1955) had noted that residential complaints and dissatisfaction are important determinants of the decision to move. Wolpert, going somewhat further, proposed that a person's tolerance for stress could be measured via a "threshold function." Once a person's stress threshold is surpassed in a particular location, that person is likely to move.

Despite the many reasons why individuals choose to change their place of residence, researchers generally agree that the study of movement behavior should focus on two major decisions: (1) the decision to seek a new residence and (2) the search for, and selection of, a new residence (Moore, 1972).

The Decision to Seek a New Residence

According to Moore, the values that individuals possess

permit them to accomplish the following:

1. to provide a set of specific *expectations* regarding the attributes of the dwelling in which he is to live. The expectations specify the level of each attribute, such as size of dwelling, which is deemed acceptable to that individual.

2. to provide a *valuation* of the dwelling in which he now lives. This valuation is based not only on such factors as the physical condition of the dwelling, the number of rooms and the size of the yard, but also on accessibility to shops, playgrounds and schools, the degree of industrial pollution, and the characteristics of the neighborhood population: in geographic terms it includes both the site and the situational characteristics of the dwelling. . . .

3. to provide valuations of specific alternatives among housing opportunities such that a *preference ordering* of such opportunities can be made. This preference ordering provides a basis for applying a rule of choice. [Moore, 1972, pp. 3–4]

Moore also suggested that a decision to move may be motivated in the following four ways: (1) decision imposed from outside the household, such as an eviction notice; (2) decision influenced by an event directly affecting the household, such as a marriage or divorce; (3) decision because of changes in housing needs or deterioration of perceived place utility; and (4) decision because of perceived higher place utilities available elsewhere.

For voluntary moves, those covered by the push and pull motives, Moore suggested a useful analytical framework (see Figure 6.2). We can assume that people periodically consider how satisfied they are with their present location, their place utility. As Wolpert noted, dissatisfaction with one's perceived place utility is likely to stimulate a decision to move. Satisfaction with a particular residence is likely to change for a variety of reasons. Older housing may show signs of deterioration, for example, or an expanding family may require more space than is currently available. Changes in the neighborhood may also influence the decision to move, as we noted earlier.

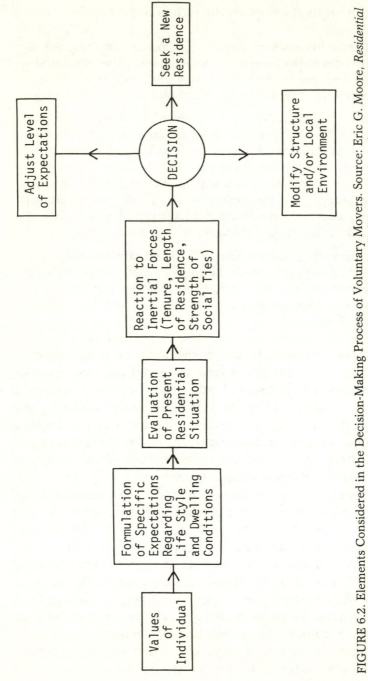

FIGURE 6.2. Elements Considered in the Decision-Making Process of Voluntary Movers. Source: Eric G. Moore, *Residential Mobility in the City*, Resource Papers for College Geography no. 13 (Washington, D.C.: Association of American Geographers, 1972), p. 5. Reprinted by permission.

On the other hand, objective measures of current conditions may seem satisfactory, but the desire to move may be stimulated by perceived conditions elsewhere. For example, new suburban neighborhoods may seem more attractive and desirable, or a person may want to be nearer to a new shopping center or golf course. However, the costs of moving—both psychological and financial—must also be considered. Leaving a neighborhood may not be easy, especially for long-time residents, because of the breaking of social ties.

The probability of moving varies with a number of characteristics of individuals, including age, education, and race. People who move generally have different characteristics than people who stay. Thus, the impact of mobility on the demographic character of origins and destinations may be different, even if the numbers of people moving out and in are the same. Areas that lose population are most likely to be losing people who are relatively younger and more educated than the general population. Between 1975 and 1978, the U.S. Bureau of the Census (1978) noted three major migration differentials, each of which deserves our attention.

Age. People in their twenties were found to be the most mobile segment of the population. They are establishing their own households, starting new jobs, graduating from school, and getting married. In their later twenties, many are buying houses, moving to larger homes as families expand, or are relocating to be nearer to schools rather than to discos or other social and recreational amenities that attract singles and childless couples. In the United States between March 1975 and March 1978, 63.4 percent of the people twenty-five to twenty-nine years old (in 1978) changed residence, compared to only 34.2 percent of the total population three years old and older (in 1978).

In the case of retired people moving to the Sunbelt states, their numbers are large only in relation to the areas they are moving into. Less than 20 percent of the people over fifty-five changed residence between 1975 and 1978. People in their forties and their teenage children had mobility rates that were midway between the extremes of the young adults and the older citizens. Middle-aged adults are more likely to be established in their careers, to be settled in a neighborhood, and to own a house; thus they are less inclined to move because they have more invested emotionally as well as monetarily in their present location.

Education. Educational attainment is also a good predictor of mobility in the United States and elsewhere as well. Between March 1975 and March 1978, 22.5 percent of people with eight years or less of schooling moved to a different house in the United States, whereas 41.5 percent of those with at least some college education moved. For most types of moves, from intraurban to interstate, people with at least some college were the most likely to move, and those with no more than an elementary school education were the least likely. The only exception to this generalization was that people with one to four years of high school were equally likely to move within a county as were those who had completed at least one year of college. People with some college education were the most inclined to move from the central cities to suburban areas and, perhaps surprisingly, also the most inclined to move from the suburbs to the central cities. The latter reflects the trend toward "gentrification," whereby older central city locations are restored and become fashionable residences for young professional people. Society Hill in Philadelphia is an excellent example.

Further educational differentials appear if distance is considered. For example, migrants with some college education are more likely to move longer distances than are people who have less education. Among movers with only an elementary education, about two out of every three moved within the same county, whereas those with some college education were about equally divided between those who moved within and those who moved between counties.

It appears that education contributes to mobility by reducing both the economic and psychic costs of moving. College-educated people often have higher salaries and are also more likely to be transferred by their employer, who usually pays the cost of the move. Better-educated people are also likely to have more information about alternative destinations and therefore are more likely to react to the pull of better opportunities elsewhere.

Race. In the United States, migration differentials by race are also significant. Between March 1975 and March 1978, blacks and whites changed residences at almost the same rate (35.4 percent and 35.0 percent, respectively). However, 26.3 percent of the blacks moved within the same county, compared to only 19.7 percent of the whites. On the other hand, whites were more likely to make long-distance moves.

Local and long-distance moves may also be viewed by looking at data for SMSAs. Whereas 22.7 percent of the blacks moved within the same SMSA, only 15.2 percent of the whites did so. Furthermore, 64.1 percent of all residence changes by blacks were within the same SMSA, and only 44.7 percent of the moves made by whites were that local. Blacks were also three times more likely than whites to move within the central city of an SMSA.

The Search for a New Residence

Given that a person has reached the stage where he or she wants to move, then it is necessary to begin a search process. Moore suggested that the search process may be considered to follow three stages: (1) establishment of evaluation criteria, (2) search for attainable alternatives, and (3) evaluation of alternatives and final selection (Moore, 1972, p. 13). Of course, the search process may lead to the decision to stay rather than to move if no place is found that provides a higher place utility than that provided by the present location.

Search behavior is conditioned by numerous factors, especially by the individual's perception of the urban area. As noted by Moore,

> The individual utilizes his perception of the urban area (with many distortions and biases contained in that perception) to organize the search. Although the majority of search activities may entail examining newspaper or real estate listings rather than travelling through the city, the outcome in terms of the vacancies encountered depends very largely on the way in

which these activities are structured and hence on the a priori perception that the individual possesses of his urban environment. [Moore, 1972, p. 13]

A model of the search procedure is detailed in Figure 6.3.

What search criteria are established depends on the initial reasons for the decision to move. In general, actual structural characteristics and situational characteristics need to be specified. For example, with rising energy costs many people are moving closer to where they work. At the same time, people need to decide how much they can afford to spend in order to attain their goals.

Perception of the City as a Factor in Migration

The search behavior of an individual is not random; it is a sampling procedure based on what the individual knows of the urban area. In smaller cities people may have first-hand knowledge of most or all of the city's neighborhoods. However, in larger urban areas first-hand knowledge is likely to be limited to areas relatively close to a person's present residence, job, school, and shopping facilities. Thus, a person's search pattern may, at least in part, be conditioned by his or her current activity pattern.

Although an urban ecosystem may be subdivided into numerous regions on the basis of such measures as income, education, housing values, or age, these measures may result in regions or neighborhoods that differ from those perceived by people who live in the city. Clark and Cadwallader (1973), for example, divided Los Angeles into perceptual regions based on the preferences of a random sample of more than 1,000 residents. Generally they found that people preferred either their own neighborhoods or neighborhoods similar to their own. A preference for beach communities and other amenity neighborhoods appeared also, but because respondents were given an income-level restraint such communities, which are expensive, were not overwhelming choices. However,

like the factorial ecological studies, it is still only a classifica-

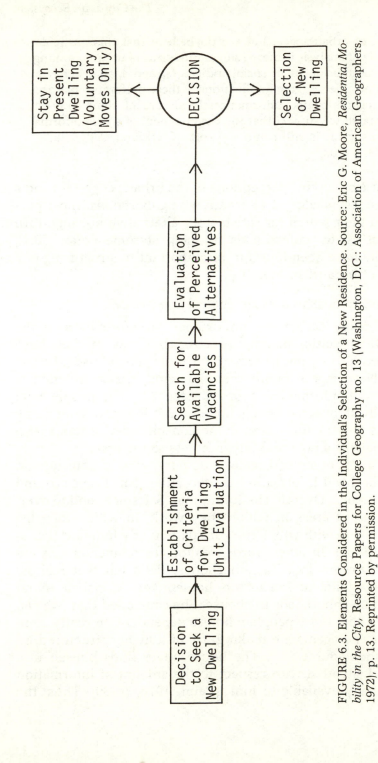

FIGURE 6.3. Elements Considered in the Individual's Selection of a New Residence. Source: Eric G. Moore, *Residential Mobility in the City*, Resource Papers for College Geography no. 13 (Washington, D.C.: Association of American Geographers, 1972), p. 13. Reprinted by permission.

tion of urban space, but we do believe that this particular mode of analysis is more relevant in terms of urban planning, the establishment of social indicators, and spatial behavior within cities. . . . the implications of these preference patterns as regards spatial information levels are of some interest, although we suspect that the development of a true information surface is still some way off. [Clark and Cadwallader, 1973, p. 703]

Because of varying perceptions of the urban ecosystem and a limited knowledge of alternative neighborhoods, most people, in their search for satisfactory alternative housing, turn to real estate professionals for help at some point. Thus, realtors have been found to be important in structuring patterns of intraurban mobility.

Realtors as Sources of Geographical Information

We noted earlier the importance of information in the mobility decision-making process, but few studies have focused directly on the way that people get and use information. Newspapers, family members, and friends are cited as important information sources, especially for people who have lived for some time in the city. But sooner or later many people looking for a new home consult a real estate agent, especially if a potential buyer is new to the area.

Palm (1976) studied realtors as purveyors of housing and neighborhood information in two cities, San Francisco and Minneapolis. Overall, she found that "Salesmen tend to over-recommend areas in which they work, in which they list houses, and with which they are particularly familiar" (Palm, 1976, p. 39). In other words, realtors' recommendations are biased toward local neighborhoods. Palm felt that realtors had a significant impact on homebuyers' decisions about which neighborhoods to choose. She concluded that "we can suggest that those people who are dependent on realty companies and agents are making use of a highly structured information source. . . . The house buyer finds himself in a limited situation with respect to the amount of information potentially available to him" (Palm, 1976, p. 39). Thus, the potential home buyer, regardless of information sources, is likely to be exposed to only a limited portion of the total number of vacancies available.

Biases in Intraurban Mobility Patterns

As we mentioned previously, potential movers do not conduct a random search for alternative housing. Researchers have found that human activitiy patterns tend to be sectorial, that is, the spatial pattern of an individual's action space in the urban ecosystem is usually wedge-shaped or pie-shaped. To a considerable extent this spatial activity pattern is a determinant of the spatial pattern of search activities for intraurban movers. Brown and Holmes (1971) in a study of Cedar Rapids, Iowa, found not only evidence of a pie-shaped search pattern for potential movers, but also that the search spaces of various socioeconomic groups were all of a similar size. What this finding suggests, of course, is that for most people a distance threshold appears to constrain their search behavior. In Cedar Rapids, Brown and Holmes found that movers had a strong tendency to move to a new location near the center of their search space. Place utility, it appears, is closely associated with a person's existing action space, and one regular determinant of intraurban migration is a distance bias.

Another bias that is also closely related to action and search spaces is a directional bias in the spatial pattern of intraurban movements. Adams (1969) analyzed intraurban movements in Minneapolis and found that people tended to move within given sectors, mainly outward from the city center though occasionally inward. Rarely did people move outside their sector or across town. Adams argued that these observations stem from people's dependence on limited mental maps or perceived images of their city. According to Adams, "Whatever their form, images control spatial activities including all kinds of movements, searches, and location choices" (Adams, 1969, p. 322). His study also disclosed "the influence of residential age structure of the city on directional bias in intra-city moves, as well as the extent to which geometrical properties of the city regulate estimated move parameters" (Adams, 1969, p. 323).

Intraurban Migration and the Residential Structure of the City

The residential structure of an urban ecosystem is constantly undergoing change. Houses are constantly being built and destroyed, neighborhoods are being revitalized or allowed to deteriorate, accessibility is constantly altered by new freeways, and people are moving from neighborhood to neighborhood. Of course, within the city changes are occurring rapidly in some places and slowly in others. For example, a downtown area may seem to remain static at the same time that changes on the city's periphery are occurring at a dizzying pace.

The mobility characteristics of a neighborhood are closely linked to changes in other neighborhood characteristics and at the same time are determined by the degree to which a neighborhood serves the needs of its residents. Moore (1972) identified four broad categories of linkage between mobility and neighborhood population change (see Figure 6.4).

Since the 1930s, human ecologists have focused attention on overall changes in urban residential structures, especially on changes in the inner city and inner suburbs as a city expands outward. Two general suburban growth theories have been developed in the literature, "the life cycle approach" and "the expansion approach." The former is concerned with changes in the central city and inner suburbs, whereas the latter is concerned with what is happening on the suburban periphery.

The life cycle view suggests that portions of the urban ecosystem pass through a well-defined cycle of population growth and decline. Aging housing, competition for space for nonresidential land users, and changing residential needs all alter the character of inner-city neighborhoods. Land for further residential development is limited or unavailable, so population growth ceases, and declines in population may set in.

The expansion view links the rate of community growth on the urban periphery to the metropolitan core. The growth of distant peripheral communities is limited by the cost and time

	Neighborhoods Experiencing Change in Selected Population Characteristics	Neighborhoods Experiencing Stability in Selected Population Characteristics
Neighborhoods Experiencing High Mobility	I a) Rapid Change resulting from ethnic, social, or racial conflict within area b) Change resulting from area being assigned high social value by specific subgroup c) Change resulting from rapid deterioration of physical environment (particularly due to location of public facilities)	II a) Inflexible housing catering to small range of household types b) Neighborhood is a transit point for inmigrants from rural and other urban areas
Neighborhoods Experiencing Low Mobility	III a) Flexible housing catering to many household types. Slow aging of population and selective outmigration by age b) Deteriorating housing with selective inmigration by socioeconomic status	IV a) Tightly structured social networks, particularly for ethnic communities, tie individual to neighborhood

FIGURE 6.4. Typical Situations Linking Mobility and Population Change at the Neighborhood Level. Source: Eric G. Moore, *Residential Mobility in the City*, Resource Papers for College Geography no. 13 (Washington, D.C.: Association of American Geographers, 1972), p. 33. Reprinted by permission.

required to overcome the distance to the metropolitan core, thus growth in peripheral communities may remain slower than in more-central suburban areas despite the attraction of cleaner air and lower housing costs.

In one recent study Guest found that "Most suburbs continue to grow, but enough suburbs are declining in population to suggest that more attention should be devoted to growth patterns within the suburban ring" (Guest, 1979, p. 413). He found that population declines were most common in two zones, one close to the urban core and the other on the outer periphery. However, he also noted an increasing tendency toward the concentration of population declines in the central suburbs. In concluding his study Guest stated that

the most striking result of this study is the importance of metropolitan age in understanding patterns of suburban growth.

Analysis of aggregate patterns obscures some pronounced differences among metropolitan areas. Metropolitan areas with older central cities are characterized by a high incidence of inner suburban population decline and peripheral suburban growth; in contrast, newer central cities have their most rapidly growing suburbs concentrated around the central cities. These patterns correspond to those reported in studies of central city–suburban differences in growth patterns among old and new metropolitan areas. [Guest, 1979, p. 413]

Although Guest did not focus on intraurban migration, we can speculate that movement is one of the major processes operating to produce the observed changes in metropolitan population growth rates.

THE DYNAMICS OF INTERURBAN MIGRATION

Migration, defined here as a permanent change of residence that crosses a county boundary, takes place primarily between urban areas. Each single movement between cities impacts two urban ecosystems, the one left behind and the one entered into. At the same time, the national system of cities is also being altered by migration because people are constantly being redistributed. Among cities, both losers and gainers can be found, and the impact of migration can be of considerable importance. In the United States between March 1975 and March 1978, 34.2 percent of the total population three years old and older changed residences. Almost half of those people, 16.1 percent, moved within the same SMSA. Another 4.9 percent moved from one SMSA to another, 2.1 percent moved from outside an SMSA to within one, 2.6 percent moved from an SMSA to an area outside one, and 8.5 percent were outside SMSAs both before and after they moved.

Why People Migrate

In a theoretical economic sense, migration is the mechanism by which human resources move to their highest-valued use, though this ideal often probably goes unrealized. Among the major determinants of migration are distance, income, and information.

It has been shown repeatedly that most migration takes place over short distances. The distance itself, however, is related to other factors that also inhibit migration. For example, distance is related to both the economic and the psychological costs of moving. Furthermore, distance is also a factor in collecting reliable information about alternative destinations. Several studies have suggested that the psychological costs of leaving friends and relatives may be significant, though they are difficult to measure.

A simple economic theory of migration is based on wage rate differentials. We could argue that migrants move up the wage rate gradient, from low-wage areas to high-wage areas. In a perfect world, migration would then serve as an equilibrating mechanism. As people left low-wage areas the smaller remaining labor supply would drive wages upward. At the same time, the growing supply of labor in the high-wage areas would tend to depress wages. Ideally, migrants would move between the areas until wage rates were equal in both places, but the world is not perfect. Imperfections exist in the market mechanism, and people are not perfectly mobile. For example, many Appalachians have chosen to stay in Appalachia despite low wages and high unemployment rates, partly because they are deeply attached to the region and partly because they are unaware of opportunities elsewhere.

Some important findings of a recent study by the U.S. Department of Labor (1977) are worth considering at this point. First, the study found that household-level unemployment or job dissatisfaction does operate as a "push" factor in migration. People who are recent arrivals in an area and have failed to immediately find employment are especially likely to move again. Second, local economic conditions, such as unemployment rates, do affect outmigration, but only among those people who are unemployed.

Third, unemployed individuals and others currently seeking work are more responsive to such economic determinants as family income, local wage rates, and expected earnings increases than are persons who are satisfied with their current jobs. Fourth, families are much more likely to move in a given time period if they moved in the recent past, mainly because of a tendency for people to return to places they recently left. Fifth, families that have moved several times previously are more likely to move again than are families that have made one or no moves recently if the multiple moves are nonreturn moves. Such people are often referred to as chronic movers.

Sixth, wives are not passive, secondary migrants but have a significant influence on the families' decisions to move. Also, contrary to the results of some studies, families with working wives are not necessarily less likely to move than are families in which the wife does not work. Families with working wives will seek locations that maximize both incomes. Finally, and somewhat surprisingly, the study found that age and education, typically among the strongest correlates of the propensity to migrate, appear to be relatively unimportant in explaining the migration of married couples when other migration determinants, many of which vary with age and education, are held constant.

Information is also important in the decision to migrate, especially information about alternative destinations. People are hesitant to move to areas about which they know little or nothing. Nelson (1959) found that friends and relatives who have previously moved from one place to another are especially good sources of information about their current locations. Often this "friends and relatives effect" leads to chain migration, reflecting a directional bias on the part of movers. The distribution of past migrants tends to be a good predictor of future migration patterns (Greenwood, 1975).

Recent Migration Patterns in the United States

The essence of American mobility is found in the following comment by Simkins. "Although it does not appear as such in any of the state seals or flags, the wheel in many ways may be considered a symbol of America; the wagon or train wheel which early carried the nation westward, or the automobile wheel that moves it now increasingly to and from metropolitan centers" (Simkins, 1978, p. 204). Since 1947 the U.S. Bureau of the Census has been annually sampling the mobility of Americans, and it has consistently found that almost 20 percent of the population changes residence each year. The United States is undoubtedly a nation on the move.

Long and Boertlein (1976) found, however, that the United States is not alone among nations in having a high mobility rate. In a comparative study of several Western nations, they found that the United States, Canada, and Australia have similar high rates of mobility. They also found evidence that, contrary to popular opinion, the American mobility rate is more likely to decrease than to increase in the future. However, by world standards the rate of geographical mobility in the United States will still be high.

Americans have always sought to better their lot in life, whether that has meant pioneers seeking "elbow room" or people in rural twentieth-century Iowa seeking the eternal sun of southern California. At the forefront of the motives for migration, of course, has been the hope of material gain, though the recent growth of the Sunbelt as a center of attraction for migrants suggests that other motives are also important. Many people seek to escape the long cold winters of the cities in the Northeast, along with smog, traffic congestion, and even high crime rates. Although an overview of migration patterns can deal only with aggregates of people, we need to remember that the motives for migration differ for different age groups and as other characteristics of people differ. For example, an upwardly mobile young executive in Chicago would be likely to move to San Diego for much different reasons than the recently retired South Dakota couple who move because they yearn for warmer winters.

Rural-Urban Migration. In 1790 the first census of the United States found that only about 10 percent of the population lived in urban areas. The United States was a young nation then, and its citizens were engaged primarily in agriculture, fishing, and mining. By 1900, however, about 40 percent of the people lived in urban areas, and by 1975 the percentage had risen to 74. During the twentieth century, urbanization has been rapid and widespread, with all regions tending toward a predominantly urban population. Rural-urban migration and urbanization, of course, have been the demographic responses to the general transformation of the United States from a rural-agrarian nation to a modern-industrial one.

Regional variations in rural-urban migration rates and urbanization during the twentieth century have been considerable. Since 1960 the overall level of urbanization has remained almost constant, but significant changes have occurred in specific regions such as the west-south-central region.

The 1970s—Changing Migration Patterns. Despite the rural-urban migration that has characterized the redistribution of people throughout the United States during the twentieth century, Americans have never been in unanimous agreement that cities, especially large ones, are desirable places in which to reside. Industrialization has tended to concentrate people in cities, primarily for economic reasons. Urban locations often mean lower costs for industries, as well as better access to service needs and to local markets. However, from the worker's viewpoint industrial concentration in urban areas means more jobs and higher wages, so to the cities they have moved. The broad overall migration patterns in the United States are apparent in Figure 6.5. Two emerging migration trends in the 1970s are of special interest and have possible long-range implications for the redistribution of people, jobs, and wealth in the United States. They are the movement to the Sunbelt and the "rural renaissance."

Movement to the Sunbelt. The Sunbelt states are those of the South and the Southwest along with California and Hawaii. Since 1970 a dramatic shift of population away from states in the north central region and the Northeast toward the Sunbelt states has occurred. The United States population grew by about 13 million between 1970 and 1977, and 40 percent of that growth occurred in the states of California, Florida, and Texas. The Sunbelt states with the highest rates of growth during that same period were Nevada, Arizona, Florida, New Mexico, Hawaii, and Texas. In early 1980, Tucson, Arizona, was adding an estimated 2,000 new residents

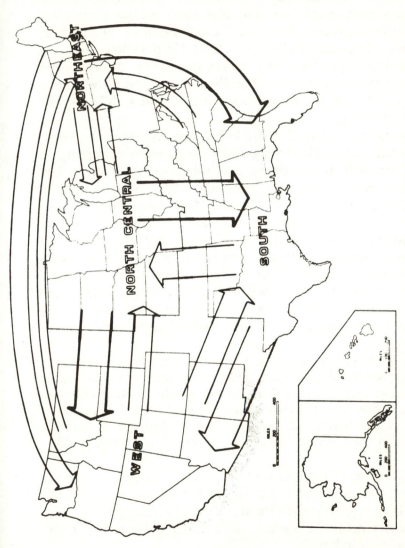

FIGURE 6.5. Region to Region Migration Flows for the United States, March 1975 to March 1977. Source: U.S. Bureau of the Census, *Current Population Reports*, "Geographical Mobility: March 1975 to March 1977," Series P-20, no. 320 (Washington, D.C.: Government Printing Office, 1978), front cover.

each month to a city with just over 310,000 people. Phoenix, Arizona, with a 1979 population of about 1.4 million, began 1980 as the thirteenth largest city in the United States. Industry is also increasingly attracted to the Sunbelt. For example, new major plants and facilities built in Phoenix in 1978 and 1979 included General Telephone and Electronics, Honeywell, Gould Industries, Intel Corporation, and the regional headquarters for Farmers Insurance. Among cities with a population of over 1.5 million, the fastest growing one is expected to be Houston, Texas, which had a 1979 population of about 1.7 million.

Regional growth during the 1970s was highest in the West. Reductions in population growth rates were occurring in many states in the Midwest and the Northeast, and a few states—Pennsylvania, New York, and Rhode Island—actually lost population between 1970 and 1977. People are increasingly moving away from the older areas of the north central and northeastern states, partly in response to environmental preferences and partly as a result of aggressive economic development in many of the Sunbelt states. Many other people are attracted to the Rocky Mountain states, where new energy development offers job opportunities, and to the Pacific Northwest, especially to Portland and Seattle.

> The Sunbelt migration, then, is part of a larger radical change in the South and the West. It is closely related to the industrial development which typifies most states in the "Southern Rim." It is a reflection of changing American lifestyles. It is part of the equalization of U.S. regions which has brought the South more in line with the rest of the nation. [Biggar, 1979, p. 27]

The impact of migration on population distribution is apparent. However, the effect on both sending and receiving areas is even greater than the numbers alone suggest, because migrants tend to be younger and better educated than the general population.

The Rural Renaissance. Perhaps for the first time in American history more people are leaving metropolitan areas than are entering them, because the long-established pattern of rural-urban migration underwent a reversal during the

1970s. Consider the following observations made by Morrison and Wheeler.

> Each year between 1970 and 1975, for every 100 people who moved to the metropolitan sector, 131 moved out. During the five years before, an average of only 94 moved out for every 100 who moved in.
>
> Many metropolitan areas, especially some of the largest ones (New York, Chicago, Philadelphia, Cleveland, Seattle, and Los Angeles, for example), stopped growing altogether.
>
> Conversely, three-fourths of all nonmetropolitan counties registered population gains from either natural increase or migration (or both), compared with only half in the 1960s and two-fifths in the 1950s. More significantly, net migration gains (more migrants moving in than out) occurred in nearly two-thirds of all nonmetropolitan counties compared with only one-fourth in the 1960s and one-tenth in the 1950s.
>
> Even nonmetropolitan areas that are far distant from urban and metropolitan influence — the kinds of places that used to be regarded as "nowhere" in the 1950s — have been registering net migration gains instead of their once perennial losses. [Morrison and Wheeler, 1976, pp. 3–4]

As one might imagine, not all nonmetropolitan areas are pleased with the prospect of increased population growth and "rural urbanization." Conflicts arise between growth advocates and those people who seek to limit growth. Land use conflicts are also common. For example, the little Napa Valley town of Calistoga, in California's famed "wine country," was confronted in 1979 with the planned development of a $20-million, 400-unit hotel complex. Proponents of the plan see it as a way of revitalizing the town and refilling tax coffers that were depleted in the wake of Proposition Thirteen. Opponents, on the other hand, see the complex as an incongruous monster that would blight the landscape and destroy the rural character of Calistoga and its environs. Elsewhere, many small-town residents fear that growth threatens to destroy the very features that attract people to small towns. For example, they point to increasing crime rates, traffic congestion problems, and even smog as the inevitable results of small-town growth.

The sudden reversal of long-term urbanization in the United States caught many people, including demographers and geographers, by surprise. Many considered that most of the nonmetropolitan growth was just a spillover from expanding metropolitan areas, but even nonmetropolitan areas far from urban centers were a part of the new trend. Spillover, of course, has been commonplace in recent decades, but a new pattern seems to be at hand. Among the major causes of the new pattern are (1) changes in communication and transportation technology that have taken away, or at least mitigated, the necessity of urban concentration and (2) the expansion of highways that allow easy access from rural to urban areas. However, regional variations in both metropolitan and nonmetropolitan growth rates may be observed. For example, the following three processes are occurring, according to Morrill (1979).

1. In the periphery of the country, generally beyond the tier of states adjacent to the core, centralization, or metropolitan growth, and small-scale urbanization are still occurring. Presumably both of these trends result from a national-scale relocation or redirection of activities from the core as well as from locally generated conditions, including research development. This zone includes most of the West and South, but it takes in some peripheral states of the Northeast as well.

2. At the scale of the metropolis, local suburban decentralization still dominates in most of the country; but in the urban industrial core, which became suburbanized in the 1920's through the 1950's, decentralization has passed to the exurban zone.

3. At a national and regional scale, increasing numbers of persons are "voting with their feet" in favor of environmentally attractive areas—some in the Northeast itself, but most in the West and South. The net effect is a redistribution from the Northeast and from metropolitan territory. [Morrill, 1979, p. 65]

The growth of retirement and recreational communities has also been a factor in nonmetropolitan growth. Early retirement, coupled with better benefits for retirees, frees an increasing number of people to seek locations based on personal preference rather than economic necessity. Wherever the elderly choose to go, of course, services are required, so jobs are created, which stimulates further growth. Not only Florida and the Southwest but also the Ozarks, the Texas hill country, and California's "gold country" in the western foothills of the Sierra Nevada are experiencing growth because of an influx of retirees.

The Migration of Blacks. Earlier we noted that there were mobility differences in the United States based on race. During the twentieth century, black migration has been a major element in internal migration. Blacks were originally brought to the South where, because of restrictions, they tended to remain. In 1900, 90 percent of the blacks in the United States lived in the South, predominantly in rural areas. However, by 1950 many blacks had left the southern rural areas, and the percentage of blacks living in the South had dropped to 68 percent, nearly two-thirds of whom lived in urban areas. The black population continued to urbanize between 1950 and 1970, with rural southern blacks moving to cities in the Northeast, Midwest, and West.

During the 1970s, significant changes occurred in the pattern of black migration. Between March 1975 and March 1977, the Northeast experienced a net outmigration of blacks in contrast to a net inmigration during the previous decade. Fewer blacks were moving into the Northeast, and more were leaving it. During the same period, the numbers of blacks entering and leaving the north central region were approximately the same, whereas the area had experienced a net inmigration of blacks during the previous decade. Most significant, the number of blacks leaving the South was about equal to the number entering it, whereas previously there had been a net outmigration of blacks. The West continued to be a net gainer of blacks.

Population Movement and the System of Cities

City systems in modern industrial nations are exceedingly complex, are constantly buffeted about by competing needs

and changing preferences, and are molded by both central-
izing and decentralizing forces. Urban dwellers depend on
mobility as a means of adjusting their needs and desires to
their perceptions of opportunities within and among urban
ecosystems. At the same time, the system of cities is affected
by the aggregate expression of individual decisions to stay or
to move, resulting in a myriad of patterns of urban change
that are at least partly regional in nature.

Although metropolitan areas have not grown as fast as
nonmetropolitan areas during the 1970s, we need to note that
the growth rates of various sizes of metropolitan areas differ
considerably. For example, the largest metropolitan areas account for most of the overall decline in metropolitan growth
rates. At the same time, growth rates in metropolitan areas
with populations under the 1 million mark were higher than
they were during the 1960s. Among the five largest metropolitan areas, only Chicago gained population between 1970
and 1977. Among SMSAs with over 500,000 people, the
fastest growing during the same time period were Houston
(25.7 percent), Anaheim–Santa Ana–Garden Grove (26.7 percent), San Diego (23.9 percent), Tampa–St. Petersburg (26.8
percent), Phoenix (29.1 percent), and Orlando (30.8 percent).

Thus, it is easy to say that migration has an impact on the
national urban system, but it is considerably more difficult to
explain and predict what changes migration will bring about.
We do know that most people moving into cities today move
there from other cities, so migration tends to represent a
trading of people among cities in various regions and size
categories. During the 1980s, migration patterns are going
to be determined not only by responses to economic opportunities but also, and increasingly, by the residential
preferences that people have.

Residential Preferences and Migration

According to Schwind, "patterns of migration presumably
are functions of, and should therefore contain information
on, both the total magnitude of population systems and the
aggregate preferences of migrants for relevant characteristics
of regions. Migrants, however, probably respond not so

much to factual statistical information about regions as to rather general perceptions of regional attractiveness" (Schwind, 1971, p. 150). Although geographers have accomplished a great deal in their studies of place preferences, most of the work that specifically relates to urban migration and city size preferences has been done by sociologists. The changing migration patterns of the 1970s have been a major stimulus to researchers to seek explanations of migration patterns other than the standard wage theory and its derivatives.

Studies of city size preferences have tended to be concerned with the need for a population distribution policy in the United States. Numerous proposals have been made – including some designed to aid depressed rural areas, such as Appalachia – to focus new migration on cities in the medium-sized range, thus decreasing inmigration to the most congested cities, and to guide the overall development of the American urban system. Fuguitt and Zuiches noted that "an important element figuring in this discussion is concern about public preferences and attitudes on desirable places to live. A policy that provides community and housing options compatible with preferences should have a greater chance of success and could be expected to lessen any discrepancy between the actual and ideal distribution of the population" (Fuguitt and Zuiches, 1975, p. 491).

One notable criticism of many of the city size preference surveys is that most of them fail to provide information about the location of the nearest cities, especially cities in the smaller-sized categories. For many people, there is a considerable difference in attractiveness between living in an isolated small town and living in a small town located within easy driving distance of a major city. Puzzled by the apparent contrast between survey results and actual migration patterns, Fuguitt and Zuiches added to a city size questionnaire a question asking those people who preferred small towns whether they also preferred that those towns be within thirty miles of a large city. What the distance-qualifying question showed was that more than half of those respondents who preferred small towns and rural areas claimed that they would like to live within thirty miles of a city of at least 50,000 population. Thus, we must be careful when interpreting the results of preference surveys that fail to include a distance-qualifying question.

It appears that the perceived quality of life in small towns is their major attraction, however romanticized the perception may be, but the lack of employment acts as a constraint on people moving to them. As already mentioned, migration into small towns often destroys the very characteristics that attracted migrants in the first place. Fuguitt and Zuiches concluded that if people all were to move to the places they preferred, no mass exodus to remote areas would occur. Most people seem to prefer the best of both worlds, a quiet bucolic residential location and the opportunities and amenities that can be provided only by a metropolitan area. A more recent study concluded that

> while size of place residential preference was only minimally related to actual population dispersal migration behavior, we have identified some residential preference attributes which characterize nonmetropolitan direction movers. A high proportion of all metropolitan area movers expressed a preference for quality schools, spacious yards, availability of entertainment, and opportunities for contact with people. However, the crucial point seems to be, what are people willing to give up in order to attain these preferences, at least some of which are associated with a nonmetropolitan environment? [DeJong and Sell, 1977, p. 141]

It appears that trade-offs between types of location must be made. Householders must decide what urban offerings they are willing to forgo in order to move to a rural or small-town location. The operation of constraints and trade-offs helps to explain the lack of a better relationship between preferences and migration patterns.

Although most studies of city size preferences have been descriptive, Laird and Mazek's is a major exception. Noting the current dissatisfaction with the more-traditional approaches, Laird and Mazek developed a location-consumer model, which they described as follows.

> The location-consumer model treats the individual as integrating his dual activities as an income earner and as a consumer of location amenities. The approach utilizes conventional utility theory to examine the individual as he selects that combination of income and location amenities (city size) which maximizes his utility. As a "location-consumer" deriving satisfaction from location amenities as well as from goods and services, the individual takes more into account than the fact that larger cities evidently provide larger incomes. He reacts to: (1) the range of choice of both private and public goods and services available in localities of different sizes, (2) the different life-styles inherent in cities of different sizes, and (3) the perceived problems associated with different sized localities, i.e., for the cities, those negative externalities lumped together under the rubric "congestion." [Laird and Mazek, 1974, p. 18]

In their model, the best location is dependent on the relationship between subjective utility functions and the particular objective income curve faced by an individual.

One major implication of that study for further research is that it is important to distinguish between income and utility. Migration models have often assumed that migrants seek to maximize their income and are indifferent to city size. Furthermore, Laird and Mazek suggested that movement to large cities should not necessarily be interpreted as revealed preferences. Using their model, the intensity of preferences may be more clearly measured conceptually by looking at the marginal rate of substitution between income and city size. Thus, their model offers a much-needed theoretical component for the analysis of place preferences and actual migration patterns. It remains now for researchers to combine this more analytical framework with the rapidly growing body of empirical studies.

REFERENCES

Adams, John S. 1969. "Directional Bias in Intra-Urban Migration." *Economic Geography* 45: 302–323.

Biggar, Jeanne C. 1979. "The Sunning of America: Migration to the Sunbelt." *Population Bulletin* 34: 1–42.

Brown, Lawrence A., and Holmes, John. 1971. "Search Behavior in an Intra-Urban Migration Context: A Spatial Perspective." *Environment and Planning* 3: 307–326.

Brown, Lawrence A., and Longbrake, David B. 1970. "Migration Flows in Intra-Urban Space: Place Utility Considerations." *Annals of the Association of American Geographers* 60: 368–384.

Clark, W.A.V. 1976. "Migration in Milwaukee." *Economic Geography* 52: 49–57.

Clark, W.A.V., and Cadwallader, M. 1973. "Residential Preferences: An Alternative View of Intraurban Space." *Environment and Planning* 5: 693–703.

Clark, W.A.V., and Moore, Eric G., eds. 1978. *Population Mobility and Residential Change*. Evanston, Ill.: Northwestern University, Department of Geography.

DeJong, Gordon F., and Sell, Ralph R. 1977. "Population Redistribution, Migration, and Residential Preferences." *Annals of the American Academy of Political and Social Science* 429: 130–144.

Fuguitt, Glenn V., and Zuiches, James J. 1975. "Residential Preferences and Population Distribution." *Demography* 12: 491–504.

Greenwood, Michael J. 1975. "Research on Internal Migration in the United States: A Survey." *Journal of Economic Literature* 12: 397–433.

Guest, Avery M. 1979. "Patterns of Suburban Population Growth, 1970–75." *Demography* 16: 401–415.

Laird, William E., and Mazek, Warren F. 1974. "City-Size Preferences and Migration." *Review of Regional Studies* 4 Supplement: 18–26.

Lee, Everett S. 1966. "A Theory of Migration." *Demography* 3: 47–57.

Long, Larry H., and Boertlein, Celia G. 1976. *The Geographical Mobility of Americans: An International Comparison*. Current Population Reports, Special Studies, Series P-23, No. 64. Washington, D.C.: Government Printing Office.

Michelson, William. 1977. *Environmental Choice, Human Behavior, and Residential Satisfaction*. New York: Oxford University Press.

Moore, Eric G. 1972. *Residential Mobility in the City*. Resource Paper No. 13. Washington, D.C.: Association of American Geographers.

Morrill, Richard L. 1979. "Stages in Patterns of Population Concentration and Dispersion." *Professional Geographer* 31: 55–65.

Morrison, Peter A. 1972. *Population Movements and the Shape of Urban Growth: Implications for Public Policy.* Vol. 5 of Sara Mills Mazie, ed., *Population Distribution and Policy.* Commission on Population Growth and the American Future, Research Reports. Washington, D.C.: Government Printing Office.

Morrison, Peter A., with Wheeler, Judith P. 1976. "Rural Renaissance in America?" *Population Bulletin* 31: 1–26.

Nelson, P. 1959. "Migration, Real Income, and Information." *Journal of Regional Science* 1: 43–74.

Palm, Risa. 1976. "The Role of Real Estate Agents as Information Mediators in Two American Cities." *Geografiska Annaler* 58B: 28–41.

Peters, Gary L., and Larkin, Robert P. 1979. *Population Geography: Problems, Concepts, and Prospects.* Dubuque, Iowa: Kendall/Hunt Publishing Company.

Rossi, Peter. 1955. *Why Families Move.* Glencoe, Ill.: Free Press.

Schwind, Paul J. 1971. "Spatial Preferences of Migrants for Regions: The Example of Maine." *Proceedings of the Association of American Geographers* 3: 150–156.

Shaw, R. Paul. 1975. *Migration Theory and Fact.* Bibliography Series No. 5. Philadelphia: Regional Science Research Institute.

Simkins, Paul D. 1978. "Characteristics of Population in the United States and Canada." In Glenn T. Trewartha, ed., *The More Developed Realm: A Geography of Its Population,* pp. 189–220. Oxford: Pergamon Press.

Smith, Terence R., et al. 1979. "A Decision-Making and Search Model for Intraurban Migration." *Geographical Analysis* 11: 1–22.

Speare, A. 1974. "Residential Satisfaction as an Intervening Variable in Residential Mobility." *Demography* 11: 173–188.

Thomlinson, Ralph. 1976. *Population Dynamics: Causes and Consequences of World Demographic Change.* 2d ed. New York: Random House.

U.S., Bureau of the Census. 1978. *Current Population Reports.* Series P-20, No. 331, "Geographical Mobility: March 1975 to March 1978." Washington, D.C.: Government Printing Office.

U.S., Department of Labor, Employment and Training Administration. 1977. *Why Families Move: A Model of the Geographic Mobility of Married Couples.* R and D Monograph 48. Washington, D.C.: Government Printing Office.

Weinberg, Daniel H., and Atkinson, Reilly. 1979. "Place Attachment and the Decision to Search for Housing." *Growth and*

Change 10: 22–29.

Wolpert, Julian. 1965. "Behavioral Aspects of the Decision to Migrate." *Papers and Proceedings of the Regional Science Association* 15: 159–169.

———. 1966. "Migration as an Adjustment to Environmental Stress." *Journal of Social Issues* 22: 92–102.

7

The Urban Ecosystem in Perspective

The preceding chapters have illustrated the manner in which the functioning of the city is analogous to processes found in a biological ecosystem. The internal structure of the city has been shown to be the product of the stimulation, interaction, feedback, adjustments, and responses of urban variables with one another.

For the biological ecosystem, general categories of systems based on a similarity of traits have been established, and each individual ecosystem within a given category will also have special features that make that particular subsystem somewhat unique. The same can be said of cities. An urban place can be viewed in general as a manufacturing city, for instance, but it is likely to be unique in some respects from other cities that are similarly classified.

The uniqueness of each urban ecosystem is owing to the subtle differences in the manner in which the variables that give life to the system interact. The physical geography of the city, its historical roots, the human mosaic, its economics, transportation, and politics are all interwoven components from which the morphology of the city evolves. The interactions among the elements of the urban system can give rise to completely different urban forms, witness Los Angeles and New York City (Figure 7.1 and Figure 7.2). One question that the urban scientists ponder is, How and why, considering the aforementioned factors, did such divergent spatial arrangements come about? Give that question a moment's thought

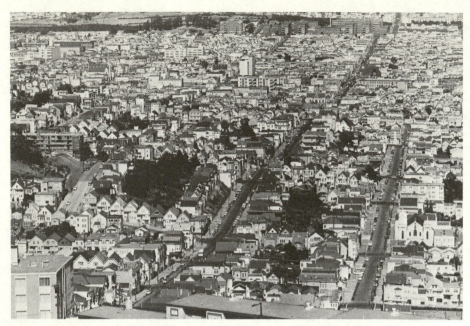

FIGURE 7.1. Low-Density City, Los Angeles. Source: HUD.

FIGURE 7.2. High-Density City, New York City. Source: HUD.

with respect to the urban areas with which you are familiar. What speculations and assumptions can be made about the workings of the urban ecosystem in those places?

THE CITY AS A WEB OF INTERACTIONS: CONSIDERATIONS BASED ON THE PHYSICAL GEOGRAPHY OF URBAN PLACES

As spatial entities, cities quite obviously impact the natural landscape. The development of urban places may dictate local changes in the physical environment. The land may be sculpted to accommodate urban activity, hills may be leveled or stream channels diverted. Conversely, the natural environment may have a great effect on the city; for example, the site of a city may be a place of substantial environmental hazard. In some instances, efforts are made to reduce the potential of such hazards—New Orleans is a case in point.

Located near the mouth of the Mississippi River, with parts of the city actually below sea level, New Orleans is subject to flooding on a fairly regular basis. A complex system of levees and pumping stations has been created in an attempt to reduce this environmental hazard. The physical geography of the city, and its location near the mouth of a vast river system, do pose environmental problems. However, it is precisely this location with respect to transportation routes that gives economic life to New Orleans. Thus, the whole complex of variables—including physical geography, transportation systems, and the economic base of the city—could be explored in great detail with respect to the roles of the variables as essential elements in the functioning of the New Orleans urban ecosystem. If we consider the historical evolution of transportation as it relates to settlement, still more components of the system can be analyzed.

The human mosaic of New Orleans has been highly influenced by the French as well as by people from the Caribbean. Location, economic activity, and the history of European colonization in North America are factors that help to explain the influence of those groups of people on New Orleans. Today, that influence is reflected by colorful traditions and ceremonies, unique areas of the city such as the French Quarter, and on the periphery of the city in the pattern of long, thin, rectangular land holdings referred to as long-lots. Whether one is studying the spatial economics or the people of New Orleans, the physical environment may be used as the central theme. In other cities, a slightly different way of looking at the physical city may be needed.

Cities contribute to alterations in the chemical composition of the physical environment. Such alteration most often occurs through pollution of the water or air. In the cities of Los Angeles and Denver, serious air pollution results from the incomplete combustion of fuel in internal combustion engines and the associated release of gases into the atmosphere. These gases are acted upon by solar energy and produce smog or the "brown cloud," as the problem is referred to in Denver.

In both Denver and Los Angeles, common culprits responsible for the air pollution problem can be found. In both cities, periods of inversion, or cold air above somewhat warmer air, occur. These inversions, discussed in Chapter 2, pose problems in Los Angeles in the summer and in Denver mainly in the winter. In considering the problem of urban smog, variables that interact with the physical attributes of each place, such as transportation, land use patterns, and the resulting general urban form, must be studied. In both Los Angeles and Denver, low-density settlement is dominant, and the mode of circulation, the movement of people within the cities, is the automobile. The automobile is the greatest contributor to the problem of air pollution in Denver, Los Angeles, and many other cities. The systems approach allows for an understanding of exactly why such problems occur and, more important, gives us a tool that may aid in solving those problems.

We have discussed, to this point, one example of how the systems approach may be used to study cities. Taking one variable, physical geography, we have used that factor as a base from which to consider its interactions with other variables. It would be possible to take any other variable—urban housing, for example—and to similarly focus all other elements in the urban ecosystem on issues related to that variable. Obviously, we have spoken in the most general terms for this review, but the systems approach is a methodology that can be used to address a question in infinite detail. The net result of this process is that we can discover the strength of the interrelationships among all the variables in the urban ecosystem.

A second method of systematically investigating the urban ecosystem would be to base investigations on urban functioning in its entirety rather than on interactions with a single variable. The reader is asked to reflect on the stages of urban development proposed by James E. Vance, Jr., that are detailed in Chapter 1. Review the processes of inception, exclusion, segregation, extension, relocation and readjustment, and redevelopment; give thought to the elements of the urban system involved at each stage; and again, analyze the interactions among those component parts. It is to be hoped that in using either methodology—focusing on a particular variable or concentrating on the general pattern—the reader will have a feeling for and an appreciation of the functioning of the city as an ecosystem.

The second part of this volume discusses the city as part of an urban system, or a group of urban places. Attention is directed to the expansion of the city, to related moves toward growth restriction, and finally, to the process of manipulating the elements of the urban ecosystem, which is referred to as the planning process.

PART 2

Systems of Cities

8

Systems of Cities

The study of urban systems may be approached in many ways, but before any approach can be chosen, there needs to be some agreement on what is meant by the terms *urban* or *urban system.* Cities interact in a variety of complex ways, creating systems of cities. Geographers are interested in the nature and structure of those interactions, particularly the spatial relationships that impinge upon these interactions. A modern industrial society is composed of cities and urban areas that are part of a complex, nested hierarchy of subsystems that range in scale from the smallest settlement to the largest urban agglomeration.

DEFINITIONS AND INTERNATIONAL COMPARISONS

Not all scholars have the same conceptual approach to the study of urban systems, and before any meaningful comparisons and analysis can be made, defintions must be agreed upon. This is no easy task. What is meant by urban? Although we touched on this in the first chapter, some review is warranted here.

Almost every country has its own definition of what is meant by urban. Because of these differences, international comparisons are difficult at best. Not only do different countries have different definitions, but in some countries the definitions have changed over time, making time-series studies difficult. Most urban definitions, however, can be included in one of four categories: size, administrative function, legal identity, or site characteristics (Peters and Larkin, 1979).

Urban, to most people, is related to the population size of an area. Little agreement exists, however, as to what population size constitutes a city or an urban area. In the United States an urban place is defined as a town that is incorporated and has a population of at least 2,500 people. In other countries the size criterion is different. For example, in Denmark an urban place is one that has a population of at least 250, whereas in India urban places must have at least 5,000 inhabitants. Because the size of minor civil divisions, such as counties, is often used instead of the size of an urban place, size definitions are often inadequate. In order for meaningful comparative studies and analyses to be undertaken, exact definitions are required.

Some countries, particularly those in Latin America, use administrative function as a criterion for urban definition. In Peru, for example, urban places are defined as capitals of all *departmentos* and *distritos* plus all towns larger than the average size of these administrative centers not possessing rural characteristics. At least two problems are associated with this definition of urban. First, how does one precisely define "rural characteristics"? Second, with this kind of definition, places that do not have administrative functions, regardless of their population size, are considered rural.

Legal identity is another criterion that is used to define urban. This method of identifying urban places can be traced back to the chartering of cities in the Middle Ages. Towns or urban areas that have a legal identity or charter are considered to be urban, and all others are considered rural, regardless of other characteristics.

Finally, site characteristics are often used in defining urban. Included as site characteristics would be such attributes as numbered streets, lighting, or a piped-in water supply. Sometimes the previously mentioned criteria, along with site characteristics, are used to define an urban place. Thus, the resulting definition of an urban place may become very complex.

The definition of urban has changed over time in the United States. No distinction was made between urban and rural places in the early censuses, and it was not until 1874, with the publication of the *Statistical Atlas of the United States,* that towns were defined. At that time a town or urban place was a settlement that had more than 8,000 inhabitants. This figure was lowered to 2,500 with the U.S. census of 1900. Massive suburbanization, which resulted in large numbers of people living outside official incorporated boundaries but still living in urban conditions, rendered the old definitions inadequate. In 1950 a density criterion for these fringe areas was adopted, which resulted in a 4.5 percent increase of the urban population.

Several other problems are associated with the definition of urban. One is the process of annexation. For example, the town of California, Pennsylvania, had a population of 2,831 in the 1950 census and a population of 5,978 in the 1960 census. A closer look at this change, however, shows that most of the growth was due to annexation. Annexation can create many problems when trying to trace population changes over time.

Another problem encountered when trying to trace population changes is reclassification. If a place had a 1970 population of 2,499 and grew to have 2,500 in 1980, then the net gain of 1 would mean that 2,500 people were subracted from the rural population and added to the urban population. Estimates are that one-third of the gain in urban population in El Salvador between 1950 and 1960 was the result of reclassification.

Defining Urban Areas in the United States

Many data units are available for analysis by the urban geographer. The concept of an extended urban area was first developed by the U.S. Bureau of the Census in 1910 with the "metropolitan district." Since that time a variety of other extended urban area units of analysis have been developed, including the municipality, the urbanized area, and the standard metropolitan statistical area.

Municipality. According to an analysis of urban systems by Bourne and Simmons, "the basic building block of every empirical concept of an urban area is the political municipality, that is, the city, town, or township" (Bourne and Simmons, 1978, p. 30). The simplest method of defining the nature of an urban system is to choose the central city of a metropolitan area, say Chicago, Philadelphia, or Boston, to represent the urban area. Using the municipality as a means of defining an urban area is relatively simple because a great deal of data are collected and aggregated by national, state, and local authorities at that level of analysis.

However, several difficulties occur in using the municipality as the unit of analysis for urban areas or systems. First, the central city, as defined by municipal boundaries, does not usually satisfy most working definitions of a city as a spatial, a social, or an economic unit. Most urban areas include areas outside the municipal boundaries of the central city. Also, some cities, several of which are in the western part of the United States – Phoenix and Santa Fe, for example – include within their municipal boundaries large land areas that will probably never be built up.

A second problem associated with using municipal boundaries is that many local and state governments change boundaries frequently by means of the annexation process or sometimes by the full integration of an area into a regional government or metropolitan area. These changes complicate analyses that are based primarily on strict municipal boundaries.

A final problem is that municipalities do not generally represent the whole labor area and therefore can generate misleading impressions. According to Bourne and Simmons,

> The industrial suburb, or a wealthy residential suburb, can exist very comfortably without the full complement of land uses, labor force, and social diversity that we expect to see in a city. These municipalities will appear as extreme points in any analysis. . . . It is only when political variables, such as the structure of government or fiscal relationships are involved that legal municipalities becomes a viable unit for urban systems analysis in their own right. [Bourne and Simmons, 1978, p. 31]

Urbanized Area. In order to overcome the conceptual and practical difficulties associated with using the municipality as the unit of analysis, the obvious response is to define the urban area in broader geographic terms that are more closely related to the functions of an urban area. In 1950 the U.S. Census Bureau developed the concept of the "urbanized area." Its definition is based upon the level of urban land use intensity as well as on a minimum population-size threshold. The purpose of developing the urbanized area concept was to provide a better separation of urban and rural populations in the vicinity of the larger cities. An urbanized area consists of a central city, or cities, and the surrounding densely settled territory. The specific criteria for the delineation of an urbanized area are as follows:

1. (a) A central city of 50,000 inhabitants or more, or (b) two cities having contiguous boundaries and constituting, for general social and economic purposes, a single community with a combined population of at least 50,000, with the smaller city having a population of at least 15,000.

2. Surrounding closely settled territory, including the following (but excluding the rural portions of extended cities):

   Incorporated places of 2,500 inhabitants or more.
   Incorporated places of 2,500 inhabitants, provided that each has a closely settled area of 100 housing units or more, and all unincorporated places recognized in the 1970 census.
   Contiguous small parcels of unincorporated land determined to have a 1970 census population density of 1,000 inhabitants or more per square mile.
   Other similar small areas in unincorporated territory without regard to population density, provided that they serve (a) to eliminate enclaves, (b) to close indentations in the urbanized areas of one mile or less across the open end, or (c) to link outlying enumeration districts of qualifying density that are not more than one and one-half miles from the main body of the urbanized area.

The urbanized area concept overcomes several difficulties associated with using the municipality as the unit of analysis,

TABLE 8.1
A Comparison of Urban Definitions

| | United States, 1970 | | |
	Number	Population	Average Size
Municipalities			
10,000 and over	2,301[1]	112,451,000	48,900
Urbanized areas			
50,000 and over	248[2]	118,447,000	477,600
Metropolitan areas	243[3]	139,419,000	573,700
Urban Population	–	149,325,000	–
Total Population	–	203,212,000	–

[1] Incorporated urban places. United States Bureau of the Census, Census of Population, 1970. Vol. 1, Characteristics of the Population, U.S. Summary, Section I, Table 6.
[2] Central city of 50,000 or more plus the surrounding closely settled incorporated and unincorporated areas. Bureau of the Census, op. cit., Table 20.
[3] Standard metropolitan statistical area includes central cities of 50,000 or more plus adjacent counties within the labor shed. Bureau of the Census, op. cit., Table 5.

Source: L. S. Bourne and J. W. Simmons, Systems of Cities (New York: Oxford University Press, 1978), p. 29.

and the largest portion of urban activity does take place in the urbanized area (see Table 8.1). Because of rapidly changing populations, the boundaries of urbanized areas do not keep pace with population changes, particularly changes that take place on the urban fringe.

Metropolitan District and Standard Metropolitan Statistical Area. Because social and economic activities in urban places are closely connected, and in many types of analyses the entire area in and around a city must be considered as a single unit, the Bureau of the Census added the concept of the "metropolitan district" to its system of area classification in 1910. This addition marked the bureau's first use of a reporting data unit for large cities and their surrounding areas. Originally, every city with a population of over 200,000 inhabitants was considered to be a metropolitan district. The concept was expanded in 1940 to include areas that contained at least one incorporated city of 50,000 people or more and contiguous minor civil divisions or incorporated places having a population density of 150 people or more per square mile.

Although the metropolitan district concept was useful in expanding the definition of an urban area, several drawbacks were associated with the concept. The primary limitation from a statistical viewpoint was that, aside from census data, little data were available for minor civil divisions. Also, prior to 1950 other area classifications were used that were defined in different ways and were not compatible with the metropolitan district classification.

In 1950 the Federal Committee on Standard Metropolitan Areas, which was composed of representatives from several federal agencies, including the Bureau of the Census, developed the standard metropolitan area (SMA) concept. The SMA was designed so that a wider variety of statistical data might be presented on a uniform basis. An SMA included one or more contiguous counties containing at least one city of 50,000 people or more. The counties had to meet certain criteria of metropolitan character and of social and economic integration with the central city in order to be included in an SMA. The primary difference between a metropolitan district and an SMA was that the metropolitan district concept was based primarily upon population density criteria whereas entire counties were included as the reporting unit in the SMA (except in New England).

In 1959 the name standard metropolitan area was changed to standard metropolitan statistical area (SMSA) to reflect the purpose and nature of the classification. The SMSA classification supplements the older farm-nonfarm, rural-urban distinctions by delineating metropolitan and nonmetropolitan areas by type of residence. Industrial concentration (labor demand) and population concentration (labor supply) are also taken into account. Since its introduction, the SMSA has been used extensively by many government agencies as a standard area for gathering, analyzing, and publishing statistics.

An SMSA always includes a city (or cities) of a specified population size (the population of the central city and the county or counties in which the city is located) and the contiguous counties when the economic and social relationships between the central city and a contiguous county meet specified criteria of metropolitan character and integration. An SMSA may cross state lines, and in New England, SMSAs are composed of cities and towns instead of counties.

The specific population criteria for SMSAs are as follows.

A. Each standard metropolitan statistical area must include at least

1. One city with 50,000 or more inhabitants, or
2. A city with at least 25,000 inhabitants that together with those contiguous places (incorporated or unincorporated) having population densities of at least 1,000 persons per square mile has a combined population of 50,000 and constitutes for general economic and social purposes a single community, provided that the county or counties in which the city and contiguous places are located has a total population of at least 75,000. (In New England, the cities and towns qualifying for inclusion in an SMSA must have a total population of at least 75,000.)

B. A contiguous county is included in a standard metropolitan statistical area if

1. At least 75 percent of the resident labor force in the county is in the nonagricultural labor force, and
2. At least 30 percent of the employed workers living in the county work in the central county or counties of the area.

C. A contiguous county that does not meet the requirements of criterion 2 is included in an SMSA if at least 75 percent of the resident labor force is in the nonagricultural labor force and it meets two of the following additional criteria of metropolitan character and one of the following criteria of integration.

1. Criteria of metropolitan character: (a) at least 25

percent of the population is urban, (b) the county had an increase of at least 15 percent in total population during the period covered by the two most recent censuses of population, (c) the county has a population density of at least 50 persons per square mile.

2. Criteria of integration: (a) at least 15 percent of the employed workers living in the county work in the central county or counties of the area, (b) the number of people working in the county who live in the central county or counties of the area is equal to at least 15 percent of the employed workers living in the county, (c) the sum of the number of workers commuting to and from the central county or counties is equal to 20 percent of the employed workers living in the county.

In the 1970 census, the Bureau of the Census recognized 243 standard metropolitan statistical areas in the United States and 4 in Puerto Rico, for a total of 247 (see Figure 8.1). So far, 288 SMSAs have been identified for the 1980 census, though population counts may qualify other places as SMSAs also.

Definitions of the standard metropolitan statistical area have evolved over time, and undoubtedly they will continue to change as the nature of urban systems changes. The primary weakness of the SMSA classification is that it uses the county as the basic spatial unit of analysis, and using the county as the unit of analysis can create several problems. For example, some counties, particularly in the western United States, can stretch hundreds of miles and cover very large areas—such as San Bernardino County in California. Also, if a small urban center is linked to an adjacent city, that small urban center's entire county would be included in the SMSA.

Although using the county as the unit of analysis creates problems, it also has strengths. According to Bourne and Simmons, "the very crudeness of the SMSA's spatial delimitation makes them relatively stable over time. They can be readily linked to other data sources and thus are useful for a wide

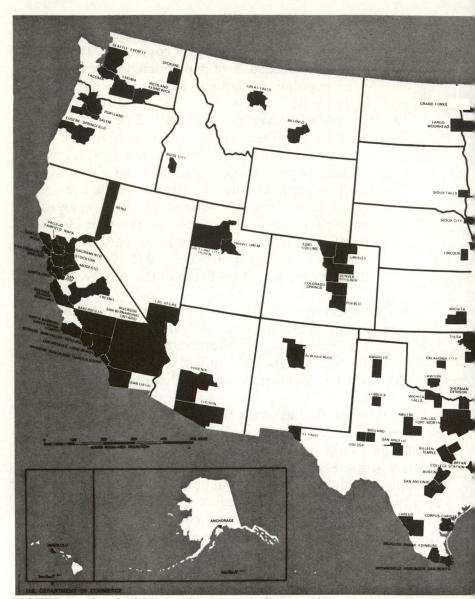

FIGURE 8.1. Standard Metropolitan Statistical Areas of the United States. Source: U.S. Bureau of the Census, *Census Geography*, Data Access Descriptions no. 33 (Washington, D.C., 1978).

BUREAU OF THE CENSUS

variety of purposes" (Bourne and Simmons, 1978, p. 34).

Standard Consolidated Statistical Areas. The standard consolidated statistical area (SCSA) is an area designed to facilitate the presentation and analysis of data for major concentrations of metropolitan populations. Each SCSA is composed of two or more contiguous standard metropolitan statistical areas that meet certain criteria of size, urban character, integration, and contiguity of urbanized area.

In 1970 only two standard consolidated statistical areas were recognized. One was the metropolitan complex surrounding New York City, and the other was the complex surrounding Chicago. In 1976 eleven additional SCSAs were designated by the Census Bureau. Each contained at least 1 million people and at least two SMSAs. The thirteen SCSAs designated so far are the following: (1) Boston-Lawrence-Lowell, (2) Chicago-Gary, (3) Cincinnati-Hamilton, (4) Cleveland-Akron-Lorain, (5) Detroit–Ann Arbor, (6) Houston-Galveston, (7) Los Angeles–Long Beach–Anaheim, (8) Miami–Fort Lauderdale, (9) Milwaukee-Racine, (10) New York–Newark–Jersey City, (11) Philadelphia-Wilmington-Trenton, (12) San Francisco–Oakland–San Jose, and (13) Seattle-Tacoma.

New Standards for Statistical Areas

The Office of Federal Statistical Policy and Standards and the Federal Committee on Standard Metropolitan Statistical Areas developed a new set of standards to define metropolitan statistical areas that were put into use after the 1980 census, which was conducted on April 1, 1980. These new criteria replaced the SCSAs and SMSAs that were used prior to the 1980 census. The new designations are as follows: (1) metropolitan statistical areas (MSAs), (2) primary metropolitan statistical areas (PMSAs), and (3) consolidated metropolitan statistical areas (CMSAs). The MSA serves as the major new unit, and its designation and implementation should be completed some time in 1982.

Definitional changes were initiated in order to provide definitions that are as consistent as possible for MSAs across the nation and to give additional flexibility in meeting the needs of various users. As with the criteria for SMSAs, an MSA is an area with a large urban population nucleus together with adjacent areas that have a degree of economic and social integration with that nucleus. The MSAs will be classified on four levels based on total population size: Level A–MSAs with 1 million inhabitants or more, Level B–MSAs with 250,000 to 1 million inhabitants, Level C–MSAs with 100,000 to 250,000 inhabitants, and Level D–MSAs with fewer than 100,000 inhabitants.

Once these new standards have been implemented, they will obviously affect the designation of central cities, the boundaries of areas, and the titles of existing SMSAs. No changes will take place, however, until the Census Bureau has released commuting and employment data for all states from the 1980 census.

A primary metropolitan statistical area is recognized if it is shown that strong internal economic and social links exist within subareas of a Level A MSA, and a PMSA is an urbanized county or group of counties (towns and cities in New England). Consolidated metropolitan statistical areas are Level A MSAs that make up two or more PMSAs.

HIERARCHY OF URBAN SYSTEMS

In order to more fully understand the urban system it is important to comprehend the complex interactions among the various nodes or parts of the system. The relationship between economic growth and cities is fairly well understood, and this relationship has led to particular types of urban system organization, particularly in advanced Western economies. Those types of system organization, as outlined by Bourne, consist of at least three levels.

1. National system–dominated by metropolitan centers that are arranged in a steplike size hierarchy. The number of centers in each level of the hierarchy increases with a corresponding decrease in the population size of the centers. This change occurs in a regular progression.

2. Regional subsystems—contained within the national system are regional subsystems of cities. Although these systems are similar to the national system, the hierarchical arrangement is not as clearly defined and is usually organized around a metropolitan area. Cities in a regional subsystem are usually smaller in size than are those in the national system and drop off more quickly in size as one moves down the hierarchy.

3. Daily urban systems—nested within the regional subsystems are daily urban systems. These systems represent the "life space of urban residents and develop as the influence of each center reaches out, absorbs, and reorganizes the adjacent territory" (Bourne, 1975, p. 12).

The interrelationship of these systems is complex and hard to simplify, and each system includes both a spatial and hierarchical dimension (see Figure 8.2). The linkages that hold these systems together have varying forms at different levels in the urban hierarchy. For example, at the national system level the linkages may not include actual movement of commodities but may include exchanges of ideas or information. At the regional level the linkages may include road traffic connections or telephone calls. The daily urban system level may include commuter or shopper movement. According to Bourne, "Over time these systems reach out to encompass ever larger proportions of the space economy and of the national territory. In so doing they have reordered the economy, life styles, and political boundaries as well as changed our image of national character" (Bourne, 1975, p. 14).

The complexity of urban systems results from the interaction among the three basic dimensions of the system—spatial, structural, and temporal. The core of the urban system for the geographer is the spatial dimension. However, in order to understand the urban system we must understand the spatial dimension in conjunction with the structural or hierarchical organization, as well as with the dimension of time.

A recent feature associated with urban systems throughout

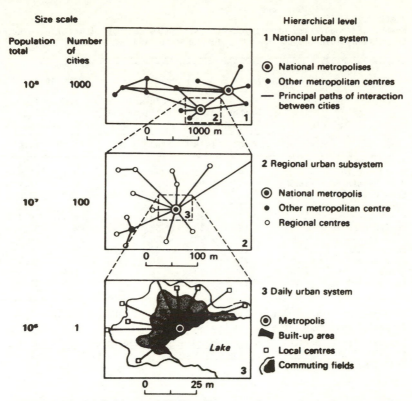

FIGURE 8.2. Definitions of Urban Systems. Source: L. S. Bourne, *Urban Systems* (Oxford: Oxford University Press, 1975), p. 13.

the world is that one city is usually much more powerful and larger than the other cities. Table 8.2 shows that almost all areas of the world have shown an increase in the number of cities with over 1 million inhabitants. The concentration of power and population in one city has led to what was referred to by Jefferson as the "primate city." According to Jefferson, "All over the world . . . the largest city shall be supereminent, and not merely in size, but in national influence. . . . A country's leading city is always disproportionately large and exceptionally expressive of national capacity and feeling" (Jefferson, 1939, p. 231).

TABLE 8.2
Number and Population of Million-Cities, and Percentage of Total Population
in Million-Cities, 1960 and 1975, in the World and Major Areas.

Area	Number of Million-Cities		Population of Million-Cities Millions		Percentage of Total Population in Million-Cities	
	1960	1975	1960	1975	1960	1975
World total	109	101	272	516	9.1	12.8
More developed regions	64	90	173	251	17.7	21.9
Less developed regions	45	101	99	265	4.9	9.2
Europe	31	37	73	93	17.3	19.3
U.S.S.R.	5	12	13	25	6.1	9.7
Northern America	18	30	52	80	26.2	32.9
Oceania	2	2	4	6	24.7	26.9
South Asia	16	34	32	88	3.7	6.8
East Asia	23	45	60	131	7.7	12.9
Africa	3	10	6	22	2.4	5.5
Latin America	11	21	31	71	14.5	21.9

Note: These estimates still correspond to earlier population
estimates and projections of the United Nations.

Source: United Nations, Concise Report on the World Population Situation
in 1970-75 and Its Long-Range Implications (New York: United Nations,
1974), p. 36.

The primate city is usually at least twice as large as the next
largest city and commonly is more than twice as significant.
Primacy can occur in both developed and developing countries, and there does not appear to be any consistent or strong
relationship between primacy and economic development
level.

The hierarchical relationship of cities can be understood by
looking at the relative size of cities within urban systems. The
relationship between rank and size of cities was formalized
by Zipf (1949) in the rank-size rule, which can be stated as

$$P_r = \frac{P_1}{r}$$

where P_r is the population of a city of rank r, P_1 is the population of the largest city, and r is the rank of the given city. An

urban system with a few large cities, a large number of medium-sized cities, and an even larger number of smaller cities would exemplify Zipf's rule. Figure 8.3 depicts a comparison of Zipf's ideal curve with the distribution of cities in the United States. According to Zipf, any deviation from the idealized pattern would indicate an improper balance in the pattern of urbanization. However, others have noted that deviations are not uncommon, and distributions should be viewed in probability terms.

The concept of the primate city and the rank-size rule have been used in international comparisons of the primacy rate—the population of the largest city compared with that of the second largest city. Thomlinson noted that

> countries with high primacy rates tend to be characterized by a low percent urban, low income, and recent political or economic dependency on another country; almost always the primate city is the national capital. . . . Most industrial countries have moderate or low primacy rates, generally traceable to strong pressures toward regionalization. [Thomlinson, 1976, p. 422]

In his classic study of city size distributions and economic development, Berry (1961) found that the rank-size rule applied mainly to the larger and more-complex countries that had a long history of urbanization. He found little relationship between economic development and the rank-size rule.

CENTRAL PLACE THEORY

The hierarchical distribution of cities according to size or function is important in determining the locational patterns of cities. However, to geographers, the spatial or areal aspect of systems of cities is paramount. What factors determine the size and spacing of cities within the urban hierarchy? Although a variety of factors determines the location of cities within the urban system, one classical location theory, the central place theory, has been developed to explain locational patterns within the urban hierarchy.

Central place theory was first formalized by the German

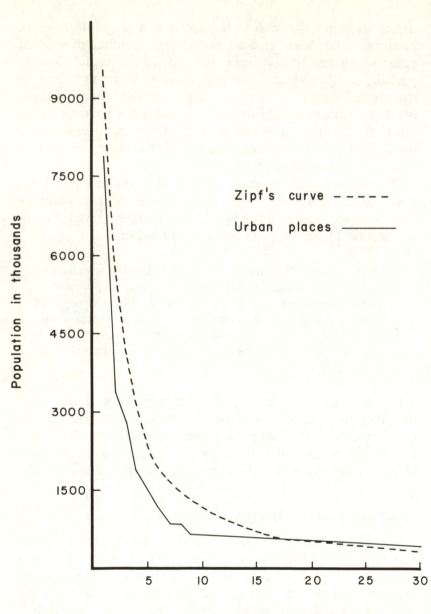

FIGURE 8.3. City Size and Rank, United States, 1970, Compared with Zipf's Theoretical Curve. Source: U.S. Bureau of the Census, *Census of Population,* "Number of Inhabitants: United States Summary," PC(1)-A1 (Washington, D.C.: Government Printing Office, 1971), p. 18.

geographer Walter Christaller in the early 1930s. His doctoral dissertation, translated as *Central Places in Southern Germany*, has become a classic work in urban geography, and it was based upon his observations in southern Germany. Central place theory is not a comprehensive theory but is primarily concerned with the locational patterns of cities relative to their secondary and tertiary activities. Market centers and the hinterlands they serve are the focus of the theory. The central places therefore serve areas larger than themselves. The trade area or market area is referred to as the hinterland, and the size of the city is a function of the demand for goods generated in the hinterland.

In the development of the central place theory, it was necessary for Christaller to make some limiting assumptions in order to specifically focus on a theory of cities as central places. Christaller assumed the following.

1. There is a uniform or homogeneous terrain with a uniform resource endowment and soil fertility.
2. There is a uniform distribution of population and purchasing power. There is homogeneity with regard to demand for goods, consumption patterns, and income.
3. All urban places of the same size are equally accessible because of a uniform transport system. This transport system allows equally easy transportation in all directions, and the costs of transportation are directly proportional to distance.
4. The producers and consumers are rational economic persons who make optimal decisions based on complete and perfect knowledge. They maximize profits and minimize transportation costs.
5. The consumers buy goods and services at the nearest center and pay transportation costs to their home as well as the cost of the goods at the center.
6. Rural demand is completely met by the minimum number of centers, and only economic restrictions limit the number of producers.

Given these assumptions, several factors must be determined. How many central places will be required to meet consumer demand? What is the most efficient spacing of central places? What will be the size of the trade or market areas?

Threshold, Range, and Order

The concepts of threshold and range are important concepts in the evolution of central place theory. In order for a firm to stay in business and in a central place, it is essential that it sell enough goods or services to meet operating costs. The minimum level of demand (price times quantity) needed to bring a firm into existence and keep it going is called the threshold. Although threshold is usually concerned with the number of people necessary to support a given function, counting people is only a substitute for measuring the actual level of demand at a shop or store.

The range of a good is the average maximum distance people are willing to travel to purchase a good. If a good is purchased by someone who lives next to the store that sells it, the cost of the good is essentially the same as the price at the store. However, for someone who lives some distance from the store, the cost of the good is the price at the store plus the cost of transport from one's house to the store and return. For example, if milk costs $1.00 a gallon and transport costs are $.10 per mile, a consumer who lives next door to the store pays $1.00 for a gallon of milk whereas someone who lives five miles away pays $1.00 plus $.50 in transport costs for a total of $1.50 for a gallon of milk. As the price of the good increases because of distance from the store, the quantity demanded will decrease. Thus, as increasing distance from the store leads to a higher price, demand will decline with distance and eventually reach zero. The range of the good is therefore the distance away from the store at which demand will reach zero. In order for a firm to stay in business, threshold conditions must be met within the appropriate range. If the threshold cannot be met within the range of the good or service, the firm will go out of business (see Figure 8.4).

Threshold and range vary according to the good or service. Goods or services that are inexpensive and frequently purchased have low thresholds, whereas expensive, infrequently purchased goods have higher thresholds. Goods with low

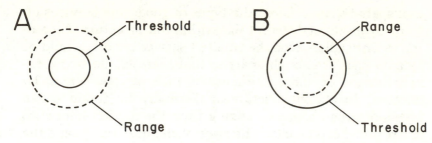

FIGURE 8.4. Firm *A* Will Stay in Business; Firm *B* Will Go out of Business.

thresholds are referred to as low-order goods, and those with high thresholds are called high-order goods. Thus, we can recognize a hierarchy of goods. Everyday commodities, such as bread or milk, are low-order goods and are usually available at nearby shops or stores. Few people would drive long distances to obtain these commodities. High-order goods or services, such as the Broadway theater, require an extremely high market threshold. Large populations are required because only a small fraction of the people want a particular good or service, such as to attend a play, at any particular time. The highest-order goods or services may require the entire country to support them.

Because goods or services can range from low to high order, the center in which that good or service is sold can also be categorized. The order of a center is based upon the highest-order good that is sold at that center. Therefore, low-order centers will offer only low-order goods, but high-order centers offer high-order goods as well as low-order goods. In other words, we can recognize a hierarchy of central places.

Central Place Hierarchy

When Christaller was developing his theory, he assumed the existence of a network of central places that included a large city, a few towns, and a large number of villages and hamlets. The theory does not address itself to the historical evolution of the central places; it assumes the existence of a central place system and deals with the characteristics of that system.

Christaller was primarily concerned with the hierarchical

and spatial structure and the types of goods and services offered by places of different size within that structure. According to Christaller, even the smallest service centers would be located just far enough apart so that there would be no encroachment of the hinterland of one service center by another. In studying southern Germany he found seven levels of urban centers, ranging from the market hamlet to the regional capital city. The sizes of the hinterlands and the distances between them increase at successively higher levels of the hierarchy. Therefore, each central place had a hinterland, and the size of that hinterland was a function of the order of the goods that could be purchased. Theoretically, the trade area or hinterland around each central place would be circular in shape; however, if the market areas were really circular, then overlaps or unserved areas would be created (see Figure 8.5). The most efficient areal market would be hexagonal in shape, because hexagons are the regular polygons that are closest to the circle in shape and eliminate both overlaps and voids.

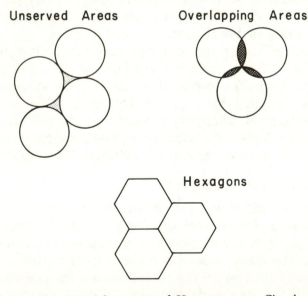

FIGURE 8.5. Advantages of Hexagons over Circular Areas.

In his study of southern Germany, Christaller postulated that service centers would be about two hours of travel time apart. (Two hours of travel time was measured in walking speed or horse speed, because Christaller's study antedated the automobile and the railroad.) This measure turned out to be seven kilometers, so the smallest service centers would be seven kilometers apart. Centers associated with the next order of central places were twelve kilometers apart. The actual distribution of towns in southern Germany at that time is depicted in Figure 8.6. Christaller's pattern is found more clearly in farm areas that were poor, self-contained, and thinly settled.

Although many of Christaller's assumptions do not hold true in many parts of the "real world," his theories are still valuable. When the real world does not agree with his featureless plain, with its geometric land use and settlement patterns, then we can investigate the differences and the reasons for those differences.

Many attempts have been made by geographers and other scholars of the urban landscape to verify the central place model, and many of the results of these efforts have been encouraging. According to Abler, Adams, and Gould, "Small centers tend to be located midway between large places. Large centers tend to be evenly spaced within market areas. The mix of goods and services available at a central place resembles the mix available in other centers of the same order and size, and differs from the mix available at centers occupying adjacent orders in the central place hierarchy" (Abler, Adams, and Gould, 1971, p. 371).

Earlier chapters treated phenomena within the context of a single urban ecosystem, whereas in this chapter we have viewed individual cities as parts of larger urban systems, or systems of cities. Spatial characteristics of city size and spatial arrangements have been presented so that we can better understand that cities do not function in isolation from each other. Connections between cities exist on local, regional, national, and often even international levels. It has also been stressed that international comparisons between cities and between urban systems are often difficult because

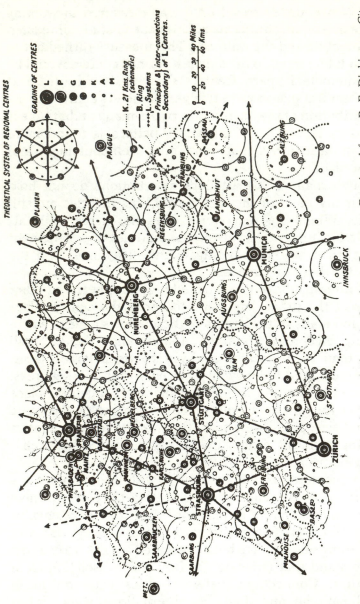

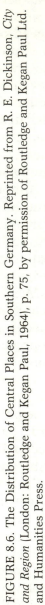

FIGURE 8.6. The Distribution of Central Places in Southern Germany. Reprinted from R. E. Dickinson, *City and Region* (London: Routledge and Kegan Paul, 1964), p. 75, by permission of Routledge and Kegan Paul Ltd. and Humanities Press.

of differences in the ways that cities are defined from nation to nation. For the United States, the various definitions used by the Bureau of the Census for urban areas of various types have been viewed in some detail.

As with all systems, what stands out most clearly in this discussion of systems of cities is their hierarchical nature. Not only is there a hierarchical arrangement of cities within a country or region, but also, and more important, that hierarchy strongly affects the diffusion of ideas and innovations as well as the size and direction of many migration streams. In turn, societal changes often initiate the need for changes in the nature of the urban hierarchy.

REFERENCES

Abler, Ronald; Adams, John S.; and Gould, Peter. 1971. *Spatial Organization*. Englewood Cliffs, N.J.: Prentice-Hall.

Berry, Brian J. L. 1961. "City Size Distributions and Economic Development." *Economic Development and Cultural Change* 9: 573–588.

Bourne, L. S. 1975. *Urban Systems: Strategies for Regulation*. Oxford: Clarendon Press.

Bourne, L. S., and Simmons, J. W. 1978. *Systems of Cities*. New York: Oxford University Press.

Christaller, Walter. 1933. *Die Zentralen Orte in Süddeutschland*. Jera: Gustav Fischer Verlag. Translated by C. W. Baskin under the title *Central Places in Southern Germany*. Englewood Cliffs, N.J.: Prentice-Hall, 1966.

Jefferson, Mark. 1939. "The Law of the Primate City." *Geographical Review* 29: 226–232.

Peters, Gary L., and Larkin, Robert P. 1979. *Population Geography: Problems, Concepts, and Prospects*. Dubuque, Iowa: Kendall/Hunt Publishing Company.

Thomlinson, Ralph. 1976. *Population Dynamics: Causes and Consequences of World Demographic Change*. 2d ed. New York: Random House.

Zipf, George K. 1949. *Human Behavior and the Principle of Least Effort*. New York: Addison-Wesley.

9

Suburbanization: Processes in the Outer City

Throughout the twentieth century, the American suburb has undergone a significant evolution in both form and function. An examination of the changes that have taken place in the suburbs of the United States in this century should be undertaken from two perspectives. First, we must consider the actual physical and socioeconomic events and processes that have served to alter suburbia. Second, we must review people's attitudes toward and perception of the suburb.

In this chapter we discuss the growth and change of the suburb, past and present, reactions to suburbia, and finally, the suburb as land use practice in the contemporary world. In such an overview, some interesting topics must be omitted. For example, we haven't the space for a discussion of the history of the suburb or for a detailed comparison between North American and European suburbs.

We may simply define a suburb as being that area surrounding a city that has a greater density of residential and commercial land use than a rural area but not the density of land use found in the central city. Within the suburbs of a major city, we find the place of transition from urban to rural.

The boundary between city and suburb may be some physical feature, but it is more often the legal or political boundary of the central or core city. There may also be a number of suburbs surrounding a single major city—one need only examine a map of the Los Angeles Basin to observe this pattern.

The suburb, as it has evolved throughout this century, is our main focus of attention, for without an understanding of the present-day suburb it is virtually impossible to truly understand the urban ecosystem.

THE EVOLUTION OF SUBURBAN AMERICA

The study of the development of the socioeconomic structure of the modern suburb is of sufficient complexity as to demand attention from an interdisciplinary perspective. At one time, the geographer's contributions to this field of study were fairly limited. The trends in academic study during the last decade, however, indicate that the geographical perspective is becoming much more widely represented and that, along with the general body of academic study on suburbia, it has undergone a significant evolution in content. A growing consensus exists among those people who investigate urban and suburban processes that a period beginning in the mid-1960s and carrying through into the 1970s is the watershed from which the definition of the suburb as simply being "sub" to the "urb" is evolving into a functional definition of the suburb as an "outer city" (Muller, 1976).

The key to understanding the evolution of the twentieth-century American suburb lies in the consideration of the extremely rapid growth and developing socioeconomic complexity of the suburb following the Second World War. Prior to the decade of the 1940s, the suburb generally served as the place of residence for specific elements of the upper-income-level urban labor force. This is not to say that the suburbs were devoid of industries or that the pre–Second World War suburb functioned exclusively as the place of residence for urban workers. It is possible, for example, to trace the history of American nonresidential suburbs from the fringe areas of preindustrial New Orleans, Philadelphia, and Boston to the nineteenth- and early twentieth-century industrial suburbs of Detroit, Chicago, and St. Louis. However, the primary function of the late nineteenth and early twentieth-century American suburb was to house the worker who was able, because of increasing efficiency in urban transportation, to live at a greater distance from the central city.

The central city of the pre-1930 era was the site of the greatest concentration of population in the urban region, and it was also the center of most of the major commercial activities. In addition, the central city was the location of any significant diversity in the social and economic composition of the population of the urban region. Conversely, the suburbs of the early twentieth century were composed mainly of whites in the upper-middle to upper socioeconomic classes who had the ability to pay the significant costs of commuting to the urban core.

In the years following the Second World War, the central city dominance in economic activity and population distribution began to erode, and the suburb began to emerge in importance. The primary cause of the developing importance of the suburb was the rapid growth of the suburban population following the war.

Patterns of Population Growth

The trends of population growth in the three major areas of American settlement—the central city, the suburb, and the rural areas—indicate the dramatic increase in the suburban population since 1940. The post-1940 pattern was fundamentally the result of the combination of a great acceleration of several established demographic trends and the development of several "new" patterns of urban settlement.

The most important demographic element in the urbanization of the suburbs was the rapid growth of population on a national scale following the Second World War (the postwar "baby boom"). This increase in the birthrate coupled with the previous waves of immigration acted to cause a sharp jump in the population of the United States.

There was a tendency for the population to concentrate in the urban areas following the Second World War, which was a continuation of a historical trend toward migration to urban areas in the United States because of employment availability. This pattern of urban inmigration was greatly accelerated following the war as many of those released from military service sought employment in urban areas.

In the decade following the end of the Second World War, much urban growth took place on the fringe areas of the cities. This trend toward suburban settlement was largely the result of the desire for increased dwelling space, life-style preferences, or freedom from perceived urban problems. The rapid growth of postwar suburbia was made possible by the widespread use of the automobile and government subsidization of housing and transportation. These topics will be dealt with in greater detail throughout this chapter.

Comparisons of actual central city and suburban growth rates indicate that in the decade of the 1930s there was a shift toward a greater percentage of growth in the suburb than in the central city. During the 1950s and 1960s, the trends first established in the 1930s were intensified to such a degree that by the mid-1970s the suburb was dominant in both growth rates and percentage growth (see Table 9.1).

Although there is substantial evidence to show that rapid

TABLE 9.1
Percentages of Urban-Suburban Population Growth Rates, 1900-1970

Decade	Population Growth Rate of Cities	Population Growth Rate of Suburbs	Population Total SMSA Growth in Cities	Percentage SMSA Growth in Suburbs
1900–10	37.1	23.6	72.1	27.9
1910–20	27.7	20.0	71.6	28.4
1920–30	24.3	32.3	59.3	40.7
1930–40	5.6	14.6	41.0	59.0
1940–50	14.7	35.9	40.7	59.3
1950–60	10.7	48.5	23.8	76.2
1960–70	5.3	28.2	4.4	95.6

Source: U.S., Census of Population, 1960. "Selected Area Reports: SMSA, Social and Economic Data for Persons in SMSA's by Residence Inside or Outside Central City," Final Report PC (3)-LD. 1960-1970. Peter O. Muller, The Outer City: Geographical Consequences of the Urbanization of the Suburbs, Resource Papers for College Geography No. 75-2 (Washington, D.C.: Association of American Geographers, 1976), p. 4. Reprinted by permission.

growth took place in the suburbs, the reasons for suburban migration have yet to be totally explored. A complete investigation into the reasons for the move to the suburb is beyond the scope of this work, but it is important to consider several of the major themes in order to appreciate the growth processes.

The Move to the Suburbs

An examination of the move to the suburbs requires a consideration of the interrelationships among a wide range of variables. These many diverse variables can be categorized into three fundamental topic areas.

1. The relationship between what has been the traditional stage in the life cycle and the need for increased dwelling space.
2. Moves caused by environmental stress and perception of life-style.
3. Increasing efficiency of transportation and the related effect on distance constraints.

The decision to move to the suburb was generally the result of a combination of these factors rather than a move inspired by any single factor.

Stage in the Life Cycle and the Need for Additional Space. The availability of land in the suburbs and the major demographic trend of large families following the Second World War were essential elements in the "suburban boom" of the late 1940s through the mid-1960s. The increasing size of the family meant an increasing need for both dwelling space and surrounding property. The land needed to meet the requirements for increased space was readily available in the suburbs. They also offered the opportunity for a life-style that, in the opinion of many, combined the advantages of living in an urban area with the perceived benefits of a more rural environment.

Image and Environment. The conception of the suburban life-style was often a major factor in the decision to locate in suburbia. Yi-Fu Tuan associated the nature of the decision to

migrate to the suburb with the search for a healthy environment and family life as well as an informal life-style.

> The city symbolized corruption and ultimate sterility. It was
> the place where men struggled for power and vain glory and
> yet succumbed to petty social conventions. The country stood
> for life: life as seen in the fruits of the soil, in green growing
> things, in pure water and clean air, in the healthy human
> family, and in freedom from arbitrary political and social con-
> straints.
> The suburb has acquired some of the values of the country.
> The ideal image of suburban living focuses now on nature and
> health, now on the family, now on the freedom to organize
> one's own life. [Tuan, 1974, p. 236]

The image of suburbia as a place to escape urban pollution
and congestion was greatly encouraged by land developers
and real estate interests, especially during the 1950s and
early 1960s.

Transportation and Distance Constraints. Regardless of the
need for space and the suburban image, American suburban
growth would not have taken place on a large scale without
the widespread use of the automobile and the development of
major highway systems. The creation of such highway
systems was largely the result of government subsidization.
The interaction between the private sector in constructing
homes and the public sector in subsidizing transportation and
housing purchases, combined with the population growth,
was responsible for the post–Second World War evolution of
suburbia.

It was not until the enactment of the Federal Aid Highway
Act of 1944 that the government began large-scale programs
of highway construction. A government program had been
established in 1916 to provide assistance to places with a
population under 2,500, and highway improvement programs had been designed to generate employment in the
1930s, but those programs had only a relatively minor impact
on the development of major highway systems (Owen, 1970).
The Federal Aid Highway Act of 1944, however, allocated
$125 million per year for three years for the construction of
highway systems in urban areas.

One of the major developments stemming from the 1944 legislation was a recommendation that called for a federally subsidized program to develop a national system of interstate highways to connect metropolitan areas, cities, and industrial areas. The result of this recommendation was the Federal Aid Highway Act of 1956, which created a national system of interstate and defense highways. A principal objective of the national interstate system was to decongest urban areas, and it was estimated that nearly 50 percent of the total expenditure went toward that goal (Smerk, 1965). Approximately 90 percent of the costs of the national interstate system were defrayed by the federal government, thus local suburban communities did not directly pay for the transportation systems that provided the accessibility essential for suburban growth (see Figure 9.1).

To assess the impact of the transportation system on suburban growth, it is essential to consider both the transportation system itself and the factor of distance from the central city

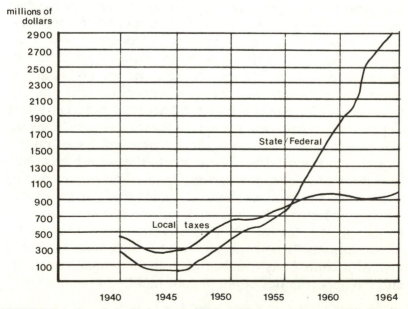

FIGURE 9.1. Trends in Financing of Urban Highways. Source: U.S. Department of Commerce, Bureau of Public Roads, Highway Statistics Division, *Highway Finances, 1921–1962* (Washington, D.C., 1964), Tables HF-1 and HF-2.

to the place of residence. Studies dealing with transportation often directly relate the development of the spatial pattern of suburban growth and urban expansion to the evolution of transportation systems. This conclusion implies a basic skeletal structure established by fixed-rail transit, for example, and an interstitial filling of this skeletal structure as methods of transportation become more personal and more flexible.

Of equal importance is the question of the distance the commuter has the ability or desire to travel from home to work place. It should be noted that the length of the commute from home to work is measurable in terms of economic costs, time, and emotional stress in addition to being measurable in linear distance. A consideration of these various measures and the perceptions of the commute to the work place is important. In the later part of the 1970s, the rising cost of fuel meant that distance began to be measured in economic terms, as it is likely to be in the foreseeable future.

The fundamental influences associated with the move to the suburb—life cycle and population increase, perception and environmental stress, and transportation and distance—must not be considered as independent and unrelated. These elements function as interworking components of a system that has created the need, desire, and ability to settle on the fringes of cities. It is interesting that employment and trade, two of the factors that have been extremely important in a historical context in drawing people to the urban region, have not been the factors that have "pulled" migrants to the suburbs. The move to the suburb has traditionally been related only indirectly to employment; that is, the suburb has been a locational choice made from a set of dwelling place alternatives and not as a direct result of employment in the suburb. This was largely the situation until the late 1960s and the 1970s, at which time the trend toward a central-city-to-suburbia shift in economic activity and job opportunities began to gain rapidly in momentum.

The Suburbanization of Economic Activity

The rapid rise of economic activity in the suburbs is one of the most important elements in the evolution of the suburb from "bedroom community" to urban place. The trend toward increasing suburban economic activity did not exist only in the late 1960s and 1970s. Rather, it was one part of the process of the changing economic function of the suburb that began when the first American suburbs served as locations for economic activities. The factor that distinguishes economic functioning in the suburbs since 1940 from that of earlier times is the magnitude of the growth in a wide variety of economic activities that followed the Second World War.

Employment Trends. One indicator of the rapid suburban economic growth is the relative proportion of the total number of jobs available in the suburb as opposed to the central city. An examination of available employment in the suburbs indicates not only that a significant increase in the proportion of suburban jobs occurred between 1960 and 1970 but also that this shift was a nationwide phenomenon (see Table 9.2).

Employment increased in the suburbs because a near-total range of types of economic activity were relocating or being

TABLE 9.2
Percentage Suburban Share of Total Jobs

SMSA	Percent Total Jobs 1960	Percent Total Jobs 1970
New York	28.8	35.9
Los Angeles	47.8	54.3
Chicago	32.2	47.5
Philadelphia	37.0	51.8
Detroit	43.3	61.4
San Francisco	44.9	50.0
Washington, D.C.	36.2	54.9
Boston	55.5	62.2
Pittsburgh	64.0	63.7
St. Louis	39.3	58.0
Baltimore	34.1	49.9
Cleveland	28.3	46.0
Houston	15.7	24.4
Minneapolis-St. Paul	23.6	41.1
Dallas	24.4	29.0
AVERAGE	37.0	47.6

Source: J. Rosenthal, "The Rapid Growth of Suburban Employment," in L. Musotti and J. Hadden, eds., Suburbia in Transition (New York: New York Times, 1974), pp. 95-100.

TABLE 9.3
Annual Percentage Increase in Population and Employment by Category, 1958-1967

Population 1960-1970	Employment 1958-1967			
	Manufacturing	Retail	Wholesale	Services
Central City				
.6	.7	.8	1.1	2.6
Suburban Ring				
2.2	3.1	5.3	7.4	6.1

Source: U.S. Bureau of the Census. Employment and Population Changes
Standard Metropolitan Statistical Areas and Central Cities. Special Economic
Reports, Series ES20 (72)-1 (Washington, D.C., 1972).

newly established in suburbia. There was, however, considerably more encouragement from most suburban municipalities for the establishment of "clean industries" (nonpolluting), which is reflected in the substantial growth in the wholesale and service sectors (see Table 9.3).

Suburbanization of Retail, Wholesale, and Corporate Activities. A wide range of factors acted to either force or induce the establishment or relocation of economic activities in the suburbs. A large and rapidly growing population meant major markets came into existence in suburbia, markets that were served by increasing numbers of retailers.

A significant aspect of the relocation of retail activity, especially since the late 1940s, was the clustering of retail establishments in "shopping centers." Suburban population growth, combined with rapidly rising retail sales, attracted great numbers of retail and service establishments to suburban shopping centers. The culmination of this pattern was in the development of the suburban shopping mall, a massive collection of shops generally centered around one or two anchor establishments, usually large department stores (see Figure 9.2). The establishment of large shopping malls produced a significant change in the pattern of retail activity in the urban region. The advent of the regional shopping mall allowed for the evolution of a noncentric pattern of major retail activity within the urban region, featuring a variety of suburban shopping areas as opposed to the once-traditional

FIGURE 9.2. Lakewood Center, Lakewood, California. Courtesy of Lakewood Center Merchants Association.

single downtown shopping district that served both the city and the suburbs.

A second aspect of the process that acted to create noncentric economic activity patterns was the phenomenon of manufacturing and wholesaling industries locating in the suburbs. The factors that influenced their locating there were mainly the upward spiral of central city land costs, congestion, increasingly difficult transportation access, and decline in the availability of all but vertical space. The suburb offered abundant land, generally at low cost, in some instances tax incentives for nonpolluting industries, and efficient transportation systems (Figure 9.3). Some suburban communities were considered to be prestigious locations, which acted as an additional pulling force to induce some types of wholesaling and manufacturing to locate in the suburbs.

The importance of a prestigious location and the corporate image were also major factors in the shift of many corporate operations to the suburbs. The suburb offered a counterpoint to the standard high-rise office building, and the availability of space made possible a variety of building types. The "campus" type of structure or the single-floor sprawling "ranch" pattern are examples of the alternatives to the high-rise, and there was the additional possibility of environmental amenities such as parklike landscaping. The corporate move

FIGURE 9.3. Suburban Transportation System. Source: HUD.

to the suburb was also influenced by the residential trends that created a managerial and an executive labor force in the suburb. All these factors, along with innovations in communication systems and the trend toward a decline in the need for "face to face" communication in many of the subheadquarter-level functions of some organizations, made the suburbs an attractive place for corporate location.

The suburban landscape of the 1970s presented a marked contrast to the suburbs of the 1930s through the early 1960s. Although census data and related research present the quantitative assessment of the evolution of the suburban function from "bedroom community" to "outer city," evidence of this change in form and function is also obtainable from simple observation. The most prominent feature of the suburban landscape of the 1940s through the early 1960s was the single-family detached home. The tremendous growth in population and economic activity that began in the 1960s and is continuing has altered the American suburban landscape

FIGURE 9.4. Recent Developments in Suburbia. Source: HUD.

in such a way that office buildings, industrial parks, large-scale shopping malls, and multiple-unit dwellings are now found along most suburban highways (Figure 9.4). The results of the evolution of the twentieth-century American suburb are apparent not only in the modification of the physical environment but also in the changing social and spatial composition of the suburb.

The Social Evolution of Suburbia

A great many indicators that reflect the changing nature of suburban social and economic structure have been identified by urban scientists. Patterns of complex social interaction in suburbia as well as an increasing diversity in social groups and economic activities are typical of the suburbs of the post–Second World War period.

Community Status and Social Interaction. In the late 1950s and early 1960s, the popular stereotype of the suburbs as the home of a rather homogeneous population of middle-class white, Republican Protestants began to give way to a more comprehensive view of the socioeconomic diversity of suburbia. Academic study that focuses on the social interaction and network linkages—both measures of social complexity—of the suburb of the 1970s reflects the growing awareness of the intricacy of suburban social and spatial organization.

The study of suburban social interaction can be organized into topic areas according to the level on which the investigation was undertaken. The broadest level of inquiry is the consideration of the degree and type of interaction at the general urban, rural, or suburban scale. Research conducted on the urban level has often been concerned with the correlation between urban problems and community size.

The analysis of social interaction on the neighborhood level has generally been considered to be the most detailed, and such analysis has played an integral part in dispelling many suburban stereotypes. One of the early conceptions of the suburb, for instance, was that social interaction on the neighborhood level was wide-ranging, frequent, intimate, and provided the major part of all social contacts. Investigation of neighborhood interaction has revealed that in reality, social contact was often fairly limited in the neighborhood and family and work-related friendships were greater factors in interaction than was mere proximity to neighbors.

Social interaction has been considered from a geographical perspective in a wide range of studies. Investigations of social interaction and the socioeconomic diversity of suburbs have revealed that there was a trend in the 1970s toward a complexity of organization and activity once associated only with the central city. The social structure of the central city, however, does remain distinctly different from that of the suburb with respect to the ethnic component of the population. This difference remains true even though by the 1970s suburbs were beginning to show evidence of a trend toward a larger, but not necessarily integrated, ethnic population.

Ethnicity, Race, and Exclusion. The nonwhite population of the suburbs has increased somewhat since the Second World War. In general, the nonwhite residents of the suburbs are not dispersed and intermixed but are highly concentrated into spatially restricted areas.

The processes of selection that maintain homogeneous areas in the suburbs have been investigated in great detail. The practices of outright discrimination in housing, exclusionary zoning, "red-lining" (refusal to loan money for home purchase in certain areas), and building requirements that eliminate all but the rich have been prevalent throughout this century. The communities surrounding Detroit, Michigan, offer a case study of the dynamics of nonwhite residential structure in the suburbs. Schnore and others discovered that the patterns found in the Detroit SMSA closely paralleled occurrences observed in the twelve largest SMSAs (Schnore, Andre, and Sharp, 1976, pp. 83–90).

If one considers the more than sixty communities surrounding Detroit in Wayne, Oakland, and Macomb counties, only six of them have a significant proportion of nonwhites. Evident in the analysis of those Michigan cities is a pattern of a very slight shift of nonwhites to suburban cities between 1960 and 1970.

Examination of the cities used in the Schnore study shows two cases of major fluctuations in the nonwhite suburban population (see Table 9.4). The city of Ecorse lost nonwhite population between 1960 and 1970, apparently because of the destruction of older housing units. Inkster saw a reduction in its nonwhite population as the result of new housing construction, which attracted whites, so the percentage of nonwhites fell.

Hamtramck and Highland Park are actually enclaves of Detroit. Schnore found that nonwhites left Hamtramck between 1960 and 1970 because, "to put it most bluntly, blacks do not find it a friendly city" (Schnore, Andre, and Sharp, 1976, p. 88). Conversely, Highland Park increased in nonwhite population because of positive social circumstances (Schnore, Andre, and Sharp, 1976).

Any attempt to determine the future of nonwhite subur-

TABLE 9.4
Size and Color Composition of Urban Municipalities in the Ring of the
Detroit SMSA, 1960-1970

	Total Population		Nonwhite (%)	
Municipality	1960	1970	1960	1970
Allen Park	36,874	40,747	*	0.6
Berkley	23,237	22,618	*	0.4
Beverly Hills+	8,644	13,598	*	0.6
Birmingham	25,415	26,170	*	0.5
Bloomfield Hills	2,294	3,672	*	1.9
Center Line	10,161	10,379	*	0.1
Clawson	14,744	17,617	*	0.4
Dearborn	111,863	104,199	*	0.4
Dearborn Heights	Uninc.‡	80,069	...	0.4
Drayton Plains	Uninc.	16,462	...	0.2
East Detroit	45,717	45,920	*	0.3
Ecorse	11,559	17,515	49.9	38.8
Farmington	6,877	13,337	*	0.2
Ferndale	31,206	30,850	*	0.7
Flat Rock+	4,694	5,643	*	0.6
Franklin	2,645	3,344	*	0.3
Fraser	7,026	11,868	*	0.3
Garden City+	37,940	41,864	*	0.4
Gibraltar	2,196	3,325	*	0.3
Grosse Isle	6,284	7,799	*	0.4
Grosse Pointe	6,594	6,637	*	0.5
Grosse Pointe Farms	12,063	11,701	*	0.6
Grosse Pointe Park	15,372	15,585	*	0.5
Grosse Pointe Shores	2,147	3,042	*	0.6
Grosse Pointe Woods	18,558	21,878	*	0.1
Hamtramck ++	29,199	27,245	16.9	12.5
Harper Woods	19,968	23,784	*	0.3
Hazel Park	25,582	23,784	*	0.5
Highland Park ++	29,900	35,444	27.3	56.9
Huntington Woods	8,634	8,536	*	0.6
Inkster	25,528	38,595	53.1	44.9
Keego Harbor	2,755	3,092	*	0.5
Lincoln Park	53,871	52,984	*	0.4
Livonia	66,562	110,109	*	0.4
Madison Heights	33,257	38,559	*	0.5

*Less than 0.05%
+Minor annexations between 1960 and 1970.
‡"Uninc." indicates that the municipality was unincorporated in 1960.
++Enclaves of Detroit.
...Data not available

Reprinted from Barry Schwartz, The Changing Face of the Suburbs
(Chicago: University of Chicago Press, 1976), p. 89, by permission of The University of Chicago Press.

banization is a most difficult task. Some people argue that as the mass-produced suburban houses of the early 1950s physically deteriorate, the accompanying potential for blight may result in a flight from the older suburbs. This possibility coupled with inner-city redevelopment could create a pattern in which lower income groups, or those otherwise restricted from housing markets, would be forced to locate in suburbs and central city sites would be highly desirable. This dynamic would be a reversal of the current pattern.

The possibility of massive black and other nonwhite suburbanization is raised by some urban scientists. Many who take that position predict that the pattern of middle-income and upper-income nonwhite movement to the suburbs will accelerate. Another school of thought is that the jury is still out on the question of nonwhite suburbanization and judgment should be reserved. Human behavior is difficult to predict, thus great danger exists in extrapolating the short-term evidence now available into long-term projections.

What happens in the long run is subject to conjecture; however recent trends of nonwhite movement to the suburbs and, in some cases, the return of whites to the central city have been documented. One of the inevitable results of non-white movement into suburbia should be the final dispelling of the myths and stereotypes that for decades have shrouded it.

Black Suburbanization Since 1970. Data from the Census Bureau's current population survey show that a turnaround in net migration of blacks into central cities has occurred since 1973 (see Table 9.5). Whereas immigration rates remained about the same for the 1970–1973 and 1975–1978 periods, the shift resulted from an increase in the rate of out-migration from the central city. As Kathryn Nelson noted,

> Because black rates of suburban immigration rose while rates of outmigration fell, there was a sharp increase in net black migration into suburbs. Black rates of migration to and from nonmetropolitan areas changed little. Therefore, the suburban immigration increase clearly reflected the increased flow

TABLE 9.5
Rates of In, Out and Net Migration for Central Cities and Suburbs by Race,
1970–1973 and 1975–1978

	Whites		Blacks	
	1970–73	1975–78	1970–73	1975–78
Central Cities				
Inmigration rate	12.4	13.7	8.1	8.5
Outmigration rate	−21.0	−22.6	−7.8	−11.4
Net migration rate	−8.6	−8.9	+0.3	−2.9
Suburbs				
Inmigration rate	17.8	17.4	19.5	25.8
Outmigration rate	−13.3	−13.2	−17.7	−13.5
Net migration rate	+4.5	+4.2	+1.8	+12.2
Nonmetropolitan areas				
Inmigration rate	8.4	8.3	3.8	4.6
Outmigration rate	−6.4	−6.4	−5.7	−5.9
Net migration rate	+2.0	+1.9	−1.9	−1.3

Source: U.S. Bureau of the Census, Current Population Reports, "Mobility of the Population of the U.S.," Series P-20, No. 262 (March 1974) and No. 331 (November 1978).

from central cities, although the percentage change appears larger for the suburbs because of the smaller black population base there. [Nelson, 1979, p. 8]

Although at first glance it appears that more blacks indeed are now sharing that American dream of a suburban home, we need to look more closely at black suburbanization patterns during the 1970s. Two trends, often interrelated, should be mentioned here. First, many blacks are moving into the older suburbs that have been or are being evacuated by whites as they seek newer suburban homes. Second, there is mounting evidence to suggest that gentrification, the movement of predominately young, white professionals into renovated central city areas, is displacing black and other minority central city residents, many of whom then choose older suburban locations.

In one recent study of black suburbanization Clay found

that "The neighborhoods in which blacks are in moderate to high concentrations (including new ones) share certain striking physical and socioeconomic resemblances to the declining central-city neighborhood they left behind" (Clay, 1979, p. 414). He noted that higher concentrations of blacks in suburban areas were associated with lower income, lower educational levels, higher unemployment rates, and relatively lower property values. Noting also that poorer blacks appear to be concentrating in suburban areas with high black concentrations, Clay suggested that "black suburban migrants become replacement cohorts in older suburbs from which large numbers of whites fled" (Clay, 1979, p. 416). The data in Table 9.6 support Clay's arguments.

During the 1970s gentrification increased as numerous central city areas were renovated and became popular residences for young whites, most of whom were professional people. Places such as Queen's Village and Society Hill in Philadelphia, German Village in Columbus, Ohio, and Capitol Hill in Washington, D.C., have had influxes of new residents that have displaced the older neighborhood residents, especially members of various minorities. Gentrification has resulted in rapidly rising house prices and taxes, along with attracting boutiques and restaurants that cater to the increasingly affluent residents. Conflicts between older minority and newer white residents have been common occurrences.

In a study of residential change in Fairmount, a small area in Philadelphia's inner city, Roman Cybriwsky found that gentrification depended on the exclusion of blacks from a neighborhood that was shifting from a working-class residential area to a fashionable one. He argued that "the most significant aspect of change in Fairmount is that for many residents the quality of life declined with the neighborhood's physical upgrading and higher socioeconomic standing" (Cybriwsky, 1978, p. 33). In Fairmount distinctive life-styles were declining. Although displacement is not currently the major cause of black suburbanization, it will remain a problem for blacks and other minorities throughout the decade of the 1980s.

Before going on, it should be pointed out that generalizations about black suburbanization must be viewed cau-

232

TABLE 9.6
Selected Characteristics of Non-South Suburban Neighborhoods by Percentage of Black Population, 1970
(percent of neighborhoods)

Characteristic	Percent Black	Type 1 None	Type 2 LE 5%	Type 3 6–14%	Type 4 15–24%	Type 5 25–49%	Type 6 50+%
1. High proportion of children (GT 40%)		35	21	15	14	23	48
2. High proportion of elderly (GT 10%)		25	35	38	51	42	22
3. Median income exceeds $10,000 per year		91	85	66	73	58	36
4. Median education is greater than 12 years		14	20	16	7	2	1
5. Unemployment rate greater than 4% (1970)		32	34	36	44	61	78
6. More than 45% of adult women in labor force		24	31	33	38	49	60
7. More than 50% of owner-occupied units valued at $25,000 or more		34	34	37	23	12	9
8. Vacancies in rental and sale units exceeds 5%		6	5	5	4	13	21
9. More than 20% of units built since 1960		54	50	42	40	26	22
10. More than 30% of the housing units built before 1939		28	53	63	71	70	61

Source: U.S. Bureau of the Census, Public Use Samples of Basic Records from 1970 Census (Washington, D.C.: U.S. Government Printing Office, 1972), p. 415.

TABLE 9.7
The Diverse Patterns of Black Suburbanization, 1955-1976

Similarity/Disparity Between Black and White Patterns Over Time

Level of black suburbanization	Increasingly wide disparities	Continued wide disparities	Decreasing but still wide disparities	Decreasing to moderate disparities	Decreasing to roughly similar	Continued similarity
High all three periods					Washington	Miami Los Angeles
Increasing to high				Atlanta San Francisco*	Cleveland Newark St. Louis	
Increasing to moderate			Baltimore	Pittsburgh Cincinnati		
Low with slight increase		Detroit Dallas Chicago			Philadelphia	
Always low	Houston	Boston New York New Orleans				

*San Francisco is unique in having both moderate levels of black suburbanization and moderate disparities between black and white movement for all three time periods.

Source: Kathyrn P. Nelson, Recent Suburbanization of Blacks: How Much, Who, and Where, Annual Housing Survey Studies, No. 1 (Washington, D.C.: U.S. Department of Housing and Urban Development, 1979), p. 27.

tiously. Within various cities patterns of black suburbanization differ. Table 9.7 provides evidence of the diversity of
patterns that exist in the level of and change in black suburbanization and the disparities that exist between blacks and
whites in their choice of suburban residences.

THE IMAGE OF SUBURBIA: FROM SUBURBAN
SADNESS TO THE SUBURBAN CITY

Why were the suburbs singled out for such unrelenting attacks during the two decades following the Second World
War by writers representing a wide range of academic disciplines? Were the suburbs of the 1950s, 1960s, and early 1970s
simply monotonous collections of upper- and middle-class
families who, upon taking up residence in a suburb, adhered
to all the expectations of the "suburban stereotype"? From the
latter question comes the question posed by Bennett M.
Berger, "Why should a group of tract houses, mass produced
and quickly thrown up on the outskirts of a large city, apparently generate so uniform a way of life?" (Berger, 1968, p.
7).

In order to deal with these questions, it is necessary to consider the suburban stereotype of uniformity of life and to
study the reasons for such generalizations and the issue of the
validity of the suburban stereotype. These are necessary considerations for preserving the "social composition" of suburbia and the protection of "suburban life-styles," often cited as
arguments in favor of growth controls in many suburban
communities. It is therefore valuable to question the validity
of the concept of the uniform suburban life-style. This investigation is important even today in order to study the impacts of growth restriction in the suburb. If the social composition of the suburb is as homogeneous as proponents of the
stereotype have claimed, then the socioeconomic impacts of
growth controls should be relatively uniform. However, if a
substantial socioeconomic heterogeneity exists in suburban
populations, then the impacts of growth controls could vary
according to socioeconomic status. Therefore, the stereotype,

true or false, becomes a worthwhile consideration for more reasons than pure academic interest.

The Suburban Sadness: Its Composition and Reason for Existence

The socioeconomic stereotype of the suburb has often been referred to as "the suburban sadness." Dobriner (1958, pp. 275-298) summarized the stereotype of the contemporary American suburb as being composed of the following ten central themes.

1. Warrens of young executives on the way up
2. Uniformly middle class
3. "Homogeneous"
4. Hotbeds of participation
5. Child centered and female dominated
6. Transient
7. Wellsprings of the outgoing life
8. Areas of adjustment
9. Beulah lands of returns of religion
10. Political Jordans from which Democrats emerge Republicans

Dobriner found that to many observers, "suburbia is the melancholia of those whose individuality has succumbed to the inexorable pressures of the organization, bureaucracy, mass culture, uniformity, conformity, monotony – the symptoms of a false egalitarianism, mistaken as social democracy" (Dobriner, 1958, p. 6).

Consideration of the popular writings of the decades of the 1950s and 1960s, as well as an investigation of the more-traditional academic literature, reinforces Dobriner's observations of the image of suburbia. Popular as well as academic literature is replete with such terms as

homogeneity; conformity; destruction of diversity; middle class; land of conformity; dullness; dormitories; materialism; protestant; philistinism; "My God all the houses look the same"; budgets that remain constantly beyond income levels; terrible anxieties; tremendously demanding schedules; women envious of the professional and social outlets available to their husbands in the city; extramarital sexual activities or drinking; relaxation at full speed; an abundance of psychosomatic ills; forced participating and homogeneity; a surface facade of health and happiness covering despair and mental disturbances; (overly) intense "Family life" weekends; preoccupation of the male with business success and the female with housewife-community success; the fragmentation of the life cycle. [Bell, 1968, p. 144]

The image of suburban "sameness" can be found, at least as a secondary theme, in works purporting to illustrate the socioeconomic diversity of the suburbs. In John Cheever's short story "The Five-Forty-Eight," the notion of repetitiveness is in evidence in the following discussion of the way suburbanites dress. "He dressed like the rest of us—as if he admitted the existence of sumptuary laws. His raincoat was the pale buff color of a mushroom. His hat was dark brown; so was his suit. Except for a few bright threads in his necktie, there was a scrupulous lack of color in his clothing that seemed protective" (Cheever, 1958, p. 94). In many other writings, both scholarly and popular, the theme of the suburban stereotype is common.

Other works clearly illustrate the propagation of the suburban stereotype. In *Crestwood Heights* (subtitled *A Study in the Culture of Suburban Life)* Seeley, Sims, and Loosley attempted to study the physical environment of the suburb as it related to the total range of psychological and social activities of the residents of Crestwood Heights, a wealthy suburb near Toronto, Canada (Seeley, Sims, and Loosley, 1967). From the front cover (which in the 1967 printing consists of caricatures of houses that are identical in shape and size, different only in color, with the expressionless face of a woman used as the front of one house) to the back cover (which claims that Crestwood Heights is like any other suburb, e.g., Scarsdale, Park Forest, or San Mateo), the residents of Crestwood Heights attempt to justify the suburban stereotype. The authors maintained, for example, that "to the people of Crestwood Heights, the career is of all concerns the most momentous. It may be called 'success,' or 'getting ahead,' or 'doing well,' whatever its name, it is thematic to the mythology of the Western World" (Seeley, Sims, and Loosley, 1967, p. 113). Throughout the book, the authors painted a picture of a community filled with inhabitants who have only the narrowest of perspectives on life and the fundamental goal of attaining the sterotyped suburban life-style.

Whether the researchers' assessments of the individuals of Crestwood Heights in particular are correct or not, a significant problem arises from the work. It would seem that for many people Crestwood Heights is not simply representative of one upper-socioeconomic-class community, but instead is typical of all of suburbia. The generalizations drawn from the work are applied not only to high-status areas but to the entire range of suburban environments. The study, in any case, has had a significant influence on suburban social science writings. Thus, it has been an important element in establishing the notion that all suburban residents hold the same values and maintain the same activity patterns.

In one of the best-known works that helps foster the stereotype of suburbia, *The Crack in the Picture Window*, John Keats attacked nearly every aspect of suburbia (Keats, 1957). Keats viewed the creation of suburbia as the work of get-rich-quick developers, who produced "identical boxes spreading like gangrene" throughout the countryside (Keats, 1957, p. xi). Keats's estimation of those who would reside in such "boxes" (Figure 9.5) is best summarized by the names he invented for an imaginary couple who move to the suburbs, John and Mary Drone.

William Whyte viewed the suburbs as "dormitories" housing the classless society who work for "the organization" (Whyte, 1956). The organization (any large employer of a collective work force) molds its workers into conformity throughout the work day. When the suburbanites return to "the front lawns of their suburbia," this process of stifling human individuality continues unabated, in part because of the lack of any real individual differences in the physical or

FIGURE 9.5. Suburban Image, Daly City, California. Source: HUD.

cultural environment of "the dormitory suburb" (Whyte, 1956, p. 300).

Whyte acknowledged the possibility that socioeconomic groups other than the middle or upper-middle classes may enter suburbia, calling suburbia the "second great melting pot." Whyte went on to conclude, however, that because suburban residents like to maintain that their suburbia not only looks classless but is classless, the non-middle classes must be transformed and assimilated.

> The organization man provides the model, and even in the suburbs where he is a minority he is influential out of all proportion to his numbers. As the newcomers to the middle class enter suburbia, they must discard old values, and their sensitivity to those of the organization man is almost statistically demonstrable. [Whyte, 1956, pp. 299–300]

The underlying theme of *The Organization Man* suggests that the product of the union between employment by the "organization" and the ecological functioning of the suburb as a place of residence has destroyed the autonomy of the individual.

Suburbia: Old Communities on New Land

The stereotype of the American suburb has been attacked as inaccurate, self-contradicting, and often illogical. The contention, found throughout *The Organization Man* and *Crestwood Heights*, that the physical environment is a causal factor in the perceived change in behavior of residents as they enter the suburbs has been thoroughly examined by Berger in his study of auto workers in suburbia (Berger, 1960). He has suggested that the suburban stereotype is actually atypical. As a counterpoint to Whyte's notion that the middle-class, church-going Republican became the model for behavioral change by the non-middle-class suburbanite, Berger found that few changes in life-style were precipitated by the move to the suburb. He argued that

> they were still overwhelmingly Democrats, they attended church as infrequently as they ever did; like most working class people, their informal contacts were largely limited to kin; they neither gave nor went to parties; on the whole they had no great hopes of getting ahead in their jobs; and instead of a transient psychology, most of them harbored a view of their new suburban home as a paradise permanently gained. [Berger, 1968, p. 435]

The underlying theme of Berger's study is best summarized in the contention that "the reported changes in the lives of suburbanites were not caused by the move to the suburb, but were the reasons for moving there in the first place" (Berger, 1960, p. 436).

Herbert Gans, in studying a particular suburban community, arrived at four primary conclusions, and he maintained that his conclusions could be "generalized to new towns and suburbs all over America" (Gans, 1967, p. 408). In observing the evolution of the social organization of a suburban community, Gans first concluded that the builder creates only the physical shell. The residents' choices as to friendships and activities involve values and preferences that new residents bring with them, therefore such choices are not a function of a particular physical environment. Second, Gans believed that the suburbanites are pleased with their homes and life-styles and, although lives were changed somewhat by the move to the suburb, the residents basically remained the same. Third, he noted that "the sources or causes of change are not to be found in suburbia per se, but in the new house, the opportunity for home ownership, and above all the population mix" (Gans, 1967, p. 409). Fourth, Gans stated that no new and unique aspects to life exist in the suburbs.

The final conclusion of Gans's work, *The Levittowners*, suggests that what happens in a community is a reflection of the people who live there, not purely the result of the physical environment or the influence of planners or civic leaders. In reporting on the evolution of Levittown, Pennsylvania, Gans reinforced the proposition that the behavioral patterns of new residents are established prior to coming to the suburbs and are not the result of the ecological organization of the suburb.

Why the Stereotype?

Given that the suburban stereotype is apparently inaccurate, why has there been such an attack on the suburbs as a place to live? A general consensus can be found among those people who study suburban phenomena that a major cause of the attack on the suburb was that the suburb failed to live up to the American dream. The American dream is traceable to the Jeffersonian ideal, the notion that the American settler should inhabit the farm and live removed from the problems and vices of the city. This theme is found throughout American literature and is typified in works such as Thoreau's *Walden*. The importance of the farm as a place to live was exemplified by Emerson, who said, "in giving him the strength and plain dignity like the face and manners of nature . . . all men keep the farm in reserve as an asylum" (Lindeman, 1954, p. 748). Hector St. John de Crèvecouer expressed the same sentiment, stating that "I therefore rest satisfied, and thank God that my lot is to be an American farmer" (de Crèvecouer, 1963, p. 27).

In *The Suburban Myth,* Donaldson made the association between the move to the suburbs and the desire for the perceived values of rural life (Donaldson, 1969). The basic premise of Donaldson's work is that the negative reaction to suburbia is largely the result of how intellectuals view the move from traditional urban settings to the suburb. Many believe that the mover goes in search of more-rural values and instead finds the conformity of suburban houses and lot sizes. Keats, for example, contrasted the repetitious housing tract with the good old days in the two- or three-story house on "Elm Street." Keats based much of his criticism of the suburb on the assumption that in going to the suburb the mover, instead of discovering a more-rural ideal, is cheated out of urban comfort. The desire to maintain at least the minimal aspects of a rural environment in the suburbs is at the heart of many of the current suburban growth restriction policies.

A second and more fundamental reason for the erroneous image of suburbia comes from a lack of understanding of the suburbs by those people who describe them. For example, it has been observed that "those who wrote about suburbia often adopted the supercilious, observer-from-Mars tone that had been characteristic of those who ventured forth in the dark slums of the nineteenth century city" (Glaab and Brown, 1976, p. 246). In addition to a general lack of detailed study of the suburbs by participant-observers, "the bandwagon effect" apparently created an atmosphere in which it became very fashionable to attack the suburbs, especially during the 1950s and 1960s.

No matter what the combination of factors was that led to the generally negative tone of academic studies of suburbia during the past twenty years, it should be understood that the negativism was in large measure responsible for the suburban stereotype. It must also be remembered that this stereotype of suburbia, although not entirely untrue in some limited cases, has been applied to a far greater range of suburban environments than was appropriate. Although criticism of the suburbs based on the social stereotype has waned, attacks on suburban development as a land use practice have intensified. The land use pattern created by suburbanization has many negative features.

SUBURBANIZATION AS A SPATIAL PROCESS

The most obvious manifestation of suburban growth is the low-density "sprawl" that covers the landscape. The pattern of alternating areas of suburban housing and open space is often referred to as "leapfrogging" (see Figure 9.6). Municipal annexation of land that is not contiguous with city boundaries is the primary cause of this checkerboard pattern.

The expansive sprawl of suburbia is costly in many respects. Each year the United States loses several million acres of agricultural land and open space on the fringes of cities to urban sprawl. The Santa Clara Valley, just south of San Francisco, California, once one of the most-productive agricultural regions in America is now virtually a total urban-suburban landscape (see Figure 9.7).

FIGURE 9.6. Variety of Suburban Land Use Patterns. Source: HUD.

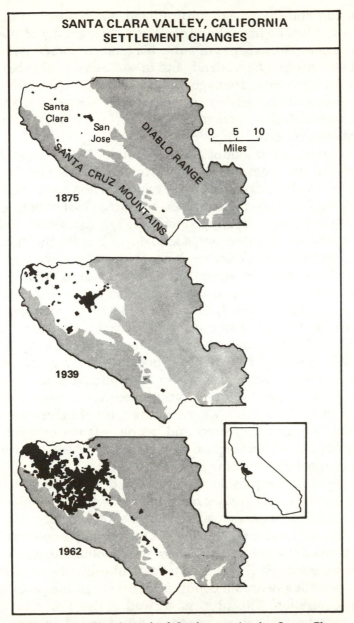

FIGURE 9.7. The Spread of Settlement in the Santa Clara Valley Since 1875. Reprinted from Jan O. M. Broek and John W. Webb, *A Geography of Mankind* (New York: McGraw-Hill, 1968), p. 399, by permission of McGraw-Hill Book Company.

In addition to lost agricultural land, vast suburban settlement has had an impact on the physical geography of the urban region. The expanse of suburbia tends to increase the effect of the urban heat island, and in some cases suburbanization has changed drainage patterns for an entire region.
Development on the fringe of a city can alter stream channels
and most definitely acts to "waterproof" the landscape, thus
increasing runoff.

Few researchers doubt that air pollution is substantially
increased by commuters who travel, often one to an
automobile, long distances from suburban homes to places of
work. Extensive commuting also consumes vast quantities of
fuel, which is becoming increasingly expensive. Public
transportation is often not adequate to handle the flow of
commuters to an urban center, so few alternatives to the
automobile exist in some cities. Suburban-to-urban commuting became an expensive proposition in the late 1970s as
the price of fuel soared, but during the 1980s economic activities are likely to continue to suburbanize.

The "flight to the suburbs," which began in the early 1950s
and is continuing, has impacted both the urban area, whose
residents were leaving, and the surrounding small towns.
The move to the suburb is often cited as a reason for the
decay of the inner city. As the desirability of inner-city residential locations decreased and people left the city for the
suburbs, a downward spiral in the attractiveness and condition of inner-city housing stock occurred.

A population explosion often occurred in the small towns
surrounding urban areas. The rapidly growing populations in
what were to become large suburbs often created great
demands on local school systems, utilities, and municipal services. Small towns on the fringe of metropolitan regions were
often transformed from compact agricultural service centers
into sprawling bedroom communities through the process of
suburbanization. This process, as well as the local residents'
reactions to such an occurrence, are detailed in the next
chapter.

It is tempting to paint a negative picture of suburban expansion as a land use practice; however, one inescapable positive

factor in the equation is that the American suburb satisfied a consumer demand. There would have been no suburban growth in the last part of this century had it not been for a favorable response by the home-buying public to the product created by the developers of suburbia.

The growth that created the suburbs has also been responsible for a rapidly growing desire on the part of many urban and suburban communities to restrict growth. As we shall see, many dramatic repercussions of growth restriction in the urban ecosystem are beginning to take place.

REFERENCES

Bell, W. 1968. "The City and the Suburb and a Theory of Social Choice." In S. Greer, ed., *The New Urbanization,* pp. 132–168. New York: St. Martin's Press.

Berger, B. 1968. *Working Class Suburbs.* Berkeley: University of California Press.

Cheever, J. 1958. *The Housebreaker of Shady Hill and Other Stories.* New York: MacFadden Books.

Clay, Phillip L. 1979. "The Process of Black Suburbanization." *Urban Affairs Quarterly* 14: 405–424.

Cybriwsky, Roman A. 1978. "Social Aspects of Neighborhood Change." *Annals of the Association of American Geographers* 68: 17–33.

de Crèvecoeur, J. Hector St. John. 1963. *Letters from an American Farmer.* New York: Signet Classics, New American Library of World Literature.

Dobriner, W., ed. 1958. *The Suburban Community.* New York: G. P. Putnam's Sons.

Donaldson, S. 1969. *The Suburban Myth.* New York: Columbia University Press.

Gans, Herbert. 1967. *The Levittowners: Ways of Life and Politics in a New Suburban Community.* New York: Vintage Books.

Glaab, C., and Brown, A. 1976. *A History of Urban America.* New York: Macmillan.

Johnson, J. H., ed. 1974. *Suburban Growth: Geographical Processes at the Edge of the Western City.* New York: John Wiley and Sons.

Keats, John. 1957. *The Crack in the Picture Window.* New York: Ballantine Books.

Lindeman, E., ed. 1954. *Basic Selections from Emerson.* New York: Mentor, New American Library.

Muller, P. 1976. *The Outer City: Geographical Consequences of the Urbanization of the Suburbs.* Resource Paper No. 75.2. Washington, D.C.: Association of American Geographers.

Nelson, Kathryn P. 1979. *Recent Suburbanization of Blacks: How Much, Who, and Where.* Annual Housing Survey Studies No. 1. Washington, D.C.: Department of Housing and Urban Development.

Owen, W. 1970. *The Metropolitan Transportation Dilemma.* Washington, D.C.: Brookings Institution.

Schnore, L.; Andre, C.; and Sharp, H. 1976. "Black Suburbanization 1930–1970." In B. Schwartz, ed., *The Changing Face of the Suburbs,* pp. 69–94. Chicago: University of Chicago Press.

Schwartz, B., ed. 1976. *The Changing Face of the Suburbs.* Chicago: University of Chicago Press.

Seeley, J.; Sims, R. A.; and Loosley, F. 1967. *Crestwood Heights.* New York: John Wiley and Sons.

Smerk, G. 1965. *Urban Transportation: The Federal Role.* Bloomington: Indiana University Press.

Tuan, Yi-Fu. 1974. *Topophilia.* Englewood Cliffs, N.J.: Prentice-Hall.

Whyte, William. 1956. *The Organization Man.* New York: Simon and Schuster.

10

Growth Restriction in the Metropolitan System

The rapid growth of population in the suburbs and the associated demand for housing have had a tremendous impact on both the landscape of suburban America and the attitudes of its residents. The proliferation of housing units and commercial establishments have presented the suburbanite with the possibility of residing in an urbanlike setting. However, many suburban residents believe that there is a distinct possibility that the quality of the suburban environment may deteriorate, the quality that some associate with good health, a clean environment, and a positive child-rearing situation. This perception has been instrumental in prompting an attitude toward suburban growth that has had profound implications for the entirety of the American urban realm, a widespread sentiment for restricting growth in the suburban communities. The goal of most growth-restriction policies has been to protect the environmental and economic stability of suburbia, to keep it a refuge from the perceived ills of the city.

There have always been practices of exclusion in the suburbs. Economic and racial segregation, both de facto and de jure, have been important parts of the mechanisms that have created suburban social areas. The current movement for restricted growth goes beyond any previous exclusion in that, theoretically, no entry into the community is permitted, although in reality, "no" means some limited number of entrants. This chapter deals with growth limitation from several perspectives: the contrast with past exclusionary zoning; why growth is controlled and how control is accomplished; where growth control is practiced and what legal issues are involved; and the impacts of growth restriction on a community.

GROWTH RESTRICTION AND MIGRATION

It is essential to clarify two commonly held, but erroneous, assumptions concerning growth limitation. First, the term most often used to describe growth limitation policies or communities that enact such policies, no-growth or no-growth communities—such as Petaluma, California—actually means some limited growth per year. The terms *growth restriction* or *growth limitation* are therefore far more accurate assessments of what growth control, as practiced in the suburban United States, encompasses.

Growth limitation does not necessarily mean any restriction on in- or outmigration as long as no net increase occurs beyond the growth ceiling. Thus, movers may enter a community as replacements for outmigrants (see Table 10.1). With this dynamic equilibrium, however, it may be possible to greatly alter the socioeconomic composition of the growth limitation community if the characteristics of the inmigrants differ greatly from those of the outmigrants. A variety of factors must be examined in the investigation of growth restriction in the urban ecosystem.

THE CLOSED SUBURB: EXCLUSIONARY PRACTICES AND SPATIAL ORGANIZATION

Policies of restricting the entry of certain groups have been practiced for a considerable length of time. Many forces have acted to create segregated and distinct social areas in cities and suburbs, using processes that range from the relative subtlety of the practices of information agents and institutional investors in excluding a particular group from an area to the most overt cases of residents in a neighborhood intimidating some potential immigrants. The strategies employed to

TABLE 10.1
Migration Rates for Several Growth-Limiting Cities and Comparison Cities Without Major Growth

| City | 1973 Population | Annual migration rates per 100 residents in 1973 | | | | | | |
| | | Inmigration | | Outmigration | | Net Migration | | |
		1970-73 (1)	1973-75 (2)	1970-73 (3)	1973-75 (4)	1970-73 (5)	1973-75 (6)	Dif (7)
Growth-limiting cities								
Petaluma, Calif.	31,700	11.3	10.0	8.3	9.5	3.0	0.5	-2.5
Livermore, Calif.	46,200	11.0	11.0	7.3	9.0	3.7	2.0	-1.7
Boulder, Colo.	75,300	11.0	12.5	9.3	12.0	1.7	0.5	-1.2
St. Petersburg, Fla.	234,000	9.3	9.0	6.3	7.5	3.0	1.5	-1.5
Boca Raton, Fla.	38,200	16.0	16.0	9.7	9.5	6.3	6.5	+0.2
Comparison cities without major growth								
San Pablo, Calif.	21,700	10.0	12.0	12.0	14.5	-2.0	-2.5	-0.5
Redlands, Calif.	37,200	9.0	10.0	9.3	10.5	-0.3	-0.5	-0.2
Waterloo, Iowa	73,900	4.7	5.5	6.0	6.0	-1.3	-0.5	+0.8
Tampa, Fla.	276,000	7.7	8.5	7.3	9.0	0.3	-0.5	-0.8
Urbana, Ill.	33,500	12.0	13.5	13.3	15.5	-1.3	-2.0	-0.7

Source: P. Morrison, Migration and Rights of Access: New Public Concerns of the 1970's (Santa Monica, Calif.:
Rand Corporation, 1977), p. 13, based on data from U.S. Bureau of the Census, Current Population Reports, "Special
Migration Tabulations Based on Administrative Records, Estimates of 1973 Population."

restrict people from moving into a community often vary with the socioeconomic status of the neighborhood.

In upper-income suburbs, the process of exclusion has been principally one of economics, reinforced by zoning and construction requirements. In the upper-income suburb, the quality of and amenities found in the housing stock and local environment generally create a high value per dwelling unit. All but the upper-income buyer are thus eliminated from purchasing a home. In addition, exclusive suburbs have created high-value dwelling units through the practice of requiring large lots, often a minimum of one to five acres, for each single-family dwelling.

The middle-income suburb, with its attendant range of house prices, is most often the target for entry. Because of the lack of protection by purely market functions, the process of exclusion in middle-income suburbia is most often "defense from within." The middle-class communities, though in other ways extremely casual in social interaction networks, have often become tightly knit alliances when it comes to discouraging nondesired inmigration.

Whereas movement into the upper- and middle-income suburbs is difficult for "nondesirable" movers, the lower- and working-class suburban sectors are often more accessible. The move into a particular "sector," as opposed to a "community," does not simply mean that movers have a free choice of locational alternatives in any desired neighbhorhood. Accessibility generally means opportunity to enter an already established, spatially restricted ethnic or racial social area within the same sector of the suburbs as the lower socioeconomic groups (Blumberg and Lulli, 1966).

The pattern of black and Mexican-American movement into the suburbs of Los Angeles, California, is a prime example of the restrictions placed on some people by the general suburban restriction process. In the Los Angeles area, blacks and Mexican-Americans who moved to the suburbs and were economically competitive with their white counterparts found themselves channeled exclusively into the southern and eastern sections of Los Angeles county (Siembieda, 1975).

Part of the restriction process often used to exclude prospective buyers from an area involves the practices of institutional investors who refuse to allocate mortgage funds unless certain specified regions of the community are selected by the mover. This practice is referred to as red lining, literally drawing a line around the area in question, and the practice has been ruled illegal. Additionally, in some cases the only information available to movers was about previously established ethnic social areas. Some ethnic groups have also faced exclusion by the individual landlord or homeowner who practiced discrimination in renting or selling.

The practices of individuals, information agents, and financial institutions have acted to restrict largely on the basis of color. Exclusion of the white home buyer from suburban regions is accomplished mainly by the force of market economics. Specifically, this restriction takes the form of large lot-size minimums and the so-called Cadillac requirements for amenities in the dwelling unit. In both ethnic and economic exclusion, the practices are designed to prevent specific people from entering a particular suburban region. Because of the massive growth of the suburban population and economic activity beginning in the 1950s, the targets for exclusion have been expanded from specific social and economic classes, races, or ethnic groups to include, in some cases, a restriction in any net increase in population regardless of ethnicity or other factors. Accompanying the change of the goals of the exclusionists was a change in the mechanisms for restricting total growth from informal local-scale practices to community-wide practices based on legal regulation.

LIMITS TO GROWTH IN THE SUBURBS

The initial consideration in a community decision to place a ceiling on growth is the issue of optimum size. The question of what is the most functional and beneficial size for a community is one that has been considered throughout history. The teachings of Aristotle, for example, reflect an early consideration of growth problems, for he foresaw that the size and area of a city could not be perpetually expanded without certain inevitable and drastic changes in urban organization.

In a historical context, the limits to urban growth were constraints resulting from the limits of an ecological system. In a preindustrial and largely spatially restricted society, the "natural" limits of the surrounding region meant that an urban area would most probably not endure if it exceeded the region's capacity to provide fuel and power, food, and water–there were, of course, some notable exceptions– (Mumford, 1956). As Western cities reached the industrial period, many of the constraints of the local region were removed as interaction and commodity flow on a broad scale became possible. The evolution of technology, industrial and postindustrial economies, and the factors that allowed for rapid population growth have facilitated the creation of cities of millions of inhabitants. This scale of urbanism is possible only when the ecological regional constraints of the past have been replaced by complex systems that function as the result of interaction and the interchange of goods on a national or even global scale.

In an analogous manner, the suburb has developed beyond the ecological limits of the past. The constraints that maintained the suburban environment as an area of transition from rural to urban have been largely reduced. The "natural" limits to suburban growth involved transportation, the monetary and temporal costs of the commute to the city, the desire to remain in the central city, and the financial ability to purchase a suburban home. During the past forty years, these constraints to suburban growth have been overcome, much like the previous reduction of the ecological constraints of the larger urban region. In the case of the American suburb, widespread use of the automobile coupled with an increasingly efficient highway system broke down suburban barriers to growth. The availability of low-cost government-insured loans and home purchase with little (or in some cases no) initial capital outlay circumvented one of the other major traditional constraints. The suburban population therefore grew virtually without restriction. The widespread concern for the rapid growth of suburban populations is in part the result of a large-scale awareness of the problems of population growth.

The rapid growth of the world's human population and the problems of providing resources for such a growing population became the focus of nationwide attention during the 1960s, and there was also a growing concern for the quality of the environment and for the preservation of environmental amenities. A concern for the environment and an awareness of problems associated with population pressures can be traced back into antiquity. However, it was not until the decade of the 1960s that these issues became a part of the awareness of virtually an entire population, as happened in America during that period. The question of environment and the awareness of the problems associated with growth are fundamental to one of the most often used rationales for the suburban growth controls of the 1970s, the desire to control population in order to preserve suburban environments.

The Rationale for Suburban Growth Control

Environmental Planning. One of the three prime incentives for limiting suburban growth, environmental protection, is the result of the collision between a developing environmental awareness and the substantial growth in the suburbs following the Second World War. Specifically, the concern for environmental preservation and the climate of fear surrounding rapidly increasing populations (on any scale from global to community), coupled with the reality of the growth of population and economic activity in suburbia, produced a desire in many communities for an immediate halt to or limitation of net growth.

The environmental argument for growth control is not unlike the "Consciousness III" of Charles Reich's futurist philosophy as described in *The Greening of America* (Reich, 1970). Reich described Consciousness III as an attitude of personal involvement that leaves behind the goals of materialism and development and replaces them with goals of personal achievement, not in terms of net worth, but in terms of net achievement for the individual. The net achievement for the suburban individual may, in part, be fulfilled by the preservation of the suburban physical environment. The desire to maintain the stability of the environmental amenities of the suburb—for example, open space, low-density development, and scenic areas—is one of the principal rationales for growth control. A second major rationale is the desire to preserve the economic stability of the suburb.

Economic Stability. A substantial consideration for the cost of living in a rapidly growing suburban area is the question of the benefits and costs of growth. If the major growth sector is in the area of single-family housing units, will those new households "pay their own way" in terms of the cost of providing additional services? Conversely, will growth be subsidized by increasing the property taxes of the entire community? It is possible to find studies that indicate a qualified "yes" to the issue of growth being economically beneficial (Associated Home Builders, 1972). In the majority of cases, however, the costs of services generally are greater than the benefits of growth if the growth is solely in single-family dwellings. The indication of studies is that development that is low density and almost exclusively nonindustrial will generally require subsidization from the community at large, often in the form of increased property taxes (Roberts and Roberts, 1975).

In an affluent community, the prospect of increasing economic costs would most probably be seen as an undesirable but not a critical problem. In a community that was chosen as a place of residence largely on the assumption that it would provide low-cost living to blue-collar and service workers, the upward spiral of the costs of living in the community could pose a major threat to life-styles. It was in precisely such a blue-collar, service-oriented community, Petaluma, California, that the problems of contending with the increased costs of home ownership combined with a proportional decrease in the efficiency of local service provisions led to the implementation of growth restriction policies.

The motivation for no-growth or limited growth policies is generally not exclusively either economic or environmental but some combination of the two factors. The third major rationale for growth control, general land use planning, has been used to influence the spatial organization of cities and suburbs for many years.

Land Use Planning. The planning process generally addresses itself to the built environment and to environmental adaptation to changing economic, social, and technological demands. Implicit in the concern for the built environment is the regulation of land use that often includes the control of development or regulation of growth. It is in this regulation of growth and development that plans and the process of formulating plans can become a part of the suburban growth restriction process.

A plan to regulate growth will often have as a major goal the protection of the economic or environmental stability of the region for which the plan was intended. This goal means that adhering to a plan as a rationale for growth control integrates planning with the aforementioned environmental and economic motivations for growth control.

Policies for Controlling Suburban Growth

Land Use Planning. The most time-honored method of controlling growth and development has been through advance or future planning. Land use planning as a growth control measure can range in scale from a situation in which vast areas of a region have been zoned for restricted growth to restrictions in building in a community or even a neighborhood. One aspect of the use of planning by a community to restrict growth is the limitation of housing starts through building quotas.

Building Quotas as a Dimension in Land Use Planning. In 1972 the city of Petaluma, California, established a policy of allowing only a certain number of housing starts in a given year in an attempt to control growth. It was mainly in the use of a set of criteria designed to determine a community-wide *numerical limit* that the planning procedure in Petaluma differed from the more-traditional dimensions of city planning. The issue was basically whether a city can decide how fast it wants to grow and whether the local municipality can then set specific growth rates.

The city of Petaluma assumed the right to set such growth standards (a maximum of 500 units per year), although the city officials were vigorously opposed by those people who contended that a city must make room for all inmigration if developers are willing to provide housing for them. Establishment of formal, regular limits to the number of housing units allowed is the second of the three major tools of growth control. The third principal method of controlling suburban growth is by resource moratorium.

Resource Moratorium and Growth Controls. The two fundamental components of growth control through resource restriction are the process of restriction through moratoria and environmental planning. Environmental planning has largely become the process of the preservation of resource quality and availability through use limitation and regulation. The scope of this resource control ranges from environmental lawsuits based on nuisance, negligence, and ultrahazardous activities to efforts to minimize pollution. The process of the establishment of a resource moratorium is pertinent to the study of suburban growth controls for this process involves a limitation to growth by the municipality or service district that refuses to supply water, sewer services, or natural gas. The distinction must be made between a resource moratorium as as function of some unique, temporary local phenomenon, such as an extreme cold spell that exhausts the supplies of natural gas or a drought that depletes water availability, and a resource moratorium as a specific, preconceived policy to restrict growth.

The rationales for growth controls as practiced in American suburban communities are the desire to adhere to a general plan, the desire to preserve economic stability, and the desire to preserve the environment. These three motivating factors are not independent and unrelated but operate as interacting and interrelated elements of a general desire to stop or drastically slow growth. In much the same manner, the methods of growth restriction, general planning, construction quotas, and resource moratoria, do not stand alone but often overlap as methods used to manage growth. We will expand upon these introductory remarks about the methods and rationales of managed growth through consideration of a case study that demonstrates the interrelationships and ecological functioning of each of the control elements and the rationale for control. Prior to discussing the case study, however, mention must be made of the effects of suburban growth controls in the United States.

GROWTH CONTROL PRACTICES IN THE UNITED STATES

Growth control policies are being established in communities throughout the United States. The trend toward an interest in community control of growth is rapidly growing in momentum. The major thrust of the research conducted on growth control has been to consider the legal aspects of growth control (Rose, 1974). A secondary aspect of research on growth control communities is an analysis of the economic implications of controlled growth. These analyses of potential economic impacts tend to be estimations for the future rather than considerations of ongoing social and economic changes within the community in question.

The potential for a change in the social and economic organization of a controlled growth community raises questions of social justice. What will be the economic impact of greatly restricted growth in a community? Will controlled growth mean an increase in housing costs that could precipitate an associated lack of residential mobility by many social groups? What will restriction do to the socioeconomic characteristics of the population of the controlled area and what impact will there be on surrounding areas? If an area of growth control is a community that has traditionally provided the low- to lower-middle-income housing, what are the implications for those income groups when growth controls are enacted?

Suburban Dynamics: Growth Leads to No-Growth

The process of decentralization and growth became a fact of life in nearly every American suburb during the 1950s and 1960s. Those trends, combined with an increasing awareness of the problems of population growth and the environmental consciousness of the residents in the 1960s and 1970s, have led to a widespread desire for protection from growth in suburbia.

Growth has become synonymous with an impending loss of life-style in a great number of suburban communities. One response to the potential loss of a life-style that many people made considerable sacrifices to achieve is the adoption of a strategy that has been used to protect the city throughout history, the development of a wall. The suburban wall is constructed through municipal ordinance and legal process, not of stone, but it serves the same gate-keeping function as the medieval wall by restricting entry into a community.

Those people who favor restricting entry generally do so with the expectation that the status quo will be maintained. The impact of restricted growth on a particular network of communities is assessed in the next section in order to ascertain whether the walling in of suburbia preserves the present or brings about substantial changes in the socioeconomic, ecological, or spatial organizations of the region.

THE IMPACTS OF GROWTH RESTRICTION: A CASE STUDY

Two California counties, Marin and Sonoma counties, compose the regional focus of this study, and they are diverse in many ways. This diversity is nowhere more evident than in the comparison of the social and economic characteristics of the respective county populations. The patterns of population growth in both space and time also demonstrate the marked contrast between development in Marin and Sonoma counties. First, we must establish the general social and economic characteristics of the study area. From that base, we will consider some of the ramifications of growth restriction. Examination of the contrast between social and economic elements of the two counties is essential, because the impacts of growth control will be shown to vary according to socioeconomic status.

The Rural-Urban Fringe

Marin and Sonoma counties constitute the north-coast corridor of the San Francisco–Oakland commuter shed (see Figure 10.1). Within the approximately ninety miles between the southern boundary of Marin County – the Golden Gate Bridge and San Francisco – and the northern boundary of Sonoma County, there is a transition in land use from urban-suburban in the south to increasingly rural. North of the city of Santa Rosa, with the exception of several small agricultural

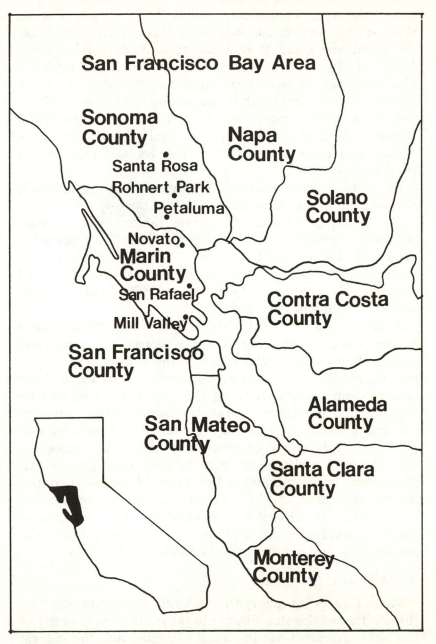

FIGURE 10.1. San Francisco Bay Area.

service centers, there is almost a complete absence of non-farm dwellings, occupations, and land use. South of Santa Rosa is the north-coast commuter shed of the San Francisco–Oakland area. As one moves southward from Santa Rosa toward San Francisco, the rural, agricultural characteristics of the land begin to give way to more-numerous and larger suburban areas. From the northern border of Marin County southward, the rural-agricultural flavor of the land is lost; patterns of suburbanization in the valleys and open space on the hillsides and ridge crests predominate.

Essential to the consideration of land use in this region is the awareness that because of zoning, open-space acquisition, publicly held lands, and terrain, the only major urban-suburban development is along the main transportation artery of the region, U.S. Route 101 (Figure 10.2). The underlying reasons for and importance of this restricted development pattern will be examined individually for both Marin and Sonoma counties.

A complete assessment of the impacts of growth control policies requires knowledge of the patterns of settlement and organization of the social areas of the region prior to the establishment of the restriction policies. A knowledge of the socioeconomic composition of the population can also be instrumental in understanding the factors that motivated restricting the net population increase. In the remainder of this chapter, the socioeconomic characteristics of the population, the local environment, and the patterns of growth germane to an understanding of the reasons for growth control will be considered. In addition, the composition and distribution of the social areas of the two counties will be established for the pre-growth-control era so that an assessment of the impact of growth controls can be made.

Marin County, California

Marin County is roughly triangular in shape with water on three sides and Sonoma County to the north. The majority of the land surface of Marin County is hilly, and the highest series of hills rises to a peak at Mt. Tamalpais (2,604 feet). The

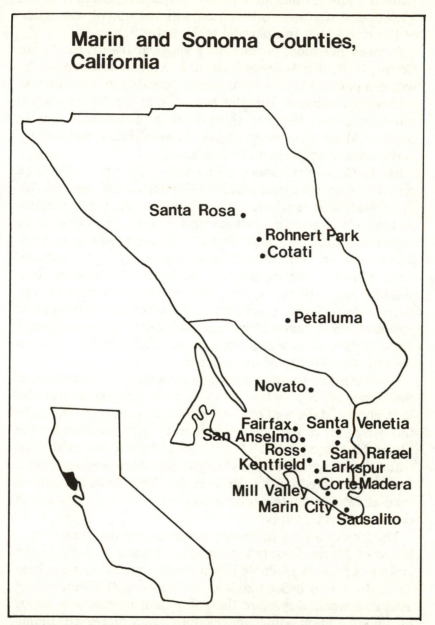

FIGURE 10.2. Marin and Sonoma Counties, California.

pattern of the various hill and valley systems generally lies in a northwest-southeast orientation with the notable exception of the ridges that run parallel to Tomales Bay.

Perhaps the most prominent geological feature of Marin County is the San Andreas fault zone, which passes under the western part of the county and is responsible for the creation and configuration of Tomales Bay. A subtle but very critical interplay occurs between the existence of the fault zone in western Marin County and resource availability, settlement, and planning and growth controls.

Marin County is located along the contact zone between two of the great crustal plates of the earth, and the San Andreas fault zone marks this boundary line. As the two major tectonic plates grind against each other, rock strata have been fractured, displaced, and along with the products of rock decomposition, intermixed in a chaotic pattern generally referred to as a melange. The importance of this subsurface activity for settlers is that the aquifer systems of impermeable rock that might otherwise be expected to provide groundwater in quantity have been broken up by the movement of the crustal plates along the fault so that little groundwater is available in Marin County.

The alternative choices for the provision of water are either the importation of water from surrounding regions or the utilization of dams and reservoirs to capture surface water. In the early part of the twentieth century, the planners for the Marin Municipal Water District opted for the use of surface water found within Marin County, and dams and reservoirs were constructed on the flanks of Mt. Tamalpais in order to take advantage of the orographic influence of the highest point in Marin County.

The lack of an out-of-county water source for the vast majority of Marin County's population means a limit to the amount of water available (from the reservoirs) at any given time. In the pre–Second World War era the amount of available water was more than sufficient to meet the needs of the population. However, as population increased dramatically following the Second World War, the amount of available water remained relatively constant, and by the early 1970s many county residents feared that there would not be enough water to supply a population that was growing in an unabated fashion. Restricting the provision of water therefore became the main instrument of Marin County's growth control plan, for it was argued that the limits of the reservoir system could support no more population growth and that seeking out other water sources was unacceptable.

Settlement Patterns: 1900–1977. The major area of settlement in Marin County since 1900 has been along the U.S. 101 corridor. The highway roughly follows the contour of San Pablo Bay in a north-south direction. Almost all of the valleys that contain the major settlements in the region open to the relatively flat shore of the bay, along which U.S. 101 is located. Since 1900 there have been three major waves of immigration into Marin County and one smaller period of influx. The earthquake and fire that virtually destroyed San Francisco in 1906 caused the first great post-1900 impetus for settlement in Marin County.

The second major post-1900 influence on Marin settlement was the opening of the Golden Gate Bridge in 1937. The bridge, which provides a surface road link between San Francisco and Marin County, was a primary factor in the development of a large-scale commuter flow from southern Marin County to San Francisco.

During the Second World War and in the years immediately following it, Marin County experienced its third major increase in population in the twentieth century. The initial population movement of this era came through interurban migration as workers relocated for employment in defense-related industries.

There was an influence on Marin settlement during the years between 1950 and 1970 that was far more subtle than the aforementioned settlement factors, but it was nonetheless important. In the post–Second World War period the "image" of Marin County as both a landscape and a life-style was projected on a nationwide basis (Exline, 1978). Typical of the literature that projected the image is this assessment of the largest Marin County city, San Rafael. "Beautiful San Rafael is an elite city where life is good the whole year round – blessed as it is by a natural setting of breathtaking charm and an economy of unlimited potential" (San Rafael, Chamber of

Commerce, 1969, p. 4). In this widely circulated work on
Marin County and San Rafael the criticisms of rapid and
large-scale growth were anticipated. "Critics will not be able
to find fault with San Rafael's swift development because it
has been tempered by the city's long, gracious traditions,
magnificent terrain, highly educated, progressive people who
have understandably chosen this garden spot for their home"
(San Rafael, Chamber of Commerce, 1969, p. 6). Additional
references are made to fortunate school children, a recreational paradise, yacht harbors, perfect climate, perpetual
spring, and a wonderful place to live, and in closing there is
the rather immodest conclusion "that here, indeed life will
always be beautiful" (San Rafael, Chamber of Commerce,
1969, p. 6). The personality of the residents of this purported
suburban paradise has similarly been captured in a variety of
popular and academic works.

Evidence of the impact of the major historical events influencing Marin County growth (and the suggested influence of
the image of Marin County as developed and circulated by
public agencies) is found in the actual growth patterns. In
1890 the total population of the county was 13,000, but the
population increased between 1940 and 1970 from 53,000 to
over 200,000 (see Table 10.2).

TABLE 10.2
Population Growth in Marin County, 1900-1970

Year	Population	Decennial % Increase	Population Density Persons per sq. mile
1900	15,702	15	30
1910	25,114	60	48
1920	27,342	9	53
1930	41,648	52	80
1940	52,907	27	102
1950	85,619	62	165
1960	146,820	71	282
1970	209,574	43	403

Source: United States Census 1890-1970; also, Marin County Statistical
Abstracts (San Rafael: Marin County Planning Department, 1974), p. 14B-3.

Population Characteristics and Social Areas. Marin is the wealthiest county in the western United States in terms of per capita income and was ranked eleventh for income in the entire United States in 1970. Marin County ranks first in California in median years of school completed and is similarly one of the leading counties in that category in the United States. These characteristics suggest a population that is high in SES attributes; however, those statistics provide no clue as to the distribution of the high-status residents.

In considering the social areas of Marin County, Lantis, Steiner, and Karinen observed that "there are virtually no lower income locales. But this is a land of the affluent, not the super rich—there are few estates" (Lantis, Steiner, and Karinen, 1977, p. 250). This is an important observation because it indicates the across-the-board nature of the distribution of the high-status areas. That is to say, based on an analysis of variables such as home value, rent, employment categories, education, and income, Marin County is composed almost entirely of high-status or relatively high-status areas. Only five census tracts in the county are "relatively low" in socioeconomic status, according to a factor analysis of the population characteristics of Marin County residents.

As is discussed in Chapter 3, the numerical relationship between the variables and the factors is much the same as a correlation coefficient; the stronger a positive relationship, the closer to 1.0; the stronger the negative relationship, the closer to -1.0. An examination of Table 10.3 makes it readily apparent that factor one is an extremely high SES factor, factor two is representative of a high median age, factor three indicates a blue-collar population, and factor four is an ethnicity factor (black). Once the characteristics of the factors have been determined, it is then possible to relate the cluster groups to the four factors. Finally, these social areas would be transferred to a map.

In plotting data for Marin County, we find that nearly all of it is composed of high or relatively high-SES areas; there are only three areas of predominantly blue-collar workers and one predominantly black area. The importance of these few relatively low-SES areas is significant.

TABLE 10.3
Varimax Rotation Factor Pattern (Marin County)

Variables	Factors			
	1	2	3	4
Home Value	.879	.471	-.316	-.629
Average Rent	.813	.510	-.412	-.610
Professional Workers	.751	.432	-.260	-.117
Managerial Workers	.422	.361		
Sales Workers		.138	.173	
Blue-collar Workers	-.612	-.350	.577	.683
Service Workers	-.183	-.212	.461	.721
High School Education	.381	.441		
College Education	.542	.433		-.170
Median Income	.791	.561	-.117	-.675
Spanish Language			.170	.115
Percent Black				.881
Percent Other				
Percent Under 18 years	-.133	-.117		
Median Age	.436	.890		

Distance Between Cluster Group and Factor Means

Cluster Group	Factors			
	1	2	3	4
1	-17.4	-11.7	7.0	31.4
2	- 4.0	- 6.8	15.8	10.1
3	2.5	22.2	- 3.0	-17.3
4	3.1	6.8	1.0	- 6.2
5	28.2	7.5	-16.0	-14.7

Distance is measured in standard deviations from the mean based on a
unit mean of 50 with a unit standard deviation of 10. For example a
value of 28.8 would represent 2.8 standard deviations above the mean.
Unless indicated, values are positive.

Based on the data generated from the factorial ecology,
Marin County can be summarized as an area of extreme af-
fluence. Areas of both the very rich (median income of well
above $35,000) and the relatively poor (median income of
under $6,000) can be found, but on balance the population
characteristics of Marin County indicate an upper-middle to
upper class that is well educated and basically white, though
there are many foreign-born people.

Sonoma County, California

The population characteristics and suburban evolution of Sonoma County are in marked contrast to those of Marin County. Sonoma County extends north and west from Marin County and San Pablo Bay, and it has a long, rugged Pacific coastline. Most of the land surface of Sonoma County is hilly, and the ridges, which trend northwest-southeast, are separated by narrow valleys. The largest areas of productive level land are in the Russian River, Sonoma, and Santa Rosa valleys. The major cities in Sonoma County are located along U.S. Route 101 in the Santa Rosa Valley.

The climate of the Sonoma County region is mild and moist, with a growing season of approximately 240 days. The combination of a mild climate, a large land area (1,010,560 acres), and the county's proximity to a major metropolitan area has greatly influenced land use in Sonoma County. Unlike Marin County, which has served as the residence for many San Francisco commuters since the turn of this century, Sonoma County has maintained its agricultural heritage. Poultry and egg production, dairying, the growing of Gravenstein apples and prunes (Sonoma County is the leading county in the United States in Gravenstein production and second in prune production), and the production of high-quality wine grapes have traditionally been the foundation for Sonoma County's economy.

Until the mid-1960s the character of the incorporated cities in Sonoma County reflected the reliance on agriculture. With the possible exception of Santa Rosa, most towns were little more than agricultural service centers. However, the mid-1960s produced a marked change in the pattern of land use and composition of the population of the Sonoma County cities along U.S. 101. By 1966 the highway was completed as a freeway that extends from San Francisco to Santa Rosa. This newly created accessibility meant the encroachment of the San Francisco–Oakland commuter shed into southern Sonoma County.

The city of Petaluma was the first city in Sonoma County to

experience the impact of a commuter population. In 1960 Petaluma was an agricultural service center that was experiencing a period of stagnation. Its population of 14,035 resided almost exclusively in the "old" section of town to the west of the freeway. During the 1960s, as access was created by the extension of the freeway and as the price level of housing in Marin County began to rise, a great surge in the construction of single-family homes in the Petaluma region occurred. The population had increased by the late 1960s to 24,870, with nearly all the new residents residing in the new tract housing east of the freeway, which bisects the city.

Social Areas of Sonoma County. The population growth in southern Sonoma County from the mid-1960s to the early 1970s was primarily due to an influx of service and blue-collar workers seeking moderately priced homes. The reasons for the choice of southern Sonoma as a place of residence generally included house price, land costs, accessibility, climate, and community atmosphere.

A great many of the families who moved to that area during that period were young families with children. The extremely low median age of the residents of the commuter cities of Rohnert Park (20.4) and Petaluma (26.4) reflects this young family trend. The median ages for Petaluma and Rohnert Park are far below the median ages of other Sonoma County and Marin County cities. The noncommuter cities of Sebastopol (median age 40.5) and Sonoma (median age 45.3) have more than 25 percent of their population over age 65, nearly triple the statewide percentage. The low median age (24.6) of the city of Cotati is partly the result of some growth through inmigration by young families, but is more the result of an influx of students who attend the neighboring state college. In 1970 the median age of Sonoma County as a whole was 29.7, slightly higher than the greater San Francisco Bay area average of 28.4. Thus, the contrast of Sonoma County commuter cities, in terms of median age, with the general region is striking.

An analysis of the social areas of the U.S. 101 corridor cities of Sonoma County reveals a pattern of socioeconomic status that is far different from that of Marin County. The population characteristics, as established by the factorial ecology based on the 1970 census, show a population of young, moderate- to low-income blue-collar and service workers (see Table 10.4).

Contrasts in the Composition of the Population of Marin and Sonoma Counties 1970: A Summary

A sharp contrast exists between the populations of Marin and Sonoma counties. The variables indicating ethnicity –

TABLE 10.4
Varimax Rotation Factor Pattern (Sonoma County)

Variables	Factors			
	1	2	3	4
Home Value	−.561	.381	.578	−.881
Average Rent	−.580	.292	.431	−.623
Professional Workers	−.648	.174	.491	−.879
Managerial Workers	−.540	.347	.188	−.636
Sales Workers	.408	.214		.268
Blue-collar Workers	.823	.233		.728
Service Workers	.804	.381		.549
High School Education	.635	.622	.440	.321
College Education	−.428	−.157	.530	−.847
Median Income	−.361	−.607	.603	−.731
Spanish Language	.103	−.316	−.442	.428
Percent Black				.137

Distance Between Cluster Group and Factor Means

Cluster Group	Factors			
	1	2	3	4
1	21.8	10.1	−18.9	−22.4
2	10.8	24.2	2.1	−11.1
3	− 3.8	2.0	4.8	4.5
4	−16.2	− 9.4	17.6	12.5
5	−20.1	−14.2	11.8	14.1

Distance is measured in standard deviations from the mean based on a unit mean of 50 and a unit standard deviation of 10. A value of −22.4 for example would represent 2.2 standard deviations below the mean. Unless otherwise noted, values are positive.

Spanish language, percentage black, foreign stock, nonwhite, and other — indicate that both areas are predominately white. The similarity in composition virtually ends at that point, because great differences exist in the socioeconomic and age structures of the respective populations.

The population of Marin County rates generally far higher than that of Sonoma County in terms of professional and managerial workers, education, and median age structure. The home values and average rents in 1970 were much greater in nearly all parts of Marin County than in almost any part of the Sonoma area.

The age structure of the population indicates a young population in most of Sonoma County and a slightly higher median age structure in Marin County. These differences in population characteristics, such as age and socioeconomic status, and the patterns of twentieth-century settlement — commuter as opposed to agricultural — have played a large part in both the variation of the rationales for growth controls in the two areas and the differences in the impact of controls.

The Effects of Growth Restriction

Growth is restricted in the study area from the Golden Gate Bridge to the city of Cotati, a distance of approximately fifty miles. This restriction means that a significant part of the commuter shed of a major American metropolitan region is now unavailable for urban or suburban expansion. In Marin County, the decision to restrict community growth evolved from a desire to preserve the physical environment. The methods of growth restriction include both broad-scale land use planning and a resource moratorium.

The residents of Marin County pride themselves on their environmental awareness and on their desire to preserve the quality of the local environment at virtually any economic cost. The ethic of environmental preservation transcends social status boundaries, as evidenced by the fact that an open space acquisition district was formed in one of the few low-SES areas of Marin County. The remarkable aspect of that special district is that it not only meant direct costs to the somewhat lower-income taxpayers but the acquisition of the open space also brought proposals for future development to a halt. This meant a loss of jobs to the many construction and service workers who help form the district.

The people of Marin County have had two fundamental opportunities to express their desire for environmental preservation by means of limited growth policies. The first chance came in the late 1960s when, as a result of a substantial public demand, the planners of Marin County began to formulate the Marin Countywide Plan. Those people who were responsible for the initial draft of the plan considered public input a vital part of the planning process, so all phases of the Marin Countywide Plan were subject to both scrutiny and final approval by the public.

As the separate components of the plan were drafted, each element of the plan was subject to public review and revision. The principal inputs to this particular type of planning process came from groups representing the major incorporated cities of Marin County and from various groups favoring environmental protection. Through the use of extensive survey research, Marin County planners determined that the special interests of the major input groups were in harmony with the general public attitude. Therefore, the largest possible consensus of opinion regarding the plan was reached, and the attitudes of the residents of Marin County served as the cornerstone of the Marin Countywide Plan.

As a result of the plan's adoption, the "inland corridor" of Marin County and most of the hillsides and ridge crests in the eastern area were excluded from the possibility of development. The vast majority of the coastal land of Marin County was also removed from possible development when the coastal area was incorporated into the federally controlled Golden Gate National Recreation Area. Through the agency of the county general plan and open space acquisition by the federal government, the western two-thirds of the county were made unavailable for development.

The residents of Marin County had a second opportunity to give support to policies of limited growth. People seeking elected positions on the Board of Directors of the Marin

Municipal Water District in the spring of 1973 were categorized as being either proponents or opponents of growth controls through the use of a moratorium on the provision of water hookups for building sites. Voters were presented with the fundamental choice of electing growth or growth restriction advocates to the five-member board. The advocates of restricted growth were elected.

The motivation for growth controls in Marin County was exclusively environmental, with restrictions being approved by the voters despite warnings of the potential of adverse economic effects. The methods of growth control included open space acquisition, land use planning, and a resource moratorium.

The implementation of, and motives for, growth controls in Sonoma County present a sharp contrast to the activities undertaken in Marin County. The primary focus of growth control activity in Sonoma County is in the city of Petaluma. Growth restriction activity in Petaluma was motivated primarily by problems associated with rapid growth and by a fear that the efficiency of the municipal services would decline. In 1950 the population was approximately 10,000. By 1960 it had increased to 14,000, and an additional increase of 10,000 between 1960 and 1970 brought the total 1970 population to 24,000. A dramatic increase in population occurred between 1970 and 1972, and in two years the population of Petaluma increased by over 5,000, bringing the total population to approximately 30,000. It was the increase of 5,000 residents in the first two years of the 1970s that caused great concern over the ability of the city to provide adequate municipal services. Additionally, many of the people who moved to Petaluma in the late 1960s and early 1970s were blue-collar workers with young children. The rapid increase in the number of school-age children led to crowded schools.

In the minds of many of Petaluma's residents in the early 1970s, there appeared to be only two choices, slow growth or a drastic increase in the city tax rate (Hart, 1974). An increase in the tax rate would have eliminated the very reason many residents had moved to Petaluma, the relatively low cost of the housing and the low property tax.

Growth limitation became the response to the problems facing Petaluma. The community desire to limit growth was not a widespread feeling that was instantaneous but came about after extensive studies of rezoning, annexation, the school system, community resources, and the tax base. The basic plan had two principal parts. First, there would be a quota on the number of dwelling units constructed. The quota allowed for 500 units a year, with half to be single-family and half multiple-family units. The plan contained a distributional element as well, calling for 300 units to be constructed west of U.S. 101 (in the old section of the city) and 200 to the east (in the primary area of development during the 1960s and 1970s). The second aspect of the quota system called for a once-a-year competition between developers, so that city planners could decide which development to approve. Those people who wished to build within the city limits were required to submit plans that would then be rated by the city planners in terms of compatibility with the social and economic goals of the city. The building quota would then be filled by the plans judged to be in the best interest of the community.

The Petaluma Plan, as it became nationally known, was enacted in 1972 and was subject to immediate challenge by building and construction interest groups. Following a series of judgments and reversals, the question of the legality of the plan as a growth control device was decided in favor of the city of Petaluma and the limited growth advocates by the United States Court of Appeals in 1975 and the United States Supreme Court in 1976.

Many questions arise when we consider the issue of controlled growth. What will be the impact of growth restriction on housing costs? Will areas of low socioeconomic status filter upward as competition in a restricted market forces high-status buyers to purchase in low-status areas? In what way will controlled growth affect the age mixture of the population?

Growth Controls and Housing Costs

It must be strongly emphasized that the rapid rise in the

cost of housing in southern Sonoma County and especially Marin County cannot be attributed solely to growth restriction. Spiraling costs of labor, land, and materials have had an impact on the cost of housing in both growth and no-growth communities. The cost of a single-family home in the controlled growth areas of Marin and Sonoma counties, however, shows evidence of a far greater increase than the cost of a single-family home in noncontrolled regions. Comparing the May 1977 median price of single-family homes in various geographical areas with the median price in Marin County provides clear evidence of the "over and above the inflation rate" nature of the price increase in a controlled growth area (see Table 10.5 and Table 10.6).

As has been previously noted, a great many factors contribute to the rapid increase in the cost of single-family homes. Extensive interviews with city and county planners, real estate agents, local government officials, and representatives of institutions that finance the purchase of homes produced but one conclusion: The substantial increase in the cost of homes in Marin County, above the national, state, and local averages, was dramatically affected by the fact that the vast majority of the land surface of Marin County is unavailable for development.

The general trend of the statements by those interviewed

TABLE 10.5
Median Prices for Single-Family Homes, May 1977

Location	Median Price of Single-Family Home in Dollars
United States	40,000
Western United States	53,300
California	56,251
San Francisco Bay Area	61,000
Santa Clara County, California	68,000
San Mateo County, California	73,000

Sources: California Real Estate (May 1977), pp. 24-25. A. Cook, "The End of Soaring Prices," New West (June 1977), pp. 28-33.

TABLE 10.6
House Prices, 1974-1978, Marin County, California

	1974		1975		1976		1977		1978		4-year increase (percent)
	Number sold	Average price	Number sold	Average price	Number sold	Average price	Number sold	Average price	Number sold	Average price	
Belvedere	39	123,715	42	183,735	51	171,375	35	212,015	27	270,595	119
Corte Madera	107	50,630	121	55,055	165	66,495	105	85,855	141	96,425	90
Fairfax	160	43,300	165	48,955	219	58,500	193	75,485	206	84,025	94
Greenbrae	58	66,600	71	75,435	95	83,610	109	102,680	112	110,335	66
Kentfield	55	96,640	68	110,665	62	125,575	83	149,310	72	171,520	77
Larkspur	69	62,540	70	72,670	88	84,250	84	114,530	84	132,045	111
Mill Valley	348	59,860	449	65,770	513	82,855	445	105,045	486	127,935	114
Novato	622	49,255	714	53,570	1,080	61,620	921	75,950	1,019	90,200	83
Ross	25	89,165	29	101,840	47	117,160	34	171,060	35	195,030	119
San Anselmo	265	53,050	270	60,535	314	71,870	297	87,280	279	106,160	100
San Rafael	733	56,700	816	61,285	966	68,750	977	84,415	1,091	97,220	71
Sausalito	57	75,845	67	85,470	115	93,020	106	112,570	111	130,460	72
Tiburon	137	86,865	163	93,775	222	113,655	156	140,650	159	199,845	130
Other Marin County	60	50,325	82	53,290	126	64,350	121	87,055	98	95,870	91
County Average	2,735	58,215	3,127	64,215	4,063	74,635	3,666	92,615	3,921	108,730	87

The average Marin County house has risen 87 percent in the past four years.

Source: Based on data from the Marin County Board of Realtors.

suggested that Marin and southern Sonoma counties were becoming nationally prominent. Marin, in particular, was felt to be one of the few "rural" communities in the United States within fifteen to twenty minutes driving time from a major metropolitan area. People also felt that San Francisco had become "the Manhattan of the West," drawing high-income executives, many of whom chose Marin as a place of residence. Finally, it was generally felt that the image of Marin County as one of the most desirable areas in the United States would act to draw potential residents to the area even though cost and availability of housing meant that movers would be spending considerable amounts of money in a highly inflated market for the most basic homes. It was the general consensus that intensive demand coupled with a restricted supply of housing was responsible for the extremely high cost of single-family homes in Marin County. A comparison of trends in house prices in the pre- and postgrowth control areas with national patterns seems to support this claim (see Table 10.7).

The demand-and-supply situation in the growth control areas created a buy-sell mind set that led to greatly inflated prices long before the market would have driven prices upward. People expected house prices to increase greatly and rapidly, thus sellers asked astronomical figures for houses, and buyers were willing to bear the cost. This process continues on into the 1980s even with high fuel costs and soaring mortgage rates.

Growth Controls and the Composition and
Transformation of Social Areas

Relatively few low-SES areas exist in Marin County, and the trend is toward mid- to low-SES groups in southern Sonoma County. In order to ascertain the impact of growth controls on social areas, families moving into the lower status areas were compared with the families who were leaving them. Occupational categories were used as the basis of the comparison. Social scientists have derived several methods of rating or assigning numerical values to job categories. One system places a value of 96 on occupations

TABLE 10.7
Price Trends in Housing, 1966-1977

Increase in the cost of a single-family home, pregrowth control period, 1966-1971

	Percentage	Actual Median Price Increase in Dollars	
		1966	1971
National rate of increase	27%	$23,800	$30,300
San Francisco Bay Area rate of increase	23%	25,900	31,000
Marin County rate of increase	19%	31,900	38,000

Increase in the cost of a single-family home, postgrowth control period, 1972-1977

	Percentage	Actual Median Price Increase in Dollars	
		1972	1977
National rate of increase	59%	$32,200	$51,300
San Francisco Bay Area rate of increase	76%	32,600	58,716
Marin County rate of increase	117%	46,000	101,000

Source: U.S. Bureau of the Census, Price Index of New One-Family Houses Sold, First Quarter, 1977, Bureau of the Census Publication C27-77Q1 (Washington, D.C.); San Francisco Area Data, San Francisco Bay Area Real Estate Research Council; Marin County Data, Marin County Board of Realtors.

such as dentist, lawyer, judge, physician, and surgeon and a value of 2 on occupations such as laborer and coal mine operator (Reiss, 1961). This system does not, of course, imply a value judgment with respect to the individual but is based on the same quantitative, nonpersonal systems that are used to determine socioeconomic status.

Residents moving out of the low-status areas had an average occupation rating of 23 (carpenters, machinists, mechanics), whereas those moving into the same areas had an average occupation rating of 66 (mid-level executives, accountants, financial officers). This difference means that the low-status areas were filtering upward in social status. Associated with this trend was an increase in income and buying power of those moving into the area. Thus, previously low-status neighborhoods became available only to the higher-income home buyer.

Additionally, the constraints placed on the supply of homes through growth restriction meant that high-income buyers would purchase homes of only marginal quality for highly inflated prices with the hope of "trading up." The prospect of building equity while residing in the north coast area, coupled with the availability of homes at costs far below those in the surrounding communities, was the primary reason nearly 90 percent of the families interviewed gave for their decision to locate in the lower-status areas.

The characteristics of those moving into the controlled growth area, based on information supplied by real estate agents, indicate a definite pattern. Home purchasers were generally between forty and sixty, had few children, had high incomes with both husband and wife working, and were white (Exline, 1978). There are obvious implications in this trend for the provision of services, school attendance, and the ability of lower-income families to compete for the purchase of a home.

Growth controls have had a substantial effect on the cost of housing and social structure in the controlled growth region. It follows that if one component of an urban regional system is disrupted, then repercussions will appear in other parts of the system. This disruption is true for the regional dynamics of housing and social structure; the changes brought about by growth controls have had a tremendous influence on the housing and social structure of the communities surrounding the region of controlled growth.

The Effects of Growth Restriction on Surrounding Communities

Rohnert Park is the city nearest to the restricted growth region (see Figure 10.2). The city came into existence in 1962, and then it was basically a collection of housing tracts featuring three-bedroom homes with one and one-half bathrooms. The people living in Rohnert Park were blue-collar workers who did not commute more than a few miles to work. The cost of housing in Rohnert Park, prior to growth restriction measures being enacted in the surrounding cities, typically was as low as could be found in the region.

Construction of single-family homes averaged about 50 units per year prior to growth controls in the surrounding area. Once growth restriction came into being in the re- mainder of the region, housing construction jumped to over 400 units per year in Rohnert Park.

Rohnert Park offered the only large-scale developable building sites in the northern part of the San Francisco Bay area, and builders created homes that attracted the lower-mid- dle- and middle-income buyers. Even with large-scale construction projects, the demand for housing outpaced the supply because of the large numbers of low-, middle-, and even some high-income groups that were either priced out of the restricted markets or excluded because of an unavailabil- ity of housing stock.

The exclusion of a wide range of buyers from the growth restricted areas had a substantial impact on what has been as- sumed to be the model of suburban social and economic structures. The traditional suburban model would have lower-income, child-rearing residents on the fringe of the ur- ban area — those who are willing or are forced to trade a long commute to the central district in order to achieve a low outlay for housing. Instead, the northern fringe of the San Francisco–Oakland metropolitan area is characterized by a population with a wide range of socioeconomic character- istics who have been excluded from locations nearer the ur- ban core by growth restriction. Rohnert Park became the locational choice for every person who could not buy in Marin County and who wanted more home for the dollar than could be found in Petaluma. Houses in Rohnert Park were suddenly selling for prices comparable with the cost of houses in the rest of the region:

The rapid growth of Rohnert Park, brought on largely by controlled growth to the south, created numerous problems. The young families of the north-coast region, many of whom were excluded from living in other areas, began to settle in Rohnert Park. This phenomenon produced a very rapid in- crease in the number of school-age children, which overloaded the existing school system. The demand for new elementary schools far surpassed the ability or desire of local taxpayers to construct schools. The matter of new school construction proved to be the first stage in a battle for growth controls in Rohnert Park. Proponents of growth argued that schools were needed to serve an expanding population, whereas opponents to growth felt that new construction would create a self-fulfilling prophecy in that with more schools there would be a demand for more construction so that those schools could be filled. One frustrated city councilperson suggested that the growth restricted communities be brought to court and be forced to pay for the impact that other cities' growth policies had had on Rohnert Park.

A second adverse impact of the rapid growth of Rohnert Park resulted from the problems created in the regional transportation system. A high percentage of the population of postgrowth-control Rohnert Park began to commute to Marin County and San Francisco. This new commuter flow, from fifty miles north into San Francisco, coupled with inadequate public transit meant greatly increased traffic congestion.

The dilemma of Rohnert Park was that the city became the community to which residents forced out of controlled markets to the south fled in order to obtain housing. Thus, the population grew far more rapidly than the city's ability to provide services. The social composition of the city has also changed markedly since the advent of growth controls elsewhere. Movers in the high-SES categories entered the Rohnert Park market, which caused a significant rise in the cost of housing as prices rose to the upper levels that prospective buyers would tolerate. When Rohnert Park was a proletarian community, the cost of housing was held down largely because developers were catering to the lower-income spectrum of the market and because there was no real competition for dwelling units. Later, a great many prospective buyers came from the higher-income groups, and the cost of housing spiraled upward.

The most profound change to occur in Rohnert Park as the result of growth controls to the south was the change in the social composition of the community. The city no longer serves solely as a place young working-class families from

Sonoma County might consider as one of several alternative locations for a home. When Rohnert Park began to function as the community that attracted the spillover from the growth controlled regions to the south, it became the locational choice for people in the mid- to high-socioeconomic classes who were excluded from the closed markets. Those inmigrants offered significantly higher bids for housing than the low-status buyer could; therefore the housing market began to escalate in price, and low-status buyers were forced to look elsewhere for housing. This process illustrates the real impact of growth controls on a surrounding, noncontrolled community.

Conclusions

It has been demonstrated that growth controls drive prices for homes upward. The most basic model of supply and demand explains this phenomenon. Potential buyers enter the housing market in ever-increasing numbers, whereas the supply of housing becomes limited because of growth restriction. Speculators act to increase this upward spiral, because they further increase the demand for housing units.

The most ironic element of the upward spiral in housing costs in the controlled growth area of this study is that the most-dramatic cost increases came in the low-status areas, which meant that outmigrants were replaced by inmigrants of a much higher socioeconomic status. Social areas in this type of dynamic housing market appear to be filtering upward toward the point at which there may well be no areas within the controlled growth region available to low- and middle-income groups.

A major change also occurred in the composition of the social areas of the controlled growth region, including a trend toward increasing homogeneity in the age structure of the population as the young and the old were priced out of the controlled region. The lack of inmigration by young or large families played havoc with the school systems in the controlled growth area.

The communities adjacent to the restricted growth areas bore many of the costs that resulted from the growth control decisions of surrounding communities. Growth in Rohnert

Park was rapid and drastic. The competition for housing between those forced to search for housing in Rohnert Park
because they were excluded from the controlled growth areas
and those attracted to the same city because it is the major
suburb of a developing city, Santa Rosa, has forced prices upward to the point where the poor and lower-income groups
are being excluded from the housing market there. Instead of
a city consisting of discrete, rather homogeneous social areas,
Rohnert Park has become a city of considerable heterogeneity in its social organization. This phenomenon of individual neighborhoods containing a great melange of social
groups is becoming common in the previously low-status
areas of Marin County as well, and it is the direct result of
movers in all social groups "scrambling" to obtain any housing
available in a tight housing market.

In an urban ecosystem, through a process of response and
adjustment to stimuli, socioeconomic areas are established
and maintained or established and transformed as a part of
the ecological functioning of the system. In this manner,
traditionally, low-income groups and the poor have been able
to secure housing as growth and transition take place in a
social space and through time. As with any functioning
system, a delicate balance between inputs and response in
the overall system must be maintained in order for the interaction that perpetuates the system to exist. When one element of the system is changed, the balance is altered, and the
system begins to respond to the introduced stimuli. It is this
process of change that has occurred in the regional housing
component of the urban ecosystem because growth controls
were enacted.

The distinct possibility exists, therefore, that the ultimate
effect of growth controls in the suburbs may be the return of
the middle class to the central city. This is not the immediate
prospect because outward movement is still possible. At
some point, however, the constraints of time, money, and
fuel resources will place a limit on the expansion of the urban
periphery, and the only alternative will be a return to the
city.

Growth controls in the suburbs of the United States are in
their infancy; restricted growth on a large scale has been in

formal existence for only half a decade. The rapid growth of all phases of American life following the Second World War, coupled with concerns for economic and environmental stability, produced the desire to restrict growth. It can be said of this no-growth ethic that we, as a society, are probably dealing with only the tip of the iceberg; growth controls have already been proposed on many levels. Dealing with the clash of these issues, a rapidly growing population searching for homes, as opposed to the desire for controlled growth, may well be one of the most critical problems facing the American urban society of the future.

Although we have painted a fairly negative picture of the impacts of growth restriction, the other side of the coin, limitless sprawl, also has undesirable characteristics. Finding the balance between the extremes in land use issues often falls to the urban planners.

REFERENCES

Associated Home Builders. 1972. *Growth: Cost Revenue Studies.* Berkeley, Calif.: Associated Home Builders of the Greater East Bay.

Blumberg, L., and Lulli, M. 1966. "Little Ghettoes: A Study of Negroes in the Suburbs." *Phylon* 27: 117–131.

Exline, C. 1978. "The Impacts of Growth Control Legislation on Two Suburban Communities: Marin and Sonoma Counties, California." Ph.D. dissertation, Department of Geography, University of California, Berkeley.

Hart, J. 1974. "The Petaluma Case." *Cry California* 9(2): 6–16.

Lantis, D.; Steiner, R.; and Karinen, A. 1977. *California, Land of Contrasts.* 3d ed. Dubuque, Iowa: Kendall/Hunt Publishing Company.

Mumford, L. 1956. "The Natural History of Urbanization." In W. Thomas, ed., *Man's Role in Changing the Face of the Earth*, pp. 382–400. Chicago: University of Chicago Press.

Reich, Charles. 1970. *The Greening of America.* New York: Random House.

Reiss, A., Jr. 1961. *Occupations and Social Status.* Glencoe, Ill.: Free Press.

Roberts, K., and Roberts, P. 1975. "Low Density Policies: The Price

Communities Pay." *Real Estate Appraiser* 41: 2.

Rose, J. 1974. "Recent Decisions on Population Growth Control: The BellTerra, Petaluma and Madison Township Cases." In J. Hughes, ed., *New Dimension in Urban Planning: Growth Controls,* pp. 178–186. New Brunswick, N.J.: Rutgers Center for Urban Policy Research.

San Rafael, California, Chamber of Commerce. 1969. *San Rafael, California.* Encino, Calif.: Windsor Publishing Company.

Siembieda, W. 1975. "Suburbanization of Ethnics of Color." *Annals of the American Academy of Political and Social Sciences* 422: 118–128.

11

THE PLANNING PROCESS

The concept and practice of planning are of vital importance to residents of a city. The process of regulating existing land use, as well as designating the future city, is welcomed by some people at one end of the spectrum of attitudes, scorned by others at the opposite pole, and little understood by most of those in between.

In introducing the study of the urban ecosystem, we mentioned the systems approach to urban planning. It was asserted that planners must consider the relationships among all possible variables (physical, social, political, and economic) if the question of how best to use the land was to be answered. Further, concepts of ecology were said to come into play in planning, for the planning practitioner must be mindful of the factors of ecological competition, balance, and succession, which are ongoing in the urban environment. Each of these concerns, the interrelationships among variables and ecological concepts, has been thematic throughout the preceding chapters. It is now our task to bring these issues into focus by considering the topic of urban planning.

In the most fundamental sense, planners attempt to manipulate the elements of an urban ecosystem to achieve a desired outcome. Planning—a scheme or program for designing, scheduling, and arranging something—is a continuing, developing process that involves many changes; it is extremely complex, and in many ways it is enigmatic.

The fruit of the planner's work, the plan, should be a source of information and an estimate for the future. In addition, a plan should describe a designed program for change and serve as a guard against the arbitrary. In creating such a document, the planner must continuously make trade-offs when manipulating the elements of the urban system in order to achieve stated goals. If economic development is the objective of a plan, growth in that sector may come at the expense of the economic and social integrity of some neighborhoods, or perhaps at a cost measured in lost environmental quality. The planner must understand such possibilities and act accordingly. It is in the realm of identifying the impact of land use decision making that planners receive considerable criticism. In the broadest sense, critics question the role of planners in the urban ecosystem.

THE ROLE OF PLANS AND PLANNERS: A HISTORICAL PERSPECTIVE

The history of urban America is one of growth and change. Following the establishment of small cities on the East Coast was the gradual development of cities in the South, North, West, and finally Far West. Once this urban network was established, growth within cities became the dominant feature of the American urban landscape. The trend toward urban growth began to accelerate rapidly following the turn of the twentieth century.

Concurrent with the growth of cities, there were changes in the physical, economic, and social structures of urban places. Technological advances in transportation and in techniques of vertical construction aided in the development of larger and more-complex cities. Urban residents in the early part of the twentieth century began to place demands on urban governments for transportation services, public services, utilities, housing, and community development that were without precedent in the United States. There was a wide range of response to the call for increasing the services to urban residents.

One school of thought, which emerged prior to the First World War, has been referred to as the reformer movement (Hancock, 1967). Proponents of this viewpoint saw in the evolving urban culture and society an opportunity for the betterment of the welfare of the urban public. Through purposeful public action, cities could become better habitats for people. Reformers felt that this task could only be accomplished through widespread manipulation and control of the elements of the urban ecosystem.

The opposing viewpoint, although not expressed in systems terminology, was basically that the city, as a system, would provide for all necessary services through the normal functioning of the system. People adhering to that thesis echoed the words of Andrew Carnegie: "The American . . . need not fear the unhealthy or abnormal growth of cities. . . . The free play of economic laws is keeping all quite right. . . . Oh, those grand, immutable, all-wise laws of natural forces, how perfectly they work if human legislatures would only let them alone" (Carnegie, 1886, pp. 47–48). Hancock observed that many city planners prior to the First World War embraced the Carnegie philosophy, "while pursuing happiness by a reversed golden rule" (Hancock, 1967, p. 291). In this environment virtually all social needs were subordinated to the demand for rapid economic development.

Not all city planners could be placed philosophically in either the economic development or social goals camps. Some planners were primarily concerned with the physical beautification of the city, and plans for public gardens and parks as well as landscaping along arterial routes came from this group.

A concern for planning the physical environment of the city as well as an interest in maximizing the public welfare can be traced back to the early 1800s. It wasn't until the second decade of the twentieth century, however, that professional planning emerged as a major factor in urban America.

The growing importance and complexity of cities in the early 1900s led to a political movement that initially, at times, transcended strict political party lines and that called for such concepts as social reform, social welfare, and constructive social engineering. During the period 1900–1920 many American cities moved from having no comprehensive plans or even zoning ordinances to having established the foundations for complex land use plans.

In subsequent decades planning became more sophisticated as new analytical techniques and more numerous and accurate data were made available to planners. Although the perceived importance of city planning would often be in a state of flux depending on who held political power, the field generally moved forward to the point at which comprehensive urban planning was considered to be vital to the welfare of the city by the 1940s.

Planning in the 1980s

Assessing the role of plans and planners in contemporary United States calls for an overview of the state of the art of urban planning at the beginning of the post–Second World War era. Although little formal comprehensive planning existed in American cities as late as the first decade of the 1900s, growth and change in the field and the ebb and flow of political support for the planning process produced the philosophical base from which post–Second World War planning practice has emerged. One element of this philosophical structure is the thinking by many planners that the goals of social and personal well-being have taken precedence over issues relating solely to growth in the economic, technological, and physical sectors. It should be noted that there is spirited debate about the contention that planning has moved dramatically in the direction of social and personal well-being.

Another component of the philosophical base is that contemporary planners are considered to have the means to identify the needs, amenities, and minimum standards of environmental quality required for a high standard of urban living. Planners can implement new community designs that preserve desirable features and bring into play new factors that work toward upgrading the quality of urban life.

Finally, planners in the 1970s and 1980s are finding greater freedom in planning for natural regions rather than being strictly confined to areas defined by arbitrary political boundaries. Transportation planning, for instance, often transcends the borders of the central city in a metropolitan area and is undertaken for the entirety of the metropolitan region. This is not to say that political problems evaporate in such a regional scheme; they do not. However, the idea of planning for the functional region involved in a problem, although in its relative infancy, has become fairly widely accepted in recent years.

Contemporary planning philosophy is the product of the three aforementioned factors: a shift in philosophical orientation toward the social and personal scale, new and more-sophisticated techniques for problem identification and designs for problem solving, and greater flexibility in the extent to which plans are formulated for a region. In addition, there are calls for a new relationship between the lay person and the planner, which say that the lay person should become educated in the planning process and provide much of the input to be used in land use decision making. The role of the lay person should be that of an agent for disseminating information about community attitudes, values, and desires. The role of the planner would continue to be "as analyst, creative designer, critic and coordinator" (Hancock, 1967, p. 302).

It would be possible to fill volumes with arguments for and against the preceding proposal for the philosophical basis of planning for the 1980s. The statements contained herein are intended to present a general overview of the intellectual inputs that influence many, but by no means all, urban planners. In counterpoint to our philosophical position are some contemporary factors that "impose strains on the persons who call themselves planners, and give rise to self-doubts" (Dyckman, 1979, p. 279).

Dyckman has identified three areas of concern that are of particular importance to urban planners (Dyckman, 1979). First, there is an ambivalent attitude toward public planning in the United States. Planners are often unsure about the degree of commitment toward their work. Support for planning fluctuates with political office holders as well as in the public's acceptance of planning. The short history of public planning and the past land use ethic in the United States may do much to explain the lack of commitment.

A second problem Dyckman defined is one common to many academic disciplines, particularly to the field of geography, and that is simply, What are the bounds of the field? Basically the search is for the key concepts and techniques that make planning, as an academic discipline, singular and unique. Active planners are concerned with the evolving body of planning theory that comes from academic planners, for it is from this theoretical foundation that new dimensions in planning will come. If the base is weak, the remainder of the structure will suffer, so the lack of a strong and unified philosophical orientation and common direction with respect to theory in American academic planning programs is considered to be a problem.

The final observation by Dyckman is perhaps the most critical. Dyckman stated:

> Planning is nothing without politics, we are told, and the nationalism of planning avails naught against the realities of politicians. Is it because planning is utopian in its vision of rational or scientific politics, or because planners are so unworldly? Do they not understand the workings of the political system? In particular, do they not understand power? [Dyckman, 1979, p. 291]

The phrase "planning is nothing without politics" should be recalled in every discussion of the process of planning. This statement can be applied to politics at any level—local, state, or national.

Let us put the political factor in perspective. In the first part of this chapter, we presented an overview of the philosophical basis of planning. The picture was one of enlightenment, concern, and improved techniques for land use analysis and decision making. The question may well be asked, Why then do we have the vast web of urban problems that confront us today? The answer lies in the realization that even with the best of intentions, little real change in the urban system is likely to take place through the planning process unless there is broad-based support and an ability to understand and function as a part of the political system. This contention is reinforced when one examines the actual process of the formulation of a plan.

THE PLANNING PROCESS

Having examined some of the purely intellectual aspects of the planning process, it is appropriate to concentrate on the applied activities that are directed toward the development of a plan. Suppose the task at hand is to create a general land use plan for an urban area.

Land Use Decision Making

The first step in the process of developing a plan is to examine the type of decision-making processes the plan will serve. In other words, how will the plan, as a document, aid in setting guidelines for land use decision making? It may be that the planners will be called upon to create a plan based upon the logical scientific method of hypothesis and testing. If this were the case, all aspects of the plan would need to be extremely specific in nature and most likely would be subject to quantitative analysis. It may be hypothesized, for instance, that a change in land use policy would stimulate economic development. The planner's charge would be to provide specific numerical examples so that the hypothesis could be examined and to project, in as exact a sense as possible, the anticipated impact of the change in land use policy. The scientific method is often used in short-range plans.

An alternative to such strict numerical analysis is the development and listing of alternatives for the varying components of the plan. Instead of searching for formal numerical proofs, planners may instead list a series of more-general alternatives based on assumptions and projections. A change in land use policy to stimulate economic growth would be discussed in fairly general and mostly qualitative terms. If zoning policy is changed, for example, (1) growth will increase dramatically; (2) however, the growth may have negative environmental impacts; (3) however, if growth is not encouraged in the economic sector, there might be negative impacts on county employment; and so on until all possible alternatives and impacts are listed. Decisions are based on what steps will bring about the most desirable results and are usually made for the long term.

The most general type of decision making comes from a designed utopia. Statements in the broadest possible terms are made about what is most desired for the future. A goal in this type of planning may include increasing local employment, decreasing traffic congestion, and having a high-quality physical environment with vast expanses of open space. How is such a complex goal accomplished? Fundamentally, all aspects do not come to fruition, but for the very long term they provide pleasant targets at which to aim.

Long-range utopian goals are attached to nearly all general plans with the hope that short-term actions may somehow, someday, bring such goals into being. In reality most American land use decision making is done for the short term and is based upon subjective decision-making processes such as determining alternatives.

The decision-making process to be used in this discussion of developing an urban general plan will be based on decision makers, such as the voting public and appointed and elected officials, choosing alternative land use schemes from a set of scenarios designed to illustrate the impacts of various land use decisions. If zoning policies are changed, for example, the plan would present several possible consequences of such decisions. Once the decision-making process has been decided upon, the plan itself must be formulated and presented as a model that will coordinate land use decision making.

Formulation of a Plan

A vast number of ways to plan are available to the planner, and the method of plan formulation used at a given time is largely the result of the target of the plan. Plans may be general and all-encompassing in nature, or a plan can be designed specifically to deal with housing, commerce and industry, community facilities, internal or external transportation facilities, recreation and open space, or a wide range of other specific topics. The concept of a plan is also related to scale. The question of the geographical unit—a neighborhood, city, metropolitan area, or region—must be considered. Given the number of topics available and the range of scales with which the planner must work, it is little wonder that there are many planning schemes. Regardless of the scope of the plan or its scale, the following elements are most likely to be found in any plan.

Definition of Interrelationships. In an ecological sense, what variables come into play in the plan and what are the relationships among those variables? Consider the topics covered in this volume: the physical environment of the city, housing, economics, transportation, suburbs, attitudes toward growth, et cetera. The variables that planners must consider are related to these topical areas.

If the complex web of variables associated with land use decision making is carefully examined in a systematic framework, the relationship of each variable to all other variables can be found. In this fashion it is possible to assess the impact of a change in or manipulation of one variable on the remainder of the urban ecosystem. In the discussion of growth restriction in Chapter 10, residents in the area of the case study should have been able to forecast the impact of restricting growth by knowing how a reduction in the supply of housing would affect economic and social variables.

The variables that make up the urban ecosystem are referred to as control variables, uncontrolled variables, or need variables. A control variable is one that can be directed or manipulated by the decision makers. Uncontrolled variables are not under the control of decision makers, and need variables describe the goals of the plan, or what is needed. The relationship of these variables can either be described pictorially or in algebraic terms (see Figure 11.1).

The figure illustrates the manner in which control variables can influence uncontrolled variables, which in turn have an impact on need variables. Further, it is demonstrated that either control or uncontrolled variables can directly influence a need variable. The second half of Figure 11.1 presents a simple diagram of some variables involved in the planning decision of where to locate a health care facility.

The uncontrolled variable in the diagram is the number of trips made to the health care center. The need variable is preventive health care, and the control variable is distance from the community. Each of the variables will affect the level of health care given in the community. If the health care center is located near the community, the number of trips to the facility will increase. If the number of children increases, there will be a corresponding increase in the need for health care, and if family income drops, there may be a decrease in

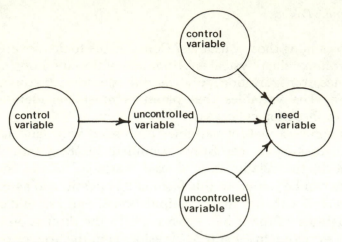

Relationship among types of variables in a system

Variables in the decision where to locate a health care facility

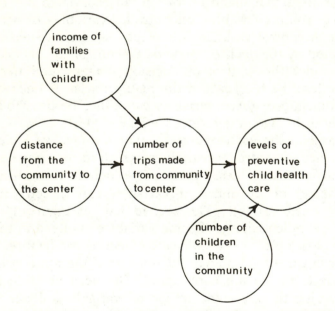

An algebraic expression of these relationships   H = f(D,I,T,C)   where
D = distance , I = income , T = trips , C = children , & H = health care

FIGURE 11.1. The Relationship Between Urban Variables. Reprinted from D. Krueckeberg and A. Silvers, *Urban Planning Analysis: Methods and Models* (New York: John Wiley, 1974), pp. 7, 8, by permission of John Wiley & Sons, Inc.

the number of visits to the health care facility (Krueckeberg and Silvers, 1974). This problem may also be modeled in simple algebraic terms (see Figure 11.1).

The planner dealing with the question of the optimum location for the health care facility would need to consider not only the variables that influence the specific location of the facility, but also how the facility would impact other activities at that location. Perhaps the facility would generate a large traffic flow or perhaps other health care institutions would locate near the first unit. It might be that land values could change in the area near the facility.

The identification, definition, and ecological analysis of variables is one of the more-difficult tasks the planner is called upon to perform. This step in the planning process is generally done in conjunction with the determination of the goals and objectives of the plan.

Determination of Planning Goals. The goals of a plan are usually clearly stated in the very first pages of the final document. Goals may be listed in a random sequence or in some order of priority, that is, the first goal listed may be what is perceived to be the most important goal of the plan. Maps may also reflect goals and are especially important to the geographer involved in planning. Map symbols can be used to describe specific points of change, or they can reflect designs for future land use patterns in general (see Figure 11.2).

Stated goals can range from being extremely specific to very general. For example,

Goal: Discourage rapid population growth while encouraging social and economic diversity of communities

Goal: Achieve a high-quality physical environment with much open space

Goal: Increase the amount of low-cost housing in the region by 3 percent per year for the next five years

Goal: Convert 5 percent of the developable but unused land in the city that is served by municipal utilities to developed land within the planning period of five years.

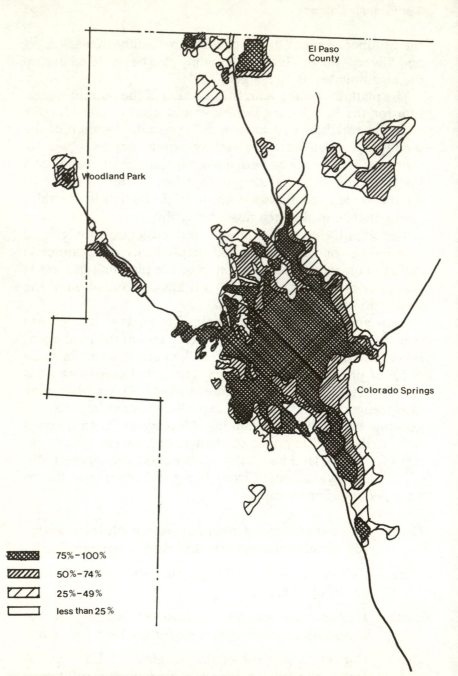

FIGURE 11.2. 1990 Percent Developed, Western El Paso County and Woodland Park, Colorado.

Goals can also be formulated through a very specific process (Krueckeberg and Silvers, 1974). For instance,

$$G = (St \times P) - Su$$

where

G = the need to be filled
St = a per capita standard
P = population size
Su = current supply

If that formula were to be used to determine the amount of agricultural open space needed in the area being planned for, the computation might take this form:

St = 4 acres per capita
P = 200,000
Su = 600,000 acres
G = (4 acres × 200,000) − 600,000

thus

G = 200,000 acres of agricultural open space needed to meet the standard

The planner now has a specific target for open space needs. The standards per capita are often fixed by the courts, government regulation, or the procedures of a particular planning office.

The goal statement reflects targets for improving conditions and at times the priorities for accomplishment. In order to determine whether or not goals are being met, standards and measuring devices are needed.

Establishment of Standards and Measurements. In devising a plan, a statement or statements describing programs that are designed to achieve goals are developed. The standards and measurements used in the evaluation of how effective the plan is in helping achieve the stated goals can be either quali-

tative or quantitative. The planner's task is essentially to identify and assess the impact of the plan on such factors as land
use and social well-being and to judge the positive or negative
aspects of each segment of the plan. It is also necessary to
consider the costs over time of the planning program and to
determine whether or not financial resources demanded by
the plan will be available in the future. Measurements can be
made to aid in both the analysis of the plan and the assessment of its cost-effectiveness.

In determining strategies for measuring the success of a
plan, the planner must determine what needs to be
measured, how the data are to be gathered, and finally how
the raw data will be statistically manipulated. In the housing
component of a plan, a likely goal is the provision of low-cost
units so that those with limited or fixed incomes can afford
housing. In order to work toward this goal, the amount of existing low-cost housing stock would need to be measured.
This measurement could be accomplished through surveys
and estimates developed by the planning department or a
similar agency, by the use of local real estate statistics, or by
the use of census information. Once the data are gathered,
statistical techniques can be used to examine the quality of
the data, to test hypotheses, to identify the relationships
among variables, or to make inferences about the relationships among the variables. Multivariate statistical techniques
such as multiple regression and factor analysis, used in conjunction with tests for statistical significance, are often employed by the planner during this step in the planning process.

In addition to taking measurements, the planner must consider the fact that standards establishing the requirements for
many activities will most likely be a factor in the plan. Standards can take the form of legal requirements, or they can be
generated by local agencies. If a new development in the
planning region will mean an additional volume of
automobile traffic, a local standard may exist that states that
for a certain increase in traffic flow a specific number of additional traffic lanes must be included in the development
plans. Standards, often stated as units needed per capita, are
incorporated into the plan.

Institution planning, such as planning for growth on a college or university campus, has largely become the product of formula computation based on set standards. As a hypothetical example, let us say that the student population increases by one hundred full-time equivalent students. This increase is placed as a variable in a formula that includes variables describing such factors as square feet of teaching space per student, the number of new faculty to be hired, and the amount of money allocated to the campus or department. Based on the formula, the increase of one hundred students would be the basis from which calculations of the exact amount of increase needed in each of the other variables would be determined. The rigid use of formulas and standards in this manner tends to make planning very inflexible. Although standards can dictate how much of an item is needed in a plan and measurements can provide data as to how much of that commodity already exists, information about the future is also needed.

Development of Assumptions and Projections. Two of the most critical aspects in the formulation of a plan that looks into the future are (1) the assumptions upon which the plan is based and (2) the projections made about future needs. In a statement of assumptions, the planner is literally assuming that what he or she believes will actually be the future needs and desires of the clientele for whom the plan is designed. It was standard practice for the urban and regional planners of the past two decades to assume that metropolitan area transportation would continue to be dominated by the automobile. Planners in the 1980s are beginning to change their assumptions about the transportation modes and related land use patterns of the future because of the rapidly rising cost of energy.

Projections are estimates of the amounts of phenomena required to meet future demands and needs. Projections can be made for such items as land use, population, travel behavior, and many other quantifiable variables. In simple terms, future trends in population might be forecast by using a logistic curve, an exponential curve, or a modified exponential curve (see Figure 11.3). Travel behavior can be projected

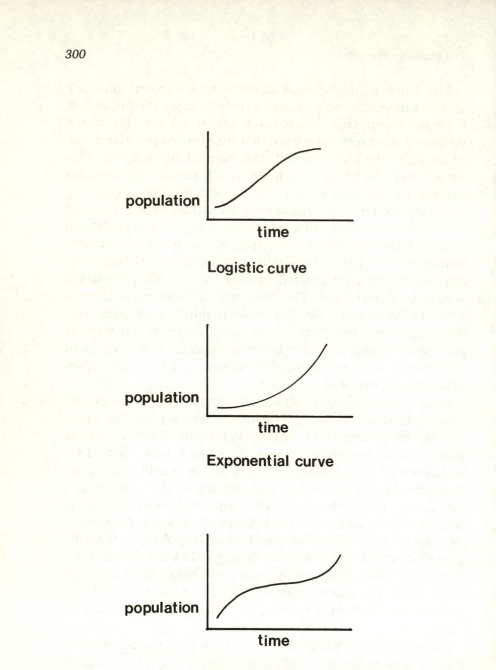

FIGURE 11.3. Growth Trends.

by using such techniques as gravity modeling (see Figure 11.4).

Projections of future land use needs are based on a variety of techniques. The use of planning requirements and simulation are two methods often employed in this task. When using planning requirements as a tool for land use analysis, a set of location requirements and space requirements are determined for a wide variety of activities. The first step in planning, once the requirements are known, is to inventory current land use practices and to estimate what will be needed in the future. Formulas, based upon standards and space needs, are then used to create a schematic diagram of future land

region of attraction

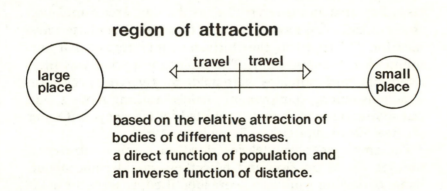

based on the relative attraction of bodies of different masses.
a direct function of population and an inverse function of distance.

the propensity to migrate between regions i and j - mathematically,

$$Mij = \frac{P_i P_j}{D_{ij}}$$

where:

    Mij = migrants going between region i and region j

    $P_i P_j$ = size of population

    D = distance separating regions i and j

FIGURE 11.4. The Gravity Model.

use that includes transportation factors, space needs for various activities, and the characteristics of the physical site. If several land uses are judged to be efficient for a particular space, the resolution of the conflict is based on the planner's estimate of the very best land use for that location (Chapin, 1965).

Simulation, specifically market simulation, is the approach to land use projection that is probably most often utilized today. Computer projections are used to simulate, or to describe, a wide range of potential land uses. A complex mathematical analysis of the various possibilities is then undertaken, and the best pattern of land use is incorporated into the plan.

One particular simulation study was done for the San Francisco Bay area and is referred to as the Bay Area Simulation Study (BASS). This model was used to simulate land use activities for 777 zones in the thirteen-county region that surrounds San Francisco Bay. The projection period was fifty-five years, and estimates were made for five-year cycles. Interactions among employment models, housing models, and transportation models were projected for every cycle (Center for Real Estate and Urban Economics, 1968).

The employment model described where new job opportunities would develop and how they would come about. Zones of declining industry were identified, as were the areas of rapid industrial growth. Behavior of consumers in the housing market was also simulated in the BASS model. Demand for and supply of housing were forecast and detail was added so that even the effect of houses being demolished in the various areas could be examined. The housing demolition model provides an example of the mathematical procedure used in the BASS simulation. The submodel indicated the number of housing units to be demolished by the type of unit, k, and where these houses were located by zone, j. The equation reads:

$$D_j^k = \text{Tot } D \left[\frac{(DR^k \cdot H^k)}{\sum_{k=1}^{6} (DR^k \cdot H^k)} \right] \left[\frac{(DR_j^k \cdot H_j^k)}{\sum_{j=1}^{n} (DR_j^k \cdot H_j^k)} \right]$$

This states that demolitions by type, by zone (D_j^k) equal total demolitions times a proportion to be allocated to type k (the middle term of the right-hand side of the equation), times a proportion to be allocated to zone j. The notational terms are:

$$\text{Tot } D = \text{Total demolitions rate (exogenously set)}$$
times total housing units in the region

DR^k = A preset demolition rate for each housing type, the relative values for k = 1, 2, 3 are 1, 2, 4, respectively, and for k = 4, 5, 6 are 2, 4, 8 respectively

H^k = is the existing housing stock by type

H_j^k = is H^k by zone

$$DR_j^{k=1,2,3} = \frac{(DD_j)^{1/4} \cdot (PM_j)^{1/2}}{HV_j}$$

where

DD_j = a density measure in zone j

PM_j = the proportion of housing units that are multiple in zone j

HV_j = an index of housing value = $(2 \cdot$ high value + middle value/total housing units)

$$DR_j^{k=4,5,6} = (DR_j^{k=1,2,3})^{1/2}$$

Thus, both of the ratio terms in the first equation find that the rate of demolition is higher in places where density is higher, multiple-family housing is more prevalent, and land values are lower. The final output of this model has a supply effect, reducing the housing stock, and a demand effect, dislocating households that must be relocated along with new households derived from the population projections (Center for Real Estate and Urban Economics, 1968, and Krueckeberg and Silvers, 1974, pp. 335–337).

By using this technique, projections can be made that are extremely specific and very precise. If this procedure is used, planners will have an accurate estimate of the impact of the destruction of existing structures on the future housing inventory in terms of both numbers of units and locations of units.

Thus far we have considered the following steps that are basic to the planning process: definition of interrelationships, determination of goals and objectives, establishment of standards and measurements by which a plan is judged, and the development of assumptions and projections about the future. The fundamental consideration in the formulation of a plan is the identification and analysis of the geographical region that is to be served by the plan.

It is essential to note that we have separated the elements of the planning process into discrete steps for the sake of discussion. In a real sense these components are incorporated concurrently into the plan, that is, standards, projections, and the interrelationships among variables may all be drawn into the plan at the same time. Each of these elements may then be refined and changed as the plan takes more definite shape. This method of proceeding is especially true for the concept of the region for which the plan is intended. Although it is the final part of our consideration, discussion of the geographic extent of the plan is a part of the planning process from the beginning and is woven into virtually all other phases of the process.

The Planning Region. The analysis of the planning region falls into two categories. First, on what scale is the plan made—for the block, neighborhood, district, central city, or the metropolitan region? Second, what are the physical, economic, social, political, and historical characteristics of the region?

For the first category, the extent of the area to be planned for is often established for the planner. It may be that a particular planning district or the political boundary of the city defines the region the planner must consider. The trend in some cases, such as for transportation and public utilities, is to plan for the entire area involved in question regardless of political boundaries.

Taking inventory of the attributes of the study region has

always been an important part of planning. It makes little sense to plan the placement of 10,000 people in a location where local water resources or the availability of developable land will allow for only a few hundred new residents. The relatively recent move to require Environmental Impact Reports (EIRs) or Enviromental Impact Statements (EISs) has created a great demand for a careful and thorough analysis of the region for which development is intended. Once a plan has been formulated, its goals defined, strategies to achieve those goals developed, and an estimate made as to the most appropriate use of the land, the most critical part of the process occurs, the implementation of the plan.

Politics and Urban Planning

In the most basic sense, the interface of planning and politics falls into two categories. The initial stage is the approval of the general plan by the appropriate government agencies and decision makers. Once a plan has been approved, the political element of the urban ecosystem is a factor in either the alteration or continued support of the plan. It is upon this latter concern that we will focus our attention.

As a hypothetical case, suppose that a general plan regulating land use has been developed for an area. The plan dictates land use through the imposition of zoning ordinances that specify the types of commercial or residential land uses that may be undertaken in various parts of the city. If a parcel of land is zoned or designated as a single-family housing region, other types of land use within that area would be prohibited unless a variance were given to allow for another land use, such as multifamily housing or some commercial activity such as a convenience food store.

A developer interested in building in this hypothetical city would need to file his or her plans with the planning department and request permission to build in accordance with the existing zoning or request a variance from the established land use policy. Once the issue of compliance with zoning were resolved, the planning department would consider the development proposal with respect to its compatibility with the physical environment, its impact on existing traffic, utilities, and schools, and a wide range of other factors. The planning department may or may not decide that the proposal is appropriate for a particular area.

How does a planning department make such a judgment? Basically, the areawide plan and the specific zoning ordinances contained within the plan act as guides in the decision-making process. A planning agency may say yes or no to a proposal based on that document's compatibility with the existing plans. It is at this point that the political power of planning departments varies considerably from city to city. In some cities the zoning ordinances are extremely well defined and literally spell out the exact parameters a development proposal must conform to in order for the proposal to be approved. In such a case, the planner has political strength by virtue of the nature of the master plan.

In other cases, zoning ordinances are very vague and leave the planner with little to fall back on as justification for a decision. In such an instance, the planner has relatively little explicit political power. These planners, however, may be in a position to greatly influence the people involved in the next step up the decision-making ladder.

Once a development proposal has gone through the planning department, it usually comes before a board such as a city planning commission. This group is generally composed of citizens appointed by elected officials. At this stage in the decision-making process, there is again an extremely wide range in the real power to make land use decisions. Many planning commissions act simply as review bodies whose principle function is to consider decisions made by the planning department. Conversely, it may be that nearly all the decision-making power with respect to approval or disapproval of plans or development proposals is vested in the planning commission or a similar government body.

In Colorado Springs, Colorado, the planning commission has virtual control over the entire land use decision-making process. Recommendations made by the first level of decision makers, the planning department, do not seem to be an influential factor in the decisions made by the city planning commission. In many other cities, the situation is essentially the reverse, with the planning department, in effect, making the decisions.

In a situation in which the planning commission makes the land use decisions, the philosophical orientation of the majority of the membership is obviously of critical importance. A commission with strong progrowth leanings may provide the incentive for industry and housing developers to locate in their particular city. An active progrowth land use decision-making body is a major component in the creation of the image of a city as being a desirable place in which to live or to locate a business. Growth potential and the so-called high quality of life available in Austin, Texas; Greenville-Spartanburg, South Carolina; Colorado Springs, Colorado; Tulsa, Oklahoma; Research Triangle, North Carolina; and Las Vegas, Nevada, have marked those places as urban areas that are expected to grow rapidly in the 1980s (Allis, 1980).

The final part of the planning process in most cities is a review and analysis of the workings of the planning department and the planning commission by the city council or some similar elected body. In most cases, this last group simply approves the actions taken by the other two decision-making units. Bringing plans and development proposals before a group of elected officials does offer an opportunity for interest groups ranging from neighborhood organizations to home builders and developers to present arguments either for or against a change in the general plan or a development proposal.

Political variables play a key role in the planning process. The most carefully thought-out plan will be of little value if people who seek variances from the plan are allowed a free hand to act without regard to the planner's design. Once a plan has been formulated, a planner may employ many strategies in order to achieve the goals of the plan.

STRATEGIES FOR URBAN PLANNING

The urban planner has a vast array of techniques for and concepts of land use control at his or her disposal. Any number of these strategies can be used in a city at any given time. The terms *environmental planning, model cities, new towns, transfer of development rights, urban renewal, planned unit development, historical preservation,* and *replanning* are a part of the planner's vocabulary. We have already explored some of the techniques for the regulation of land use in discussing zoning and growth control techniques. We will briefly review three further concepts of urban planning; urban renewal, planned unit development, and transfer of development rights.

Urban Renewal

Urban residents are undoubtedly familiar with the term *urban renewal.* Historically, efforts in the United States to improve living conditions in cities led to the Housing Act of 1937 from which the concept of urban renewal evolved. A series of housing acts followed the 1937 legislation, and each brought more federal money to the task of rebuilding cities.

Urban renewal programs work in three fundamental ways. First is the preventative tool of conservation. Housing areas that are said to be suffering from urban blight or deterioration are examined, and deficiencies in the housing stock are noted. Methods are designed and plans are implemented to correct the problems. The criteria used in the determination of urban blight conditions are drawn from federal standards that pertain to the minimum requirements for the physical condition of a house. If a house or neighborhood has become seriously blighted, the second aspect of urban renewal is activated, specifically, rehabilitation.

Rehabilitation became an important concept with the enactment of the Housing Act of 1954. In the process of rehabilitation, money is loaned to the owner of the property to bring the unit up to federal standards (Figure 11.5 and Figure 11.6). The basic concepts of urban planning are important in the rehabilitation process, for in order to qualify for financial assistance, goals for change must be established and standards must be observed in the reconditioning process.

The final aspect of urban renewal is redevelopment. The core areas of cities are the most likely targets for redevelopment (Figure 11.7 and Figure 11.8). In the redevelopment phase, an agency at some level of government assumes

FIGURE 11.5. Site for Urban Renewal. Source: HUD.

FIGURE 11.6. Urban Rehabilitation. Source: HUD.

FIGURE 11.7A. Redevelopment in CBD (Before). Source: HUD.

FIGURE 11.7B. Redevelopment in CBD (After). Source: HUD.

FIGURE 11.8A. Changing Urban Skyline (Before). Source: HUD.

FIGURE 11.8B. Changing Urban Skyline (After). Source: HUD.

ownership of the land, clears it of existing structures, and aids in rebuilding the area. The following are typical goals of a redevelopment project.

1. Create neighborhoods with living conditions that are safe, clean, quiet, and visually pleasing
2. Provide high-quality public transportation
3. Create community facilities such as parks and neighborhood centers

The standards of quality for neighbhorhoods, transportation, or community facilities are set by the federal government.

Urban renewal projects are often incorporated into the general master plan of cities as subunits of the entire plan. The goals, objectives, standards, and projections of urban renewal projects generally coincide with those same elements of the general plan. Urban renewal provides a means by which a nonlocal agency can greatly influence the planning and land use activity of a city. A second planning strategy, planned unit development, is a method that enables local planning officials to control land use.

Planned Unit Development

Planned unit development (PUD) is a planning scheme that calls for the creation of what are essentially complete miniplans for any development proposal or alteration of the existing general plan. A PUD code may specify requirements such as the relative percentage of land that must be "green space" (with lawns or other vegetation) or driveways and streets and what percentage can be used for the buildings. In many cases PUD codes call for at least 60 percent of the land to be open space of some type.

In addition to open space requirements, a PUD code may set specific standards designed to preserve environmental quality and to minimize the impact of proposals on transportation systems, schools, and public utilities. PUD codes attempt to ensure that a development will not adversely impact the aesthetic quality of an area, property values of existing residences, or the nature and character of the neighborhoods near a proposed development.

Planned unit development regulations are enforced through zoning ordinances. A person proposing a development on a parcel of land that is PUD zoned must adhere to all the regulations if the proposal is to be approved. In using PUD as a tool, very strict standards can be established that have the ultimate effect, in theory, of ensuring that all proposals are well thought-out and carefully designed. This is a theoretical statement, for in some cities the PUD codes are vague and essentially little more than old zoning under a new label. In those cities, variances from the requirements of a PUD code are generally given freely. At the other end of the spectrum, PUD codes can regulate virtually every aspect of what is to be developed and variances are rarely given. In cities with strong PUD codes, only development that is considered to be in harmony with the goals of the city is allowed.

Planned unit development goes beyond the traditional concept of zoning because of the potential for all-encompassing regulatory powers. A parcel of land that is simply zoned for four or five units per acre for single-family dwellings or ten to fifteen units per acre for multiple-family structures is not very well regulated other than for population density. Development on that same parcel of land under a strong PUD code could be closely regulated and the potential impact of the development on the surrounding neighborhoods or the entire city could be carefully scrutinized.

In our earlier discussion of attitudes toward planning, we saw that some people saw that planning and unnecessary land use regulation are unwarranted in the city, whereas others feel that such controls are essential to the welfare of the urban place. These same arguments apply toward strong PUD zoning. Controversy over the desirability of strong PUD ordinances is found throughout the academic writings on urban planning. Our final example of the methodologies used by planners is also highly controversial.

Transfer of Development Rights

Urban renewal and planned unit development are primarily concerned with the central areas of a city. Transfer of development rights (TDR) involves land use both on the urban periphery and in the more central regions of the city.

Transfer of development rights is a system that was developed in response to the conversion of agricultural land on the edge of cities to urban or suburban land use. Estimates vary, but some people have estimated that up to four square miles of agricultural land are converted to urban use in the United States per day. This conversion leads to urban sprawl and makes urban planning a very difficult task.

Essentially, TDR is a system that separates the rights to develop the land from the land itself. A TDR procedure allows a landowner to sell or transfer his or her right to develop land in a specific area. One type of TDR is exemplified by the person who owns fifty acres of prime agricultural land on the edge of a city and who was planning to sell that land for subdivision and development. That person may instead sell the *rights,* not the land itself, to build on the land to a government agency, which may keep the land as open space or may control the timing and nature of development on the land.

In the early 1960s, the concept of the TDR system was proposed by Gerald D. Lloyd (Lloyd, 1961). By the early 1970s some states, Maryland for instance, had passed legislation that was designed to develop a system for the transfer of development rights. The initial system used in many states is to create "a market for development rights in which owners of developable land must buy development rights from owners of preserved open space land as a prerequisite for development" (Rose, 1975, p. 186). All land is considered developable at first, following which time some parcels are designated as open space and some as developable land. A person building on land designated as developable has to pay a person owning land designated as open space in order to compensate that person for his or her lost development rights. It is not difficult to imagine the outcry that has resulted from this arrangement. The fundamental question we have to consider is, Do people have the right to use their land in any way they deem appropriate? The question of whether the public or the individual should benefit from the use of the land has been asked throughout American history and has sparked considerable controversy.

The most appropriate use of the land in and near cities will continue to be in the spotlight. Concern for open space and environmental quality, when combined with the alarming loss of prime agricultural land and other factors, makes the "right of the use of land" one of the more difficult philosophical problems that urban scientists will face in the coming decades. In the concluding chapter, we review the urban ecosystem concept from the perspective offered throughout this work. We also consider the roles of the urban scientist and the layman alike in shaping the urban future.

REFERENCES

Allis, S. 1980. "Company Towns." *Wall Street Journal,* March 14, pp. 1 and 17.

Carnegie, A. 1886. *Triumphant Democracy.* New York: Charles Scribner's Sons.

Center for Real Estate and Urban Economics. 1968. *Jobs, People and Land: Bay Area Simulation Study.* Berkeley, Calif.: Center for Real Estate and Urban Economics.

Chapin, F. Stuart, Jr. 1965. *Urban Land Use Planning.* 2d ed. Urbana: University of Illinois Press.

Dyckman, J. 1979. "Three Crises of American Planning." In R. Burchell and G. Sternlieb, eds., *Planning Theory in the 1980s,* pp. 279–295. New Brunswick, N.J.: Center for Urban Policy Research.

Hancock, J. 1967. "Planners in the Changing American City, 1900–1940." *Journal of the American Institute of Planners* 33:5: 290–304.

Krueckeberg, D., and Silvers, S. 1974. *Urban Planning Analysis: Methods and Models.* New York: John Wiley and Sons.

Lloyd, Gerald D. 1961. *Transferable Density in Connection with Density Zoning.* Technical Bulletin No. 40. Washington, D.C.: Urban Land Institute.

Rose, G. 1975. "A Proposal for the Separation and Marketability of Development Rights as a Technique to Preserve Open Space." In G. Rose, ed., *Transfer of Development Rights,* pp. 186–199. Rutgers, N.J.: Center for Urban Policy Research.

12

Urban America: Problems and Prospects

We live in an urbanizing world. The United States in particular is a highly urbanized country. In the urban environment, people often tend to regard themselves as figures on the landscape rather than as shapers of the urban ecosystem. The city is frequently viewed as simply a collection of buildings and streets. There is often little realization that the city is no mere haphazard collection of those artifacts but rather is the result of a process that reacts to the whole complex of human wants and interests that defines and organizes human activity. In order to understand the dynamics of a metropolitan region, the intellectual, political, economic, social, and psychological traits of human groups must be figured into the analysis.

A knowledge of how a city functions can enable people to realize the true potential for the average urban resident to become a shaper of the landscape. This possibility became evident to some degree after the turn of this century with an increasing public demand for urban services and planning. The potential is currently extremely apparent in the growth control movements found in the United States. The case study of growth restriction in suburban communities presented in Chapter 10 describes the manner in which informed, organized people can exert control over their own destiny. In a similar vein, the chapter on urban planning was designed specifically to demonstrate the actual applied aspects of the process of plan formulation, and the placement of the section on planning at the end of the volume was to allow for a presentation of an overview of the elements of the urban ecosystem before suggestions were made as to how the system might be regulated and designed.

It is hoped that the information contained in this volume has helped the reader develop skills in the analysis of both the urban ecosystem and the manner in which cities in a system of cities interrelate. The anticipated result of such skill development is that one can become not just a figure on the urban landscape but a critical observer and perhaps a factor in the process that shapes cities. Citizen input and the resource pool made available by the intelligence and experience of a vast number of people will be of critical importance in solving the urban problems of the future. How, for example, will the problem of the lost agricultural resource be reconciled as agricultural land is converted to urban uses? Prime farmland is a precious commodity; once it has been urbanized it is lost to agricultural use, and similar amounts of comparable agricultural land are not likely to suddenly appear at another location. Growth controls have been proposed as one solution to this problem. If growth is restricted, where will the large number of people just entering the home-buying stage of the life cycle find a place to live?

These are important questions because the desire to restrict growth is on the increase. Dealing with the clash of issues that result from a rapidly growing population searching for homes as opposed to the desires of many communities for controlled growth may well be one of the most critical problems facing the American urban society of the future. If the rapidly upward spiral of fuel costs is brought into play, the issue becomes extremely complex. There are certainly no simple answers to such complicated problems. It is our contention, however, that the use of a systems methodology could provide a powerful tool for problem solving.

The systems approach is not proposed solely because of its potential for urban analysis and problem solving. When used as a technique for observing the functioning of cities, the systems approach helps put the city into a perspective that is often used solely for the natural landscape. The awareness of the beauty and harmony found in nature can be transferred to the city. It then follows that the urban area will take on new forms and meanings for the observer trained in ecosystem analysis. It must also be remembered that the method of analysis and concepts of urban study suggested in this volume may be employed in the observation of cities of any size and cultural context.

It has been our goal to make the reader aware of the ecological functioning of cities and the part all urban residents may play as part of the urban ecosystem. We hope this volume has kindled an interest in, and will lead to a continued study of, the matchless diversity found in the urban landscape.

Glossary

Basic economic activities: Activities located within a city that serve areas and persons outside that city.

Bid-rent gradient: A curve that illustrates the relationship between distance and the cost of land. The concept is often used to illustrate the economic competition or "bidding" between land uses at a particular distance from the central business district.

Building quota: A strict numerical limit of building permits that are issued in a given period of time. This practice is used to restrict growth and encourage development practices in harmony with general civic goals for growth.

Centrality: Being central or located at the center of a collection of entities. The central business district (CBD) is an example of this concept. A location near the center of a city, a grouping of like economic activities, or a population concentration is an important consideration in the decision of where to establish many urban activities.

Central place: An important urban node that serves a surrounding region. The size of the service region is related to the size of the central place.

Central place hierarchy: The organization of central places into a hierarchical structure with a few large places at the top of the structure and many smaller places on the lower levels. The largest places offer the greatest range of goods and activities and serve the greatest area.

Chain migration: A person who has moved to a place influencing others to move to that location. A chain or linkage of information about a place is responsible for this type of migration.

Cluster distribution: The clustering of like or similar activities. Many cluster distributions may be present in a city; for instance, a cluster of activities related to the electronics industry or a cluster of financial institutions.

Concentric land use zones: An important theory of urban social and economic structures holds that the city is composed of concentric circles of specific land uses and that these circles surround the CBD.

Directional bias: The belief that a bias or preference in direction exists in the way people perceive a city. Specifically, people know the city most completely along the lines they travel most often. This journey pattern is generally focused on the trip from home to CBD, thus a bias may exist along that corridor.

Distance: The space existing between points. Distance may be measured as linear, in terms of economic costs, by the use of time, or by the perception of the difficulty of a trip between points.

Distance bias: A concept that is based on the assumption that people know their local area in greatest detail and that the knowledge of the urban environment decreases with distance.

Dust dome: The circulation of pollutants in the atmosphere above a city. The heat produced by an urban area tends to create a pattern of air movement that can cause pollutants to be trapped in the urban area creating, literally, a dome of polluted air.

Ecological analysis: The use of the concepts of ecological study, primarily analysis of the interrelationships among elements of a system, to study urban places.

Ecological processes: Processes such as the invasion, succession, and dominance of plant types found in an ecological succession used in analogous form to describe the dynamics of social areas in cities.

Ethnic community: A social group within a culture and its specific place of residence.

Exclusionary practices: Practices that tend to restrict the free movement of people into various communities. Such activities act to perpetuate socially and economically segregated areas.

Externalities: Advantages that occur due to the concentration of like types of industry in one location.

Factorial ecology: A multivariate statistical technique used to locate and analyze the social areas of cities.

Feedback: Any information that describes the results of a process.

Filtering: Generally, the process through which housing stock changes from high-income ownership to the place of residence for people in other economic groups.

Gravity model: A model that formalizes the relationship between the size or importance of places, the distance between places, and the deterioration of interaction with distance.

Interurban migration: The movement of people between cities.

Intervening obstacles: Factors that reduce the amount or efficiency of interaction between two points. Such obstacles can take many forms.

Intraurban migration: The movement of people within cities.

Land rent: Basically, the value of land for any specific purpose when all factors such as local environmental attributes and distance from the center are considered.

Land use planning: The formalized process of determining the best use of land for the present and estimating the most appropriate future use of land.

Multiplier effect: The magnifying effect of basic employment; that is, for each job in the basic sector, other jobs are created to serve the basic workers.

National urban system: The system of cities in a national political unit and the relationship among cities in the hierarchy of such a system, especially in terms of economic activities.

Nonbasic economic activity: Goods and services generated in non-basic activities are consumed within the city. Nonbasic activities are often referred to as service activities.

Outer city: The complex of industrial and residential suburbs of the 1970s and beyond in their role as urban places on the fringe of the city.

Petaluma Plan: The generally applied term for the city of Petaluma, California, Growth Control Ordinance. This ordinance was precedent setting in the United States in allowing cities to limit growth.

Place utility: The attributes of a location that make that place important when compared to surrounding locations.

Planned unit development (PUD): A planning scheme that calls for comprehensive analysis and coordinated planning for development projects.

Planning region: All areas that will affect or be affected by a plan.

Primate city: If a country has only one large city, that urban place is referred to as a primate city.

Pull factor migration: Forces that act to attract movers to a given area.

Push factor migration: Circumstances that act to force movers to leave a given area.

Range: The distance people will travel to obtain specific goods and services.

Rural-urban fringe: That area of transition of land use from urban to rural functions.

Rural urbanization: The trend toward urban-type development far beyond traditional city limits and suburbs.

Sector theory: The theory that assumes that urban social and economic areas can be organized into wedge-shaped sectors with the CBD as the point of origin.

Social area analysis: A method for delimiting and examining the social areas of cities.

Socioeconomic status (SES): A summary of a person's or a group's level of education, income, type of employment, and home value or rent. Generally stated as high, medium, or low.

Spatial distribution: The arrangement of phenomena on the earth's surface.

Spatial interaction: The pattern of linkages and exchanges between points on the surface of the earth.

Standard metropolitan area (SMA): Used to define urban areas in the 1950 census. (See standard metropolitan statistical area.)

Standard metropolitan statistical area (SMSA): Used to define urban areas since 1960. An SMSA includes at least one central city and the surrounding counties where 75 percent of the population is engaged in nonagricultural activities.

Suburb: The area at the edge of the city. A place of transition from urban to the rural-urban fringe.

Suburban sadness: Used to describe the stereotypes of suburbia often found in literature of the 1950s and 1960s.

Threshold: The minimum number of people required in order for a specific good or service to be available.

Urban climatology: The study of the microclimate associated with cities.

Urban ecosystem concept: Consideration of the city functioning as a biological ecosystem. Using the processes found in nature, through analogy, to study the city.

Urban heat island: A product of the changes in the physical environment brought about by urbanization. Cities continually produce and retain heat, which in turn creates microclimates in cities.

Urbanism: The life-styles and culture of those living in an urban area.

Urbanization: The process of becoming urban in nature or character.

Urbanized area: The inclusive area of city, suburb, and rural-urban fringe.

Urban morphology: The form and structure of the city.

Urban renewal: The process of redevelopment of cities, especially inner cities.

Zoning: Land use regulation in which the types of activities that may be undertaken are defined for all parcels of land.

Index